MW00654928

MILID Yearbook 2015

A Collaboration between UNITWIN Cooperation Programme
on Media and Information Literacy and Intercultural Dialogue,
and the International Clearinghouse on Children, Youth and
Media at NORDICOM

Media and Information Literacy for the Sustainable Development Goals

Edited by Jagtar Singh, Alton Grizzle,
Sin Joan Yee and Sherri Hope Culver

For Pilar Pacheco
with profound regards
Jagtar Singh
Lead Editor
08/3/2016

MILID Yearbook 2015
Media and Information Literacy for the Sustainable Development Goals

Editors:
Jagtar Singh, Alton Grizzle, Sin Joan Yee and Sherri Hope Culver

A collaboration between UNITWIN Cooperation Programme on
Media and Information Literacy and Intercultural Dialogue,
and the International Clearinghouse on Children, Youth and Media
at Nordicom, University of Gothenburg

ISBN 978-91-87957-13-0 (printed version)
ISBN 978-91-87957-17-8 (pdf version)

Published by:
The International Clearinghouse on Children, Youth and Media
Nordicom
University of Gothenburg
Box 713
SE-405 30 Göteborg

Cover by:
Daniel Zachrisson

Inlay by:
Duolongo

Printed by:
Ale Tryckteam AB, Bohus, Sweden 2015

Editorial Advisory Board

Content

Foreword

Getachew Engida, Deputy Director-General, UNESCO.

As we move towards 'knowledge societies', timely access to relevant, useful and quality information, including development information, is critical for making informed decisions and improving the lives of people.

With the convergence of new communication technologies with media, the ascent of the Internet and social media, as well as the growing use of computer and mobile devices, the promises of information and media have increased manifold. This opens new horizons for every woman and man to exercise their rights to freedom of opinion, expression and access to information – to be actors in, and beneficiaries of, sustainable development.

However, to enjoy these benefits, every citizen needs to be equipped with adequate devices and affordable connectivity. Without this, the gap between the information rich and the information poor will continue to grow – contributing to development gaps that would be unsustainable.

Through its leadership, in Broadband Commission for Digital Development, on ICTs and disabilities, and for gender empowerment, UNESCO is working across the board to encourage policies to overcome the hurdle to inclusive development. Media and information literacy is a flagship of our work. On all sides of the digital divide, everyone needs the necessary competencies to access, evaluate critically, interact with and produce useful, timely and relevant information. For this, individuals must be media and information literate. UNESCO approaches media and information literacy (MIL) as a composite concept, reflecting the symbiosis between information and the media generated by the new technology. MIL covers a range of competencies – from finding and evaluating the credibility of online information, through to how to react to attempts to shape young people's identities by social media and advertising. MIL encompasses knowledge about the significance of the right to privacy in the digital age, as well as interactions with talk radio, online etiquette and intercultural respect. This is, indeed, a dynamic field, responding to a fast changing world.

In this context, the first edition of the MILID Yearbook was published in 2013 with the theme, "Media and Information Literacy and Intercultural Dialogue". The 2014 edition of the yearbook was on "Global Citizenship in a Digital World." The present edition has a timely and highly relevant theme – "Media and Information Literacy for the Sustainable Development Goals."

The contents of the yearbook have been organized into five sections, to present 31 carefully chosen and edited articles on education, sustainable development, and freedom of expression, interreligious and intercultural dialogue, media and other information providers, gender equality, persons with disabilities, linguistic diversity, environment, health and agriculture. I see this yearbook as a reference for all who are interested in promoting MIL across frontiers as tool for open and inclusive development.

UNESCO is working consistently to promote MIL and empower people with competencies for surviving and thriving in this highly complex world. We have prepared a MIL toolkit (including MIL Curriculum for Teachers; Global MIL Assessment Framework; and MIL Policy and Strategy Guidelines) for the stakeholders. We have initiated the UNESCO-UNAOC MILID University UNITWIN Network Programme for promoting teaching and research in media and information literacy. And we have initiated the Global Alliance for Partnerships on Media and Information Literacy which is gaining ground across different regions of the world. Four regional chapters have been launched. National level MIL networks are also being supported by UNESCO. The Media and Information Literacy University Network of India (MILUNI), is one such example. UNESCO is deeply committed to scaling up and out such lessons – by involving teachers and youth at the grassroots level, and national and state governments at the top level. Results are becoming visible day by day.

It is our firm belief that MIL can contribute to the progress of individuals and societies by developing necessary knowledge, skills, attitudes, and confidence among children, youth, women and men, senior citizens, and persons with disabilities. The greatest resource of any country is human ingenuity and creativity. MIL can help to ensure a level playing field for one and all. I sincerely hope that the MILID Yearbook 2015 would contribute its share in this regard. I congratulate all the contributors and the partners who have helped us put together this knowledge resource.

Getachew Engida
Deputy Director-General
UNESCO

Preface

The MILID Yearbook is a peer reviewed academic publication and a joint initiative of the UNESCO-UNAOC University Cooperation Programme on Media and Information Literacy and Intercultural Dialogue (MILID). The cooperation programme was launched in 2011 within the framework of the UNESCO university twinning programme (UNITWIN). The MILID university network now consists of 17 universities from all regions of the world.

MILID Yearbook 2013 and 2014 were published in cooperation with the Nordic Information Centre for Media and Communication Research (Nordicom). The theme of the MILID Yearbook 2014 was "Global Citizenship in a Digital World."

The objectives of the Yearbook are to:

• Strengthen and deepen the knowledge concerning MILID on global, regional and national levels including the frame on human rights and democracy

• Widen and deepen the knowledge concerning MILID

• Widen and intensify the collaboration and exchange on media and information literacy between the partner universities

• Visualize and stimulate research and practices within as well as outside the UNITWIN Network in the field of MILID while promoting a more holistic perspective.

In the year 2000, governments and development partners all over the world agreed on eight global development targets called the Millennium Development Goals (MDGs). The year 2015 is a pivotal year as it marks the end of the period during which the MDGs were to be reached and the year in which new global development targets are to be set. These new targets are referred to as the Post-2015 Sustainable Development Goals (SDGs). This process is in its highest gear with ongoing debates and consultative meetings/initiatives globally both online and offline. While much progress has been made, achievement of the MDGs has been mixed across countries. The centrality of information and communication to development is irrefutable. The MILID Yearbook provides a case for media and information literacy (MIL) as a tool for open and inclusive sustainable development. It draws on research findings, theories and practices of MIL, and the development focusing on the following theme and sub-themes. Theme of the 2015 MILID Yearbook is, "Media and Information Literacy for the Sustainable Development Goals."

Key Sub-themes are:

- Governance, citizenship and freedom of expression
- Access to information and knowledge for all citizens
- Development of media, libraries, Internet and other information providers
- Education, teaching, and learning – including professional development
- Linguistic and cultural diversity as well as intercultural and interfaith dialogue
- Women, children and youth, persons with disabilities and other marginalised social groups
- Health and wellness
- Business, industry, employment and sustainable economic development
- Agriculture, farming, wildlife protection, forestry and natural resources conservation as well as other areas.

The Yearbook Includes 31 Articles Organized into the Following Five Sections:

- Sustainable development through teaching and learning (nine articles)
- Media organizations, information providers and freedom of expression (nine articles)
- Linguistic diversity, interreligious and intercultural dialogues (five articles)
- Gender equality and persons with disabilities (four articles)
- Advancing knowledge societies: environment, health and agriculture (four articles)

It is obvious from the above listing that there has been greater response this year to the sub-themes related to sustainable development through education, media organizations, information providers, and freedom of expression. These sub-themes are covered in 18 articles in this yearbook. The remaining three sections offer articles on linguistic diversity, interreligious and intercultural dialogue, gender equality, persons with disabilities, environment, health, and agriculture.

Besides this preface, the foreword, introduction and the contributors' list add further value to the yearbook. For the editors, 2015 MILID Yearbook has proved to be a great learning and networking experience.

The 2015 edition of the MILID Yearbook displays how media and information literacy can be helpful in facilitating progress and achievement of the sustainable development goals. It is sincerely hoped that the articles in this yearbook will go a long way to sensitize the stakeholders about the role and value of MIL in sustainable development of one and all across frontiers.

It is a matter of profound satisfaction for us that in spite of working in different continents and varying time zones, we could successfully coordinate with the authors, the editorial advisory board members, and the publisher. We are deeply grateful to all the contributors for facilitating the publication of this yearbook.

Jagtar Singh
Alton Grizzle
Sin Joan Yee
Sherri Hope Culver

Introduction

Towards a Global Media and Information Literacy Movement in Support of the Sustainable Development Goals

Mr Ban Ki Moon, Secretary-General of the United Nations in his synthesis report, *Road to Dignity by 2030* notes, "The year 2015 offers a unique opportunity for global leaders and people to end poverty, transform the world to better meet human needs and the necessities of economic transformation, while protecting our environment, ensuring peace and realizing human rights… Member States [national governments] have recognized the importance of building on existing initiatives to develop measurements of progress on sustainable development that go beyond gross domestic product." (Road to Dignity, 2014, p. 3, 37).

The United Nations have proposed 17 Sustainable Development Goals (SDGs) as below:

Goal 1   End poverty in all its forms everywhere

Goal 2   End hunger, achieve food security and improved nutrition and promote sustainable agriculture

Goal 3   Ensure healthy lives and promote well-being for all at all ages

Goal 4   Ensure inclusive and equitable quality education and promote lifelong learning opportunities for all

Goal 5   Achieve gender equality and empower all women and girls

Goal 6   Ensure availability and sustainable management of water and sanitation for all

Goal 7   Ensure access to affordable, reliable, sustainable and modern energy for all

Goal 8   Promote sustained, inclusive and sustainable economic growth, full and productive employment and decent work for all

Goal 9   Build resilient infrastructure, promote inclusive and sustainable industrialization and foster innovation

Goal 10	Reduce inequality within and among countries
Goal 11	Make cities and human settlements inclusive, safe, resilient and sustainable
Goal 12	Ensure sustainable consumption and production patterns
Goal 13	Take urgent action to combat climate change and its impacts
Goal 14	Conserve and sustainably use the oceans, seas and marine resources for sustainable development
Goal 15	Protect, restore and promote sustainable use of terrestrial eco-systems, sustainably manage forests, combat desertification, and halt and reverse land degradation and halt biodiversity loss
Goal 16	Promote peaceful and inclusive societies for sustainable develop-ment, provide access to justice for all and build effective, accoun-table and inclusive institutions at all levels
Goal 17	Strengthen the means of implementation and revitalize the global partnership for sustainable development

Over the past decade, there is increasing recognition and acceptance that tech-nological advancement and explosion of media[1] and other information provi-ders,[2] including those on the Internet, have made it urgent for all citizens to acquire media and information competencies. Survival in knowledge societies requires that women, men, children and youth, in general, all citizens, have the competencies to purposefully navigate the flood of information, decipher media messages they come across, create and participate in media and interact online despite their race, gender, age, beliefs, ability or location. This rapid growth in technologies and media has opened up new forms of citizen engagement. Wo-men/girls and men/boys use of social networking platforms has created a vir-tual second world. Meanwhile, a large number of studies show that citizens do not have the competencies to effectively exploit the opportunities provided by this virtual world and at the same time minimize the potential risks. The risks are connected to the reliability of information, privacy, safety and security is-sues, and potential abuse of media, the Internet and other information sources. At the same time, freedom of expression and freedom of information as well as access to information and knowledge, which include freedom of the press and free Internet, are indispensable to good governance, accountability, tack-ling poverty and improving development, in general. The importance of these freedoms, enshrined in the Universal Declaration of Human Rights, to citizens' participation is unquestioned.

UNESCO holds that media and information literacy (MIL) is essential to em-power citizenries all around the world to have full benefits of these fundamental human rights and freedoms as well as enable sound social discourse. It also enables citizens to be aware of their responsibilities in the context of the freedoms mentioned above. These include the responsibility to demand quality media and information services and to use information and technology ethically. This is very much in tune with Goal 16 of the SDGs which reads as, 'Promote peaceful and inclusive societies for sustainable development, provide access to justice for all and build effective, accountable and inclusive institutions at all levels.' MIL empowers citizens, including children and youth, with competencies related to media, information, ICT and other aspects of literacy which are needed for the 21st century. These competencies include the ability to: access, find, evaluate, use the information they need in ethical and effective ways; understand the role and functions of media and other information providers such as libraries, museums and archives, including those on the Internet, in democratic societies and in the lives of individuals; understand the conditions under which media and information providers can fulfil their functions; critically evaluate information and media content; engage with media and information providers for self-expression, life-long learning, democratic participation, and good governance; and updated skills (including ICT skills) needed to produce content. Different programmes at UNESCO are relevant to the range of aspects of MIL competencies. For instance, MIL when connected to cultural competencies can contribute to furthering intercultural dialogue, cultural and linguistic diversity and facilitate a culture of peace and non-violence. In an era of interconnectedness and interdependence, social literacies underpinned by MIL are necessary for harmonious living. This is also echoed by the Goal 16 of the SDGs.

To broaden the reach and impact of MIL initiatives globally, UNESCO and partners established the Global Alliance for Partnerships on Media and Information Literacy (GAPMIL) in June 2013. The GAPMIL was established in cooperation with and the involvement of UNESCO, UNAOC, UNICEF, Open Society Foundation, IREX, European Commission, Government of Nigeria, and the Swedish International Development Cooperation Agency (SIDA) through a call for interest which was distributed to stakeholders groups globally. Close to three hundred organizations responded and agreed to be associated with GAPMIL. This was followed by a three-month online debate and culminated with the gathering of partners and debates in Nigeria from 27-29 June 2013, during the Global Forum for Partnerships on MIL, incorporating the International Conference on MIL and Intercultural Dialogue. Other development partners are also invited to join GAPMIL. In fact, GAPMIL substantiates the spirit of Goal 17 which intends to strengthen the means of implementation and revitalize the global partnership for sustainable development. This process was necessary to enhance co-ownership and galvanize consensus on what shape the GAPMIL should take. A great number of contributions by MIL experts all over the world have been brought through these debates in order to prepare the GAPMIL Framework and Action Plan.

The Following Principles Underpin the Gapmil Framework and Plan of Action:

- Convergence – a joined-up approach; a theoretical convergence that embraces a blending of media literacy and information literacy as a combined set of competencies; also a practical convergence where journalists and information/library specialists and their related activities meet;
- MIL is seen as essential to citizens engagement, good governance, intercultural dialogue and development;
- Rights-based approach, programmes targeting both citizens who have rights to MIL and those bearing the duty to provide MIL programmes;
- Women/men and boys/girls, people with disabilities, indigenous groups or ethnic minorities should have equal access to MIL;
- Prioritizing empowerment over protectionism;
- Culture and linguistic diversity approach;
- A balance of joint actions and organisation, country or region specific actions.

GAPMIL is a ground-breaking initiative to promote international cooperation to ensure that all citizens have access to media and information literacy competencies. Organizations from over eighty countries have agreed to join forces and stand together for change under this platform. Drawing upon over 40 years of UNESCO's experience in MIL, it has become absolutely essential to establish more enduring partnerships that are necessary to amplify the impact of MIL. GAPMIL is needed to give greater impetus for fostering media and information literate citizenries in the context of Millennium Development Goals (MDGs) and SDGs.

To this end, GAPMIL as a joint initiative of UNESCO and other key stakeholders, seeks to globally connect MIL to key development areas and articulate key strategic partnerships to drive development.

Gapmil Promotes Relationship Between Mil and Key Development Areas, Including:

1. Governance, citizenship and freedom of expression;
2. Access to information and knowledge for all citizens;
3. Development of media, libraries, Internet and other information providers;

4. Education, teaching, and learning – including professional development;

5. Linguistic and cultural diversity as well as intercultural and interfaith dialogue;

6. Women, children and youth, persons with disabilities and other marginalised social groups;

7. Health and wellness;

8. Business, industry, employment and sustainable economic development;

9. Agriculture, farming, wildlife protection, forestry and natural resources conservation as well as other areas.

GAPMIL enables the MIL community to speak and address, with a unified voice, certain critical matters, including the need for policies and programs that promote media and information literacy as a means to open and inclusive development. In an information driven world, information and knowledge become the life blood to development and good governance. Just as it was essential to the implementation of the MDGs, MIL – which requires that people of all levels of society acquire skills to access and critically evaluate information and to effectively engage with media of all forms – can have a significant impact on the achievement of the SDGs. Universal Primary Education is Goal 2 of the MDGs. This goal seeks to "ensure that by 2015, children everywhere, boys and girls alike, will be able to complete a full course of primary schooling."[3] Goal 4 of the SDGs also intends to 'ensure inclusive and equitable quality education and promote lifelong learning opportunities for all.' Part of the overall education of children includes supporting young people to become active citizens as they navigate the plethora of information and media messages that they encounter, and as they explore the potential positive and negative aspects of information and media content. GAPMIL is committed to supporting children and youth in their efforts to engage in meaningful participation in our world dominated by information, media and technology. The overall aim of GAPMIL fits into Goal 8 of the MDGs which emphasizes the role of developed countries in aiding developing countries and sets objectives and targets for developed countries to achieve a 'global partnership for development' by supporting fair trade, debt relief, increasing aid, access to affordable essential medicines and encouraging technology transfer.[4] This is reiterated by the Goal 17 of the SDGs, to 'strengthen the means of implementation and revitalize the global partnership for sustainable development.'

In this regard, GAPMIL assists Member States in articulating national MIL policies and strategies – integrating these with existing national ICTs, information, media and communication, and education policies/strategies and regulatory systems. It also encourages and supports Member States in developing relevance in local projects and government partnerships, particularly in countries and regions where MIL is a novel or developing concept. This includes encouraging Ministries of Education to develop standard MIL Curriculum to be incorporated into educational systems. Furthermore, national governments will be supported to monitor and evaluate MIL initiatives through the use of the Global Framework of MIL Indicators developed by UNESCO. GAPMIL also assists and supports Member States in setting up and monitoring MIL goals and targets in respect to MIL; providing MIL training for all citizens at the country and regional levels. It fosters partnerships with UN agencies, other development organizations, the private sector including business enterprises, training institutions, faith-based institutions and civil society organizations, including the media, libraries, archives and museums (on and offline), adopting a multi-sectoral approach with clearly defined roles for coordination at different levels.

GAPMIL encourages universities and other training institutions to develop and launch certificate, diploma, bachelor, master and doctoral programmes in MIL to develop a cadre of MIL experts in all regions and countries. It will pursue training of trainers in MIL for capacity development reinforcement and advocacy as well as raise awareness by sensitizing governments as to the importance of MIL as a tool to enhance citizens' participation in knowledge societies, freedom of expression and quality media. In line with Goal 5 (Achieve gender equality and empower all women and girls) of the SDGs, GAPMIL believes that gender equality is critical in consolidating the democratic momentum and imperative for the global development drive. UNESCO and UNAOC have created the UNESCO-UNAOC UNITWIN Global Chair on Media and Information Literacy and Intercultural Dialogue ("UNESCO-UNAOC MILID UNITWIN").

UNESCO-UNAOC MILID UNITWIN's Specific Objectives Include:

- Act as an Observatory for critically analyzing: the role of Media and Information Literacy ("MIL") as a catalyst for civic participation, democracy and development; for the promotion of free, independent and pluralistic media; as well as MIL's contribution to the prevention and resolution of conflicts and intercultural tensions and polarizations.

- Enhance intercultural and cooperative research on MIL and the exchanges between universities and mass media, encouraging MIL's initiatives towards respecting human rights and dignity and cultural diversity.

- Develop within the participant universities educational and media production practices that contribute to dissolving prejudice and intercultural barriers and favour global dialogue and cooperation among citizens as well as social and political institutions around the world. In addition to the international dimension, these practices will be reflected at the local level in the eight cities or neighborhoods in which the partner universities are located.

- Promote global actions relating to MIL (including adaptation of the UNESCO MIL Curriculum for Teacher Education and other relevant tools, publications, congresses, seminars, teaching resources, and faculty and students' exchanges) that could contribute towards stimulating dialogue and understanding among people of and within different cultures and societies.

- Create a virtual centre to research on, and study and develop MIL initiatives aimed at the creation of projects and publications linking universities and research centres.

- Promote and support other global media initiatives that could reinforce civic participation through open, free and independent media and information systems that favour intercultural dialogue and cooperation.

- Encourage and support citizen participation as well as educational and cultural institutions whose initiatives promote media and information literacy, cooperation and intercultural dialogue (UNESCO-UNAOC UNITWIN, 2014). In fact, the UNESCO-UNAOC MILID UNITWIN is the research arm of GAPMIL.

Similarly, "the objective of MILID Week is to shine the spotlight on the importance of media and information literate citizenries to foster inter-cultural dialogue, and mutual understanding. It underscores how interwoven media and information competencies (knowledge, skills and attitude) and intercultural competencies are. The initiative is planned within the framework of the UNITWIN Cooperation Programme on Media and Information Programme Literacy and brings together universities representing all regions of the world and many other stakeholders who are involved in MIL and intercultural dialogue. Activities include debates, research and the MILID partners meeting." (Media and Information Literacy and Intercultural Dialogue Week, 2014). Gender equality is broadly seen and understood as a key issue in the pursuit of democracy, governance and development. GAPMIL is committed to supporting women in meaningful participation in our world which is driven by information, media and technologies which are male dominated.

Advances in media and information technology in the last decade have facilitated a global communications network and process that have both positive and negative impacts on women and young girls. Around the world, little attention is paid to the coverage of women in the media. MIL can fill the gap to enhance women's presence and participation in the media. GAPMIL realizes the crucial role in supporting women media professionals, in creating alternative media spaces for the expression of women's perspectives on the world, and in critiquing offensive or stereotypical media content.[5] GAPMIL believes that women should be empowered by enhancing their skills, knowledge and access to information technology. This will strengthen their ability to combat negative portrayals of women. It supports women's education, training and employment to promote and ensure women's equal access to all areas and levels of the media; research into all aspects of women and the media and encourage the development of educational and training programmes, including media and information literacy projects for girls.[6]

The SDGs[7] seek to build on the MDGs. For the SDGs to be successful, it has to be an "inclusive and transparent intergovernmental process open to all stakeholders."[8] The key to this success will be engagement and participation. This can be enhanced through the GAPMIL process which seeks to make citizens active agents of change. While there is an intrinsic value to people being empowered and claiming their right to be heard, their participation and ownership is also essential to achieving successful and sustainable development outcomes.[9] Capacity building is important to advance the SDGs. The emerging development agenda looks set to encompass a set of goals that are more complex, transformative, interdependent and universally applicable than the MDGs. If the implementation of this kind of agenda is to be successful, capacities like the ones being promoted by GAPMIL are at the core.[10]

In this context, the MILID Yearbook provides a case for media and information literacy as a tool for open and inclusive sustainable development. It draws on research findings, theories and practices of MIL and developments focusing on the theme and sub-themes (see the preface for details) identified for the 2015 MILD Yearbook. This year, there has been an overwhelming response to the sub-themes related to sustainable development through education, media organizations, information providers, and freedom of expression, linguistic diversity, interreligious and intercultural dialogue, gender equality, persons with disabilities, environment, health, and agriculture. But because of the constraints of space and time, only 31 best of the best articles could be accommodated in the yearbook. In fact, the 2015 edition of the MILID Yearbook displays how media and information literacy can be helpful in facilitating progress and achieving the sustainable development goals. It is earnestly hoped that the articles published in this yearbook will certainly sensitize the stakeholders about the roles and goals of MIL in the sustainable development of one and all across frontiers.

UNESCO UNAOC GAPMIL

This introduction is an adapted extract of the Framework and Action Plan of the UNESCO-led Global Alliance for Partnerships on Media and Information Literacy (GAPMIL).

References

Road to Dignity by 2030, (2014). http://www.un.org/disabilities/documents/reports/SG_
    Synthesis_Report_Road_to_Dignity_by_2030.pdf Accessed on 14 May 2015.
*UNESCO-UNAOC UNITWIN (2014) on Media and Information Literacy and Intercultural
    Dialogue.* http://www.unaoc.org/communities/academia/unesco-unaoc-milid/
    Accessed on 15 May 2015.
Media and Information Literacy and Intercultural Dialogue Week, (2014). http://www.
    unescobkk.org/communication-and-information/freedom-of-expression-democracy-
    and-peace/media-and-information-literacy/milid-week/ Accessed on 15 May 2015.
United Nations Educational, Scientific and Cultural Organization (UNESCO)
United Nations Alliance of Civilizations (UNAOC)
Global Alliance for Partnerships on Media and Information Literacy (GAPMIL).
    http://www.unesco.org/new/en/communication-and-information/media-
    development/media-literacy/global-alliance-for-partnerships-on-media-and-
    information-literacy/

Notes

1   The use of the term "media" here refers to two dimensions. Firstly, there is the news
    media as an institution, the "fourth estate", having specific professional functions that
    its constituents pledge to fulfil in democratic societies and which are necessary for
    good governance and development. This includes radio, television and newspapers,
    whether online or offline, as well as includes journalistic content on the Internet.
    Secondly, there is media as the plural of the term "medium", and which here refers to
    multiple communication modes such as broadcast and cable television, radio, news-
    papers, motion pictures, video games, books, magazines, certain uses of the Internet,
    etc. MIL encompasses engagement with all these modes. For its part, UNESCO is
    particularly concerned with information and news, and focuses less on other content
    such as entertainment, interpersonal communications, and advertising.

2   The use of the term "information providers" here refers to the information manage-
    ment, information agencies, memory, cultural and Internet information organiza-
    tions. It includes libraries, archives, museums, documentation centres, information
    management institutions, not-for-profit and for-profit information providers, net-
    works and companies which provide range of services and content online and other.

3   http://www.un.org/millenniumgoals/ Retrieved 24 April, 2015

4   Background page, United Nations Millennium Development Goals website. Retrieved
    21 April, 2015

5   GAPMIL's statement on the occasion of the International Women's Day, March 8,
    2015 http://www.africmil.org/gapmils-statement-on-the-occasion-of-the-internation-
    al-womens-day-march-8-2015/ Retrieved 22 April, 2015

6   Ibid

7   Sustainable development goals: https://sustainabledevelopment.un.org/index.
    php?menu=1300 Retrieved 23 April, 2015

8   Ibid

9   Ibid

10 Ibid

Sustainable Development through Teaching and Learning

Explore, Engage, Empower Model:

Integrating Media and Information Literacy (MIL) for Sustainable Development in Communication Education Curriculum

Jose Reuben Q. Alagaran II

With the ushering in of the Post-2015 Development Agenda, there is a need to review existing curricula to make them more responsive to sustainable development goals. As future media practitioners, students need to access, understand, use and share needed information to promote sustainable development. How then should media and information literacy (MIL) in communication curriculum be taught so that it reflects the ideals of the Post-2015 Development Agenda of the United Nations? This conceptual article attempts to provide some new perspectives on integrating media and information literacy in the communication curriculum through a new model – the Explore, Engage, Empower Model.

Keywords: Triple E's of MIL, curriculum, sustainable development

Introduction

Curriculum development has always been challenged with the emergence of new ideas and perspectives on how to best train students. These new perspectives are not only brought about by the developments in information and communication technologies, but also changes in the content and pedagogy of subject courses. The Bachelor of Arts in Communication curricular program is no exception, especially in the formation of future media practitioners who are expected to be the game-changers in the promotion of free, independent, and pluralistic media.

With the ushering in of the Post-2015 Development Agenda, there is a need to review existing curricula to make them more responsive to sustainable development goals. As future media practitioners, students need to access, understand, use and share needed information to promote sustainable development. How then should media and information literacy (MIL) in communication curriculum be taught so that it reflects the ideals of the Post-2015 Development Agenda of the United Nations? This conceptual article attempts to provide some new perspectives on integrating media and information literacy in the communication curriculum through a new model – the Explore, Engage, Empower Model.

The Explore, Engage, Empower Model

Since its inception as a composite concept by UNESCO, media and information literacy has come of age. Apart from the pioneering MIL Curriculum for Teachers (UNESCO, 2011), UNESCO has developed a set of indicators to assess how MIL is developed as part of national policies and programs and a set of competencies to guide lesson development, implementation and assessment in schools. Education, through formal and non-formal means, is instrumental in promoting freedom of expression and access to information as necessary preconditions to achieve the goals of the Post-2015 Development Agenda.

As defined by UNESCO, "Media and information literacy is a set of competencies that empowers citizens to access, retrieve, understand, evaluate and use, create as well as share information and media content in all formats, using various tools, in a critical, ethical, and effective way, in order to participate and engage in personal, professional, and societal activities" (UNESCO, 2013, p. 29).

This definition implies that there is a need for skills progression in MIL for today's students as part of lifelong learning to contribute meaningfully to personal, professional, and societal development. This set of competencies must be reflected in national education policies to guide curriculum development and promote it as a framework in crafting institutional and program outcomes among educational institutions.

The skills progression has been simplified as illustrated in the author's Explore, Engage, and Empower Model, or the "Triple E's of MIL Model" for easy recall.

Figure 1. Explore, Engage, and Empower Model of media and information literacy (MIL)

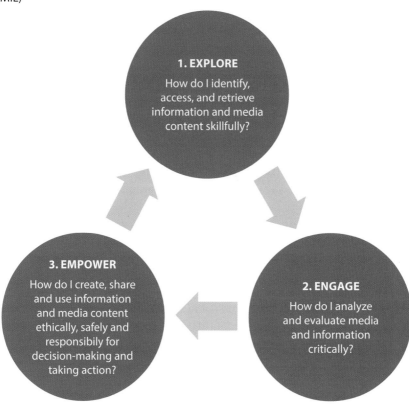

The media and information literacy competencies can be grouped into three major practical applications: explore, engage, and empower.

1. To *explore* is to identify, access, and retrieve information and media content skilfully;

2. To *engage* is to analyze and evaluate media and information critically; and

3. To *empower* is to create or produce, share or communicate, and use information and media content ethically, safely, and responsibly for decision-making and taking action.

The **Explore, Engage and Empower Model** (The Triple E's of MIL) provides a general process framework for understanding and practicing media and information literacy. When teachers and students **explore** media and information, they search or find out how they can locate, access, and retrieve information and media content using different tools and techniques. This requires functional skills in the use of technologies. Likewise, teachers and students need to recognize and identify a need for information to make sure that this is going to be useful and relevant for them and for their audience before they search for it.

When teachers and students **engage** with media, they critically analyze and evaluate media and information content in terms of media language through codes and conventions, and representations of gender, ethnicity, race, sexuality or religion. They need to evaluate the credibility, accuracy, and reliability of media information and content by checking its authorship, purpose, and the techniques used to entice audiences. Finally, they **empower** themselves when they create, share, and use information and media content wisely, ethically, safely, and responsibly to improve their personal, professional, and social lives. They produce media materials and messages for different media platforms within the bounds of legal and moral orders to aid decision-making for most of life's concerns (Alagaran, 2015). This model encapsulates all the relevant competencies that students in the digital age must be able to acquire in a more concise and straightforward fashion. Likewise, this highlights empowerment as the ultimate level of practicing MIL skilfully and applying it in our everyday lives, especially in the exercise of our universal rights and fundamental freedoms.

How then do we integrate this model of MIL skills progression in the development of communication curriculum? How will this contribute to the achievement of the goals of Post-2015 Development Agenda?

Integrating MIL in the Curriculum to Promote Sustainable Development Goals

MIL can be both a content area and a process in the communication curriculum. It can be a topic for discussion in subjects like communication issues, communication and society, and communication research. It can also be a process through activities introduced in media production and management courses.

As a content area, MIL can be discussed as a concept and discussions may focus on why it is relevant. On the other hand, MIL as a process enables students to explore websites, libraries, archives, popular media and other information providers, analyze and evaluate media and information content, and produce and share communication materials, campaigns, plans, and strategies.

Specifically, MIL may promote sustainable development goals through awareness and understanding of development issues such as education, governance and human rights, poverty, climate and energy, health, women empowerment, water and sanitation, food and agriculture, peace and stability, and infrastructure and technology. These issues can be addressed as part of class activities that encourage students to explore traditional and new media, engage with media and information, and empower themselves through the creation and sharing of media messages and information products.

The succeeding matrix provides some class activities which may guide communication educators and students in the use of MIL to promote sustainable development goals. The communication course subjects are clustered into four major groups: theory (including fundamentals); research; production; and management (including media laws and ethics).

MIL Skills	Communication Courses			
	Theory (Including Fundamentals)	Research	Production	Management (Including Laws and Ethics)
Explore (access and retrieve)	Discuss Post-2015 Development Agenda in introductory courses and the role of communication in promoting it as part of national development. Access the different genres or traditions of communication models and theories through different search engines and share to class the experience. Then search sites for lecture videos and other multimedia materials on development issues and programs and create web folders.	Access studies based on positivist, interpretive, cultural and critical communication research traditions. Discuss why these research studies are important in the development of national development policies for education, ICT, governance, business, and civil societies, among others.	Search for Youtube videos on development issues. Check which organizations produced these videos and find out what other materials are available in the library, through archives, or other sources on these issues. Share with class what you have discovered in terms of sources on these issues and how they can be accessed.	Interview media managers about access to information as it applies to development stories. Find out if they are having an easy or difficult task in accessing this information and how they manage such situations. Ask them about their experiences in accessing government data and other information. Write an interview story and submit this as an article for publication.

MIL Skills	Communication Courses			
	Theory (Including Fundamentals)	**Research**	**Production**	**Management** (Including Laws and Ethics)
Engage (analysis and evaluate)	Discuss the communication dimensions of these development programs. Find out whether there are information, education, and communication (IEC) campaign materials produced. Relate them with the communication models and theories retrieved and discuss how the development issue and program is framed and communicated based on existing communication theories.	Analyze print and audio-visual campaigns, news stories and online materials about development issues based on media analysis questions. Find out how the development issues are presented in terms of codes and conventions and media representations. The findings will form part of a broader study on deconstructing development issues.	Assess these materials in terms of authenticity and reliability of information. Determine the sources of information used, how the issues are presented in the videos and the purpose on why they have been produced for a particular audience. Evaluate both content and technical aspects of these videos from a human rights lens.	Based on the interviews, evaluate stories based on the experiences and practices of a media person and a government representative about access to information. Check what are considered public and private documents and reflect how the nature of the documents will affect a media person's desire to report the truth in line with freedom of expression.
Empower (create, use, and share)	Produce another set of materials on the same development issue or program. Compare the existing with the proposed and revised communication materials. Use and share these materials with colleagues through social media. Get feedback from friends and colleagues of other cultures and review topics that they consistently talk about and why.	Use the results of this study to develop action plans on communicating sustainable development programs. Write an article on what you have found out and post this on Facebook or send this to media organizations.	Attempt to produce these materials in another platform or medium. Reflect on what you have discovered about understanding the medium as a source of media messages and information content. Invite your classmates to express their views on the issue and how a change in platform affects the presentation of the development issue.	If you found out that media managers are denied access to certain records, check the existing laws on access to information and freedom of expression. Then reflect on how such laws or the lack of them influences decision-making in the monitoring and implementation of development programs.

Implications to GAPMIL Learning and Development Activities

The Global Alliance for Partnerships on Media and Information Literacy (GAPMIL) must regularly meet to discuss areas for partnerships in learning and development, specifically formal and non-formal education activities. MIL experts in different regions and countries must work together to address specific development agenda that should be covered in international conferences or workshops on MIL to be organized in the regions. Even diploma, college or graduate programs must include discussions on MIL as it relates to sustainable development. This is important as every region has specific development concerns to be prioritized especially on issues related to human rights, governance, climate change, poverty, health, among others.

References

Alagaran II, J. R. (2015). *Discovering Media and Information Literacy*, Draft Lesson for Media and Information Literacy Class, Quezon City: Miriam College

Global Alliance for Partnerships on Media and Information Literacy (GAPMIL) Framework and Plan of Action, (2013). Paris: UNESCO

UNESCO (2013). Global Media and Information Literacy Assessment Framework: Country Readiness and Competencies, Paris: UNESCO

UNESCO (2011). Media and Information Literacy Curriculum for Teachers, Paris: UNESCO

The MILID Dividend: A Conceptual Framework for MILID in the Glocal Society

Thomas Röhlinger

This article suggests a structure model for MILID itself: its components and their inter-relations and dynamics. It is very interdisciplinary, as A. Grizzle (UNESCO) suggested in the 2014 Yearbook edition. The concept discussed links MILID to a wide range of social systems that are essential both for the success of MILID and for the success of the post-2015 agenda. It enriches MILID with sociological insights, namely from the following theorists: N. Luhmann (system theory), N. Chomsky (propaganda, political economy of mass media), J. Galtung (theory of imperialism), J. Servaes (Communication for Sustainable Social Change) and combines it with several other theoretical elements, e.g. from peace education and environmental studies. An approach called "MILID Dividend" is introduced; and further-more a contextual environment called "MILID+" that may be helpful to observe and explain the failures and successes of MILID. This structure may be used as an element of a larger system to detect, prove, develop and sustain the positive impacts and potentials of MILID for local and global society in a scientific way. Some practical implications of the model are also outlined, as well as some strategic and political recommendations for MILID in the post-2015 era.

Keywords: MILID+, children's media, civil society, social change, MILID dividend, MILID strategy

General Set Model: MIL, MILID and MILID+

The interrelations between MILID and its components are neither fully clear nor consensual: Is MIL a part of MILID or the other way around? Also: What about the context? I suggest the following simple model, based on mathematics set theory:

Figure 1. General set model: MIL, MILID and MILID+

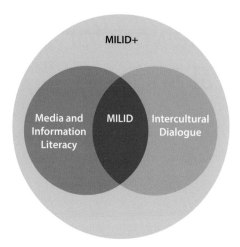

A) The sphere of MIL (Media and Information Literacy)

B) The sphere of ID (Intercultural Dialogue)

C) The common intersection that is called MILID (Media and Information Literacy AND Intercultural Dialogue)

D) The dynamic common global environment that is surrounding A, B and C. This environment shall be called MILID+. The "+" sign is a symbol for two aspects:

- MILID in interrelations with its glocal (global + local) context
- MILID creating a positive glocal dividend; a "plus"

The MILID+ Dividend Process Model

Figure 2. The MILID dividend process model

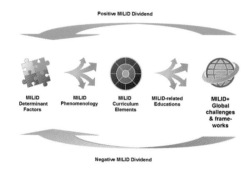

Primacy of Global Challenges: Contextualization of MIL/MILID

Before one can focus on MIL and MILID itself, one should consider MILID+, the global context of the issue. In this context, one can see global challenges (war, poverty, climate change), but also global chances: e.g. the frameworks of international agreements. This is necessary to understand the mission, methodological tools and dynamics of MILID. Among these frameworks are the common ground built by the UN Millennium Development Goals/Sustainable Development Goals (SDGs) But this context also includes more central documents like:

• Universal Declaration of Human rights

• UN Declarations of the Rights of the Child

• UN Decade "Learning for Sustainable Development" and follow-ups

• UNESCO Declaration Cultural Diversity

• UN Decade of Biodiversity

In all those fields, leading organizations report significant deficits concerning awareness and implementation: millions of children out of school (UNESCO)[1], dramatic global loss of languages and hence cultural diversity (e.g. UNESCO World Report 2009, p. 69), climate change and loss of biodiversity (WWF)[2], violations of human rights (Human Rights Watch)[3] and children's rights (UNICEF)[4] in dozens of states worldwide. This is why a "primacy of the global challenges" is proposed.

The Determinant Factors

Both MIL and international dialogue separately and combined as MILID are influenced, if not determined by other spheres of reality.

   All these systems have their own system logics, processes and genetic codes that may not be congruent with those of MIL and MILID systems. They may support MILID, disturb it, change it or be irrelevant, depending on a complex set of circumstances.

   Among these influential spheres are: history, anthropology, biology, psychology, technology, science, physics, geography, setting (venue), demography, economy, semiotics, politics, culture and ecology.

MILID Phenomenology

Media content, media organizations, media processes etc. take certain forms. Our model allows us to see these forms, the MILID phenomenology, in a broad context. The phenomenology of media (for example: children's media) consists of elements like the following: goals of communication (information, propaganda, dialogue), participants (e.g. members of formal/informal education, media, parents, peers); codes, modes (sound, visuals, music, text); target groups, journalistic forms, time and timing, locations of production, dissemination, reception, use; degree of citizen participation (e.g. children).

The question of ownership (private/public/civil-society/community-owned) of the media facilities, content and distribution channels is an especially important aspect. For instance, the main and primary purpose of commercial TV by definition is producing *privately owned profit for the owners*; whereas the main and legal purpose of MILID-related NGO's is production of *social* capital for the community, e.g. by empowering children. This leads to fundamental differences concerning content, children's participation etc; according to respective criticism of Gaschke (2011) in the field of children and Herman & Chomsky (1988) (political economy of mass media).

Towards a MILID Strategy Framework and Model Curriculum

One can begin a discussion about the MILID framework by starting with the Global Alliance for Partnerships in Media and Information Literacy (GAPMIL) and more specifically with The UNESCO Media and Information Literacy Curriculum for Teachers and the ecology of different literacies (UNESCO, 2011, p.19): information literacy, media literacy, advertising literacy etc. These remain as important elements, but the focus expands to bring in several other elements, such as ecological literacy.

In the next step, MIL is combined with intercultural dialogue, expressed in the term MILID. There are several definitions of intercultural dialogue, e.g. the European Institute for Comparative Cultural Research defines it as "process that comprises an open and respectful exchange or interaction between individuals, groups and organisations with different cultural backgrounds or world views".[5]

However, the defining process is still ongoing[6].

In the context of MILID with its connotation of "intercultural" and hence "cultural", I propose to define media and information in a broader sense than in the MIL context:

- Media, in MILID context is everything that carries or has the potential to carry information. This includes e.g. all art forms in history; the human body as media (Faulstich, 1997) and the natural environment, "ecological literacy"[7] or "nature literacy" (Pyle, 2002, p. 312).

- Information is every "difference that makes a difference" (Bateson, 1981, p. 582). For instance, children have very different understanding of what is news than adults.

- Literacy of intercultural information is of central relevance.

Hence, I propose to extend the MIL curriculum towards a an even more holistic MILID strategy framework and a respective model curriculum; e.g. enriched with elements of ecological literacy for urban children and youth suffering from so-called "nature illiteracy" and even "nature deficit disorder"[8] to give them a deeper understanding of the interrelations between cultural and natural processes[9], environment and peace etc.

MILID in the Context of Related Educations

With this step, the gap between the global challenges mentioned above and the capacities of MILID can be closed. The missing links are numerous sub-disciplines of education that are related to one or more of the global challenges: the MILID-related educations (see Figure 2) of peace, environment, sustainable development, children's and human rights, global citizenship, languages, empathy/emotional intelligence etc.

All of them have their roots in different sciences, e.g. peace and environmental studies, (inter)cultural and political sciences, economics, psychology, medicine. This makes clear that MILID can only be successful if it is truly interdisciplinary and not reduced to social media, news journalism or coding.

Also, it shall be clear that these specific educations need significant amounts of quality time, organizational resources and financial resources in order to be successful.

This may lead to conflicts inside the MILID community e.g. with approaches emphasizing technical digital media skills. From our global practical experience, I want to state that digital media technical skills alone can turn into weapons when not trained on the solid foundations of intense education in the spirit of peace, empathy and intercultural dialogue.

MILID has to balance these conflicts. It has to blend a perspective to what is needed on a local level with what is most functional to manage the aforementioned global challenges.

Positive and Negative MILID-Related Communications and their Impacts on MILID+

In the perspective of the international frameworks of SDGs, children's rights etc., the model outlined in Figure 2 allows one to differentiate between "positive" or "constructive" and negative and even "pathological" communication.

"Positive" MILID-related communications shall be defined here as functional for the global challenges mentioned above; effectively contributing to the production of social capital by contributing to sustainable social change, defending good practice or preventing harm to already made achievements towards the mentioned global challenges.

"Negative" MILID-related communications would be the opposite.

Moreover, one can link these communications to determinant factors and the media phenomenology above, in order to find explanations for dysfunctional and even "pathological" communications and to find options for change.

One can also identify a "neutral" zone, e.g. media based small talk without significant social impact.

The MILID Spiral and the MILID Dividend

These communications – constructive, negative or neutral – feed back to society; they create a certain impact on the social, educational, political, and ecological subsystems. This impact is where communication is influencing/changing (a part of) reality.

Project cycle management tools are useful here: in our case, the project is to apply MILID in order to change the social reality in line with the global challenges above. The impact of the project can be observed and measured as the difference between the state of reality before and after the MILID intervention: for example, the level of violence in a region, number of school drop-out children etc.

And this impact, in turn, is changing the determinant factors for future communications and actions. This is where the MILID process cycle closes. In best case, one could even speak about a MILID spiral: one does not see a circular repetition but an even larger round on each new level. MILID begins to pay for itself. Thus, our MILID spiral is creating a sustainable added value to society that could be called MILID dividend.

The MILID Balance Sheet

To be more specific, several dividends in social sub-systems like education, environment, peace building, and diversity have been observed. All these dividends contribute to the MILID balance sheet. Here are the economical dimensions of this approach, beginning with the potential positive side: The dividend from ending violence alone could reach trillions (sic!) of dollars worldwide, according to the comprehensive study *Economic Costs of Violence Containment* by the Institute for Economics and Peace (2014) [10].

But the implementation and use of MILID and its elements of media, intercultural dialogue etc. are critical conditions to end violence and reach peace. Other significant dividends could be realized e.g. in environment, diversity and education – but again, only in connection with proper and intense use of MILID. These positive dividends could also function as power stations for sustainable job creation.

These are central arguments for MILID in the political prioritization and global agenda setting. The global MILID community should use them in strategic and coordinated form.

Of course, one may also observe downward spirals, e.g. in regions of armed conflicts, in areas with destroyed environments or in so-called failing states. Here, the MILID dividend observed would be on the negative side of the balance sheet; representing a loss of social capital.

One can measure damage done by natural disasters. But to the authors' knowledge, there exists no standardized model to measure the damage done through misuse of MILID tools yet; nor does one know exact methods to translate this into economical facts and financial numbers communicable to the political system. It is recommended that work be done on these scientific deficits. One methodological proposal to start with is transferred from peace studies:

One can at least estimate the budgets for dysfunctional and damaging communications and compare them with the budgets that are needed to compensate these damages with functional communication. One can hence calculate the accumulated financial budgets invested for:

- nationalist, militaristic or authoritarian propaganda

- propaganda of uncivil society, e.g. extremist political or extremist religious groups, criminal organizations

- advertisements with the potential to cause damage in populations, e.g. children's health problems (von Feilitzen & Stenersen, 2014).

As a result, one can see the large financial dimensions of these multiple problems and compare them with the scarce resources on the positive side of the MILID balance sheet.

These imbalances can also be expressed in numbers of active workforce in respective operations or in numbers of audience reach on both sides of the balance sheet.

In the past, one was not able to argue for change on the basis of hard economic facts. But a MILID balance sheet with such figures, examined on scientific basis, can help to clearly define and demand the financial budgets and other resources needed to combat, avoid or re-balance the negative input with positive educational work and content, on both a local and global level.

The Complete MILID+ Model

As the last step, the proposed model has to be seen as dynamically changing in the dimensions of space and time: A functional MILID strategy in one region at a certain time can turn into an epic failure in other regions or times. This means there is the need for a cautious and culture sensitive introduction of digital media in remote areas.

Now, all elements of the MILID+ model are presented, showing that MIL and MILID can only be understood, applied and improved in their full context. One can see the complex structures related to MILID and the vast variety of sciences that have to be involved. It also becomes clear that this is a dialectic process: improving MILID+ practices improves reality; and better circumstances in reality are the basis for improved MILID+ practice.

Conclusions

The Primacy of MILID

MILID+ is of great relevance for the global society and its children. But it needs scarce resources of time, personal, finance and technology. This is a matter of setting political priorities accordingly – on a local, national and global level. This may be referred to as the primacy of MILID.

The Primary Serving Function of MILID Towards Global Agreements

The primacy of MILID represents an important privilege – but in turn, MILID's global character also creates a high responsibility for MILID: to focus on serving the fulfillment of the mentioned central global agreements. This may be referred to as the "primary global serving function of MILID".

MILID-Based Inversion of the Burden of Proof

Chomsky and Hermans "political economy of mass media" approach, critizised propaganda of governments and profit-driven influence of corporates in the public/mediated sphere (Chomsky & Herman 1988, pp. 1-35) With this reference, one may draw the inverse conclusion, again with the example of children:

Media related offerings to children that violate global agreements concerning SDGs, peace etc. are likely to directly or indirectly reduce the positive social impact of MILID. It is hence necessary to scientifically examine the legal, ethical and educational legitimation to target children. Respective producers and owners should be made legally and financially accountable and should not be licensed if they violate agreements. This follows Gaschke's call to "inverse the burden of proof" towards the media producers and owners targeting children (Gaschke 2011, p. 247).

Like Gaschke and much earlier Chomsky and Herman (1988, p. 307), one may demand more support for public and civil society media to enable the MILID-related activities globally needed.

MILID+ as Corner Stone of Global *Res Publica*

In summary:

- MIL gives us a common global alphabet, to "read each other".

- MILID gives us a common language, to "understand each other".

- MILID+ helps us to "help each other". It seems to be an emerging glocal cultural technique that gives us the holistic perspective and the practical tools for sustainable glocal change, using the power of media and intercultural collaboration. MILID+ can hence be seen as a corner stone of emerging global *res publica*. MILID+ achievements shall be treated and saved as global common goods.

Researchers and practitioners are invited to apply and develop MILID+ as a living document.

References

Bateson, G. (1981). *Ökologie des Geistes. Anthropologische, psychologische, biologische und epistemologische Perspektiven*. Frankfurt a.M.: Suhrkamp.

Feilitzen, C. v. & Stenersen, J. (2014). *Young People, Media and Health: Risks and Rights. Yearbook 2014.* The International Clearinghouse on Children, Youth and Media, Gothenburg: Nordicom.

Faulstich, W. (1997). *Das Medium als Kult*. Göttingen: Vandenhoeck & Ruprecht

Gaschke, S. (2011). *Die verkaufte Kindheit: Wie Kinderwünsche vermarktet werden und was Eltern dagegen tun können*. Bonn: Bundeszentrale für politische Bildung

Galtung, J. (1971). A Structural Theory of Imperialism. *Journal of Peace Research* 8(2), pp. 81-117. Thousand Oaks, CL: Sage Publications, Ltd.

Herman, E.S. & Chomsky, N. (1988). *Manufacturing Consent*. The political economy of the mass media. New York: Pantheon.

Pyle, R.M.: Eden in a Vacant Lot. In: Kahn, P.H.; Kellert, Stephen R. (2002). *Children and Nature: Psychological, Sociocultural, and Evolutionary Investigations*. p. 305-325. Cambridge, MA: M.I.T. Press.

Institute for Economics and Peace (2014). The Economic Cost of Violence Containment. Retrieved from: http://www.visionofhumanity.org/sites/default/files/The%20Economic%20Cost%20of%20Violence%20Containment.pdf

Luhmann, N. (1996). *Die Realität der Massenmedien*. Wiesbaden: VS Verlag für Sozialwissenschaften.

Mayer, C.-H. (2008). *Trainingshandbuch Interkulturelle Mediation und Konfliktlösung*. Münster: Waxmann.

Servaes, J. (2008). *Communication for Development and Social Change*. Thousand Oaks, CL: Sage Publications Ltd.

Wilson, C.; Grizzle, A.; Tuazon, R.; Akyempong, K.; Cheung, C. K. (2011). *The UNESCO Media and Information Literacy Curriculum for Teachers*. Paris: UNESCO.

Notes

1. http://www.uis.unesco.org/Education/Pages/oosc-2014-progress-stalled-on-reaching-upe.aspx
2. http://www.wwf.de/living-planet-report/
3. http://www.hrw.org/world-report/2014
4. http://www.unicef.org/sowc2014/numbers/
5. http://www.interculturaldialogue.eu/web/intercultural-dialogue.php
6. See e.g. open source project Open Lines http://openlines.labforculture.org/display.php
7. http://en.wikipedia.org/wiki/Ecological_literacy
8. See e.g. http://www.education.com/topic/nature-deficit-disorder/
9. See e.g. UNEP http://www.unep.org/civil-society/Portals/24105/documents/publications/Cultural_Diversity_and_Biodiversity_part%201.pdf
10. http://www.visionofhumanity.org/sites/default/files/The%20Economic%20Cost%20of%20Violence%20Containment.pdf

From Information Skills for Learning to Media and Information Literacy

A Decade of Transition in South Asia: 2004-2014

Jagtar Singh

This article presents in brief the developments in the field of information research skills in South Asia from 2004 to 2014. Besides, describing the "Empowering 8 Problem Solving Model" and the "HIL Model", the article reports on the International Federation of Library Associations and Institutions (IFLA) and UNESCO supported workshops held in Sri Lanka, India and Bangladesh in 2004, 2005, 2008, 2011 and 2012 along with an International Media and Information Literacy Survey (IMILS) undertaken to generate baseline data on information seeking behaviour of graduate students. The article also highlights the formation of the Media and Information Literacy University Network of India (MILUNI) and outcomes of the UNESCO funded MIL National Consultation held at India International Centre (IIC), New Delhi from November 11th-13th, 2014. Besides, it also reports the progress of the MIL Curriculum under the e-PG Pathshala Project of the Government of India.

Keywords: paradigm shift, information skills for learning, media and information literacy, Empowering 8 Problem Solving Model, HIL Model, e-PG Pathshala

Introduction

With the convergence of computer and communication technologies and ascent of the Internet, the traditional constraints of space and time stand collapsed and information is available to information seekers 24X7 provided they are able to pay for it and competent to access the needed information critically and ethically. In fact, with so much unfiltered information in the public domain available via the Internet, the end user is completely bewildered and unable to determine the quality of publically available information. This I have realised during my interaction with my students during recent past. Library and information professionals (LIPs) and faculty members are working on various interventions to empower information seekers with information research skills. Media and information literacy is one such intervention being promoted by the NGOs, such as UNESCO, IFLA (International Federation of Library Associations and Institutions) and other associations and educational institutions. This article reports India's leadership role in promoting media and information literacy in South Asia and also developing collaboration and partnership with international bodies such as UNESCO and IFLA. The transition story in South Asia began with an IFLA/ALP (Action for Development through Libraries Programme) Sponsored Regional Workshop on 'Information Skills for Learning' hosted by the National Institute of Library and Information Sciences (NILIS), University of Colombo at Galadari Hotel betweenNovember 1ˢᵗ-5ᵗʰ, 2004. The 'Empowering 8 Problem Solving Model' was developed in this workshop to meet the information seeking requirements of students in Asia and the Pacific.

Paradigm Shift

Information and communication technology (ICT) has made a profound impact on all types of libraries. Today the elite are immensely benefited by the power of digital and virtual libraries. At the same time we are very much worried about the future of non-elite libraries and the info-poor. The future of these libraries is dependent both on external and internal changes. The ICT is providing the LIPs with both opportunities and challenges. In fact, there is a paradigm shift from standalone libraries to library and information networks; from printed publications to digital documents; and from ownership to access. This transition is the result of the impact of ICTs, the Internet and the World Wide Web on different types of libraries. If we look around, many educational, social, economic, cultural, political, and technological changes are taking place. In the context of libraries and information centres (LICs), economic and technological changes have made a profound impact. Economically speaking, LICs are faced with a diametrically opposite situation with growing electronic resources and services on the one hand, and declining library budgets and library use on the other. There is a tremendous pressure on the LIPs to justify the need for their existence in view of the fact that the library users are moving away from the libraries. It is high time to ascertain why this is happening and what is the way out to bring the users back to the fold of libraries. Perhaps we have failed to come up to the expectations of the end users. It is high time to sensitize information seekers about the value of library resources and services in achieving their educational, professionals, social and personal goals. In order to develop critical thinking and independent learning among them, they must be equipped with media and information literacy skills.

Gaps and Divides

In today's world, we are surrounded by many gaps and divides. There is gap between the tacit knowledge and the explicit knowledge, between theory and practice, between the competent and the incompetent. Similarly, there are many divides, such as the divide between the rich and the poor, the rural and the urban residents, the male and the female, the elite and non-elite. All these gaps are potential perils for the sustainable development of nations worldwide. But the capacity gap is the biggest gap. In the information economy, it can be bridged only by equipping the stakeholders with media and information literacy skills. The art of accessing information has seen many vicissitudes. In the library users' context, it started with library orientation and moved to media and information literacy through library instruction, bibliographic instruction, user education and information literacy. After the adoption of Fez Declaration, UNESCO is promoting MIL as a composite concept and LIPs are also falling in line with the thinking of UNESCO. An effort has been made in this article to report this transition which started with the Colombo workshop in 2004 and culminated in the formulation of Media and Information Literacy University Network in India (MILUNI).

Transition Overview

The developments in the field of information research skills from 2004 to 2014 in South Asia are presented briefly in this paragraph. The biggest achievement in the field was creation of the "Empowering 8 Problem Solving Model" at an 'IFLA Sponsored International Workshop on Information Skills for Learning' hosted by the National Institute of Library and Information Sciences (NILIS), University of Colombo, Sri Lanka at Galadari Hotel in 2004. Dr. Pradeepa Wijetunge has also prepared information literacy modules for graduate programmes in Sri Lanka (Wijetunge & Manatinge, 2014; Boeriswati, 2012).

The name "Empowering 8 Problem Solving Model" was suggested by the author of this article and was unanimously approved by all the workshop participants. Lot of money has been spent on developing this model, but unfortunately because of lack of proper marketing, this model has not gained ground in the Asia and the Pacific region. Dr. Pradeepa Wijetunge has developed information literacy modules but now these need to be expanded to include the media component as well. Besides India, Sri Lanka and China, this model has not been widely adopted even in South Asia. Something needs to be done by IFLA to promote its use as it has spent a lot of money on it.

Empowering 8 Problem Solving Model

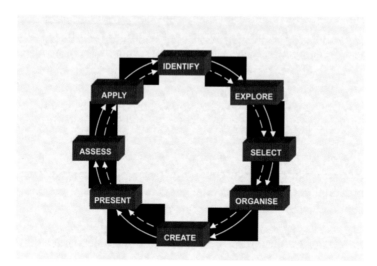

Source: Wijetunge & Manatinge, (2014)

The 'Empowering 8 Problem Solving Model' is developed to support problem-based learning, project-based learning, and resource-based student-centred learning. The starting point in this model is to 'identify' the information problem and then move through the cycle to the eighth stage, i.e. to 'apply'. The two arrows in this model represent a librarian and a teacher, respectively. It means, both a librarian and a teacher have a critical role to play in solving a student's problem with this model. In fact, media and information literacy is required to focus not only on media and bits of information, rather it should teach the art of fishing from troubled waters or finding a needle from the haystack. In the Internet era, there is lot of information pollution in the public domain. Therefore, the haystack of recorded knowledge is growing and the needle of pertinent information is moving away from the information seekers. Only media and information literacy can empower the stakeholders with necessary competencies to evaluate information and separate the gold of pertinent information from the rusted iron of useless information. In the Internet era, we need to develop information seekers as experts in information seeking like a hunter who can shoot a moving target.

In 2005, the second phase of 'UNESCO/IFLA Sponsored Regional Workshop on Information Skills for Learning' was held at Punjabi University, Patiala. The workshop participants were exhorted by His Excellency General (Retd.) S. F. Rodrigues, Governor of Punjab and Chancellor, Punjabi University, Patiala to resolve the contradiction between the social purpose of empowering the masses with information skills and elitist approach of holding conferences, seminars, and workshops in air conditioned rooms. He advised them to reach out the information poor people across the globe and do something concrete to equip them with information skills and other job-related necessary competencies (Information Skills, 2005). Again in 2008, Punjabi University, Patiala hosted a 'UNESCO Sponsored Train-the-Trainers (TTT) in Information Literacy Regional Workshop'. Valuable recommendations of this workshop were highly appreciated by UNESCO and used in its prestigious publication entitled *Understanding Information Literacy: A Primer* by F. W. Horton, Jr. (Train-the-Trainers, 2008). A special issue of Defence Scientific Information and Documentation Centre (DESIDOC) *Journal of Information Technology* (DJLIT) on "Information Literacy" was edited by Prof. C. R. Karisiddappa and published by the DESIDOC (Jagtar, 2008). Research findings of a study on students' awareness of health information initiatives by the governments of India and Bangladesh were presented in Gothenburg, Sweden (Jagtar & Begum, 2010). Besides, an IFLA Sponsored Regional Workshop was organized in three phases during this period by East West University, Dhaka, and Jagtar Singh served as lead resource person for this workshop (Train-the-Trainers, 2011; Health Information, 2012). Again in 2012, under the leadership of Jagtar Singh, an International Media and Information Literacy Survey (IMILS) was undertaken to generate baseline data on information seeking behaviour of graduate students. About twenty countries of Asia and the Pacific participated in this survey. This project was funded by UNESCO. The findings of this survey were published in the UNESCO MILID Yearbook 2013 (Jagtar & Horton, Jr., 2013).

At Punjabi University, Patiala and Kurukshetra University, Kurukshetra, PhDs were awarded on: Information Literacy; Resource-based Student-centred learning, and Health Information Literacy (Begum, 2014; Bhupinder, 2014; Navkiran, 2014). University of Delhi Library has also started an informal information literacy training programme. Similarly, Indira Gandhi National Open University (IGNOU), New Delhi has also developed an appreciation course in information literacy to be started from the year 2016.

Leadership and Collaboration

There is great difference between a leader and a manager, as well as competence and competencies. A leader facilitates change but a manager maintains the status quo. Similarly, competence means complete mastery and competencies means a set of skills. These can be hard as well as soft skills. Competence comes with experience. However, before that we must have commonsense and formal education. Then the LIPs must internalize strategic professional learning as a lifelong learning process. LIPs must be equipped with cultural literacy and information skills for learning to create the ripple effect among the faculty and students. Similarly, a sense of responsibility and accountability along with team spirit, motiva-

tion, and interpersonal skills should also become a part of their mind, body, and soul. Only that way, the LIPs can make sense of the web-based chaos.
Here one is reminded of the following lines:

> *Where is the wisdom?*
> *We have lost in knowledge.*
> *Where is the knowledge?*
> *We have lost in information.*

The Rock (T. S. Eliot)

HIL Model

Source: Navkiran, (2014)

HIL in this model stands for 'Health Information Literacy'. This model, developed by the author of this article, has eight stages. A naïve information seeker will have to start from the stage one, i.e. 'defining information need' and move up to the eighth stage, i.e. 'using the information ethically and legally'. An expert information seeker may start from any stage in this eight stages' cycle. In this model, teachers, doctors and librarians have a pivotal role as facilitators in assisting the information seeker to get quality information on time. This model has been designed both for the information seekers and the intermediaries.

In fact, hallmark of media and information literacy is to develop critical thinking and independent learning among the stakeholders for obtaining their personal, professional, education and social goals. In this context, both the 'Empowering 8 Problem Solving Model' and the 'HIL Model' have a significant role to play. But for that both the models need be publicized widely across globe.

In 2014, Media and Information Literacy University Network for India (MILUNI) was formed and a Media and Information Literacy-National Consultation (MIL-NC) (funded by UNESCO) was held at India International Centre (IIC), New Delhi with the following objectives:

1. To advise Government of India on MIL policy and strategy

2. To develop a MIL competency framework

3. To develop MIL curriculum as per national aspirations
   (UNESCO-led Indian, 2014)

The tangible outcomes of the MIL-NC are given below:

The draft 'Policy and Strategy Paper' has been prepared and sent to UNESCO for comments. Institute of Mass Communication (IIMC), New Delhi has taken the responsibility to develop the 'MIL Competency Framework.' Modules for the 'MIL Curriculum as per National Aspirations' have been finalized and now the content is being created under the Ministry of Human Resource Development (MHRD), Government of India's (GOI) e-PG Pathshala Project (e-PG Pathshala, 2015). The course contents are given below:

Paper Name: Media and Information Literacy

Table 1: List of modules

S.No.	Module Name
I	**Fundamentals of Media and Information Literacy**
1	Media and information definition, need and purpose, role of MIL in the society
2	Theories and models for media and information literacy
3	MIL policies and strategies
II	**Media and Information Literacy Indicators**
4	Media literacy indicators and information literacy indicators
5	IL standards
6	ML standards
III	**Media and Information Ethics and Laws**
7	Media ethics
8	Information ethics
9	Right to information and privacy
10	IPR and plagiarism (ICT)

S.No.	Module Name
IV	**Media Convergence: Development and Trends**
11	Technology convergence
12	Content convergence
13	Mobile technologies (tablets, mobiles)
14	Interactive multimedia tools
V	**Data Literacy**
15	Open data, big data, data visualization tools, data analytics, data repository, data protection
VI	**Information Searching and Browsing**
16	Search engines and search strategies
17	Open access information : DOAJ, ROAR, OpenDOAR, DOAB and etc.
18	Subject gateways, portals, and headlines grabbers
VII	**Social Media**
19	Role of social media in the society
20	Social media platforms and tools
VIII	**Research Metrics**
21	Research metrics tools
22	Bibliographical citations
IX	**Evaluation of Information**
23	Criteria for evaluation of documentary information
24	Criteria for evaluation of web resources
25	Media content analysis (film, television, advertisement, ownership pattern, international flow of media of messages)
X	**Information Sources and Library Skills**
26	Types of Information and information resources
XI	**Construction of Media Messages**
27	Media message

Besides, course components have also been prepared by the University of Uttrakhand (UOU) and the Foundation for Responsible Media (FORMEDIA) for basic and extended level training of stakeholders. Two training programmes were conducted by the (UOU), Haldwani in India (Uttrakhand Open, 2015). These are reported by Neelima Mathur in her article in this yearbook. These course components have also been translated in Hindi language. In 2015, Dr. Jagtar Singh has been assigned the work of preparing the MILID Yearbook 2015 as a lead editor along with three other co-editors. South Asian Library Conference is going to be held at Lahore, Pakistan from 12-13 October 2015. In this conference, special attention will be paid to media and information literacy. Effort will be made to involve UNESCO experts and officers through Skype conversation.

Conclusion

The real power of any nation is not its money or natural resources; rather it lies with its human resources. Hence, a nation that puts premium on its human resources is bound to lead other nations. Similarly, the value of knowledge and information lies in use. Education, experience, learning and pro-active attitude, and media and information literacy are the four pillars of progress. If we are really committed to nation building and peaceful co-existence, then there should be no compromise on quality of education and integration of media and information literacy to support lifelong learning and promote the use of knowledge and information in decision-making and problem-solving. Every effort must be made to bridge the widening gap between 'tacit knowledge' and 'explicit knowledge.' In fact, media and information literacy is the best tool for, as well as the lifeline of lifelong learning. To promote MIL across frontiers, we will have to adopt a bottom-up approach. We will have to reach out the info-poor and marginalized sections of society to empower them with the MIL skills. Governments, associations and NGOs have a pivotal role to play. Same is true about other friends of media and information literacy. Let charity begin from home.

References

Begum, D. (2014). Awareness and Application of Information Literacy in Select Private Universities of Bangladesh: A Comparative Study. Unpublished Ph.D. Thesis Punjabi University, Patiala.

Bhupinder Singh (2014). Information Literacy for Resource-Based Student-Centred Learning in India: A Case Study. Unpublished Ph.D. Thesis Punjabi University, Patiala.

Boeriswati, E. (2012). The implementing model of Empowering Eight for information literacy. *US-China Education Review* A 7, 650-661.

e-PG Pathshala (2015). http://epgp.inflibnet.ac.in/about.php

Health Information Literacy (2012). Workshop on Health Information Literacy, 20 July 2012, East West University, Dhaka, Bangladesh. Retrieved from http://lib.ewubd.edu/hil1%282011%29

Information skills for learning: Part II Empowering 8 International Workshop, 3-7 October 2005. Patiala: Punjabi University.

Jagtar Singh (2008). Sense-making: Information Literacy for Lifelong Learning and Knowledge Management. *DESIDOC Journal of Library and Information Technology*, 28(2), March, 13-17.

Jagtar Singh & Begum, D. (2010). Student Awareness of Health Information Initiative of the Governments of India and Bangladesh: A Study of Punjabi University, Patiala and East West University, Dhaka. Articles of the 76th IFLA World Library and Information Congress, 10-15 August 2010, Gothenburg, Sweden. Retrieved from http://conference. ifla.org/past-wlic/2010/100-singh-en.pdf

Jagtar Singh & Horton, Jr., F. W. (2013). Media and information literacy survey: research habits and practices of university students. In Carlsson, U. & Culver, S. H. (Eds) *MILID Yearbook 2013: Media and Information Literacy and Intercultural Dialogue.* Gothenburg: The International Clearinghouse on Children, Youth and Media, pp. 286-291.

Navkiran Kaur (2014). Role of Medical College Libraries in Health Information Literacy in Punjab and Chandigarh: An Analytical Study. Unpublished Ph.D. Thesis Punjabi University, Patiala.

South Asian Library Conference on Journey through Print to Digital Information & Beyond, 12-13 October, 2015, Lahore University of Management Sciences, Lahore. Retrieved from http://www.pla.org.pk/conference-chair.html

Train-the-Trainers (2008). Workshop in Information Literacy for South and Central Asia inaugurated in India. Retrieved from http://portal.unesco.org/ci/en/ev.php-URL_ID=27746&URL_DO=DO_TOPIC&URL_SECTION=201.html

Train- the-Trainers (2011). International Workshop on Health Information Literacy, 27-30 July 2011, East West University, Dhaka, Bangladesh. Retrieved from http://lib.ewubd. edu/iwhil2011

UNESCO-led Indian (2014). National MIL Consultation from November 11-13, 2014. Retrieved from http://uou.ac.in/miluni

Uttarakhand Open University (2015, February 20) organises workshop in association with UNESCO. [video file] Retrieved from https://www.youtube.com/watch?v= Ihu3jjYgTpc

Wijetunge, P. & Kalpana, M. (2014). Empowering 8 in practice: information literacy programme for law undergraduates revisited. *Annals of Library and Information Studies,* 61, March, pp. 24-32.

Media and Information Literacy Education: Fundamentals for Global Teaching and Learning

Carolyn Wilson & Tessa Jolls

New approaches to learning, including "connected learning", have gained currency world-wide as educators have recognized that students learn in the context of a networked, global media culture. In a post-2015 world, media and information literacy (MIL) provides a common denominator through which citizens can connect – an idea anticipated and articulated through the work of pioneers Marshall McLuhan, Len Masterman and Barry Duncan. This foundational work provides a pathway to teach in a systematic way that is consistent, replicable, measurable and scalable on a global basis – and thus, timeless. This article will outline how the work of these pioneers continues to define our understanding of MIL, and provides recommendations for sustainable MIL programs for teachers and students now, and beyond 2015.

Keywords: connected literacy, media and information literacy, Len Masterman, Barry Duncan, Marshall McLuhan, key concepts, media literacy, post-2015 development agenda, Aspen Institute, critical thinking, heuristic learning

The Post-2015 Development Agenda of the United Nation's highlights several goals that are fundamental for equity, inclusion and relevance in education. While the goals could be described by some as ambitious and perhaps even idealistic, they nevertheless remain essential for ensuring a just society as we imagine the educational landscape beyond 2015. The need for education and professional development for teachers, inclusive access to learning technologies and the Internet, and access to knowledge and skills development for all citizens, are just a few of the priorities that have been identified (UNESCO, 2015). While many look to the field of media and information literacy (MIL) to envision ways of implementing these priorities, it is also important that we look to the history of MIL to build upon the foundations in MIL theory and practice that have been proven to be effective. While it may seem counter-intuitive, it can be useful at times, to borrow from communications expert Marshall McLuhan (1969), to look forward "through a rear-view mirror".

MIL and New Approaches to Education

New approaches to education are arising to meet the demands of the post-2015 agenda. With the advent of the Internet and social media, it is now possible to provide education opportunities that offer a radically different approach from the "factory model" of education in closed classrooms that has long prevailed in many parts of the world. "Connected learning" is an approach that calls for education to provide youth with opportunities to engage in socially- supportive learning that is also personally interesting and relevant, while connecting academics to civic engagement and career opportunities. Additionally, core properties of connected learning experiences are described as "production-centered," using digital tools to create a wide variety of media, knowledge and cultural content, with shared purposes for cross-generational and cross-cultural learning geared toward common goals and problem-solving (Aspen Institute, 2014, p. 31). These characteristics are closely aligned with the skills that citizens need and that employers cite as desirable for workplace readiness, such as professionalism/work ethic, oral and written communications, teamwork/collaboration and critical thinking/problem solving (Lotto & Barrington, 2006).

To address these widespread sentiments, as well as the profound changes being called for in the world of education, the Aspen Institute released a comprehensive report called "Learner at the Center of a Networked World" (Aspen Institute, 2014, p. 16). The report identifies five essential principles for creating safe, optimized and rewarding learning experiences for young learners:

- learners need to be at the center of new learning networks that extend outside schools;

- every student should have access to learning networks, insuring that every student has connectivity, and access to hardware, applications, digital- age literacy and high-quality content;

- learning networks need to be inter-operable, so that education resources are not isolated in separate silos and that innovation can be shared;

- learners should have the literacies necessary to utilize media as well as safeguard themselves in the digital age;

- students should have safe and trusted environments for learning, which will protect children's safety and privacy online.

The report calls for a different approach for acquiring content knowledge and competencies – namely, that "*all learners and educators need a sufficient degree of media, digital and social-emotional literacies to learn through multiple media confidently, effectively and safely. Every student must have a chance to learn these vital skills*" (Aspen Institute, 2014, p. 36) [emphasis added].

The relevance of media and information literacy to the post-development agenda is further illustrated by the description of MIL provided by UNESCO (2014): "Media and Information Literacy recognizes the primary role of information and media in our everyday lives. It lies at the core of freedom of expression and information – since it empowers citizens to understand the functions of media and other information providers, to critically evaluate their content, and to make informed decisions as users and producers of information and media content."

However, for media and information literacy to have an impact on education, MIL skills must be valued, articulated and taught in ways that are consistent, replicable, measurable and scalable globally – thus becoming sustainable and timeless (Jolls & Wilson, 2014). Very few of today's teachers grew up themselves learning through a media and information literacy lens, and unless professional development is scaled up and delivered in a way that is accessible for the many rather than the few, the likelihood of transforming teaching and learning is greatly diminished.

Foundations for MIL Education: the Work of McLuhan and Masterman

In many regions, media and information literacy has existed largely outside the education mainstream, and as a result there has been little formal exploration of how to teach it effectively either in graduate schools of education or in school districts. Tomorrow's teachers need the opportunity to learn about media and information literacy theory, to develop pedagogical approaches for exploring new MIL technologies, and to develop critical frameworks that can be used in the analysis and evaluation of media content and information available in today's world. New approaches to learning also demand openly networked, online platforms and digital tools that can make learning resources abundant (Aspen Institute, 2014, p. 31). But technology itself is only one part of the equation. The work of helping teachers develop MIL programs for students in a systematic, consistent and research-validated way is an enormous task, given the relatively young state of the field and the challenges of using media in the classroom. Yet in our efforts to move forward, our work can be informed by the foundations for media and information literacy that have already been established and proven. Because MIL has been rarely institutionalized in education systems, there is often little understanding of the foundation and basic concepts of media and information literacy, including how these concepts evolved, and what their contribution can be in a post-2015 world (Jolls & Wilson, 2014).

In North America and other parts of the world, the underlying foundation for MIL rests on the groundbreaking work of Marshall McLuhan, a Canadian whose work in the 1940s through the 1960s called attention to the profound impact of media and information technologies on our lives, our culture and our future. McLuhan foresaw that technology would shrink the world and expand it at the same time. He predicted how various technologies would eventually merge to create what we now know as the Internet. He used the phrase the "global village" to describe the impact of this merging, including the priority and value that would be placed on the exchange of information and possibilities for intercultural dialogue (McLuhan, 1964). Through his famous phrase "the medium is the message", he articulated his idea that the form through which information is conveyed is as important as the content of the message (1967). According to McLuhan, because each medium has its own technological "grammar" or bias, each inevitably creates and shapes a unique message, even if each is conveying the same information about the same subject. Ultimately, McLuhan saw that technology would come to act as an extension of ourselves, shaping and influencing the way we think, act and relate to one another (1964).

In the U.S. and Canada, the foundations of the MIL discipline continued to be developed through the work of Len Masterman in England and Barry Duncan in Canada, acknowledged by many educators as the founders of media and information literacy as it is known in North America today. This foundation includes the basic principles for media and information literacy introduced by Masterman in 1989 and the ways in which these were taken up by Duncan and his Canadian colleagues in their Key Concepts. The Key Concepts, first introduced in the 1989, remain central to media and information literacy education in Canada today (Wilson & Duncan, 2008). Building on the work of their Canadian colleagues, the American version of the Concepts was introduced in 1993 and continues to underpin the work of educators across the United States (Thoman, 1993). The development of media literacy in both of these countries reinforces the importance of a fundamental paradigm and conceptual framework for media and information literacy education today (Jolls & Wilson, 2014).

But it was when Masterman first published his ground-breaking books, *Teaching About Television* (1980) and *Teaching the Media* (1985), that the basic pedagogy for media and information literacy was first articulated, which enabled these disciplines to be developed further in North America and taught systematically to elementary and secondary students.

According to Masterman, there is a key factor which underpins the discipline of media and information literacy. "The central unifying concept of Media Education is that of representation. The media mediate. They do not reflect but represent the world. The media, that is, are symbolic sign systems that must be decoded. Without this principle, no media education is possible. From it, all else flows" (Masterman 1989).

Masterman anticipated how, in a world where content is infinitely available, it would be essential for educators to provide their students with heuristic approaches to learning. This approach is well suited to the type of teaching and learning needed in an age driven by algorithms, as Masterman observed in a 2010 interview for the *Voices of Media Literacy* project: "…you can teach about the media most effectively, not through a content-centered approach, but through the application of a conceptual framework which can help pupils to make sense of any media text. And that applies every bit as much to the new digitized technologies as it did to the old mass media… The acid test of whether a media course has been successful resides in the students' ability to respond critically to media texts they will encounter in the future [including those they are creating]. Media education is nothing if it is not an education for life" (Masterman, 2010).

As Masterman identified new tenets for media education, he continued his quest to describe – through a process of inquiry – how media operate. While Masterman uses television as his example here, the questions he is posing could just as easily be applied to radio, social media or print:

> …*if we are looking at TV as a representational system, then the questions inevitably arise as to who is creating these representations. Who is doing the representing? Who is telling us that this is the way the world is? That their way of seeing is simply natural? Other questions emerge. What is the nature of the world that is being represented? What are its values and dominant assumptions? What are the techniques that are used to create the 'authenticity' of TV? How are TV's representations read and how are they understood by its audiences? How are we as an audience positioned by the text? What divergent interpretations exist within the class?*

(Masterman, 2010)

Masterman's questioning led him to identify how media operate as symbolic "sign systems", and he articulated ideas about the constructed nature of media, purpose, authorship, media techniques and formats, bias, omissions, power, lifestyles, values and points of view. He developed and applied a systematic framework to address all media in his second book, *Teaching the Media* (Masterman, 1985).

Building on the Foundations: Global Developments in MIL

Masterman's approach and the concepts of media literacy provide a framework necessary for understanding how media operate as a system for representation. As Masterman said, "What existed up until about the 1960's, where it existed at all, was a study of the media that was highly fragmented and split around different established subjects, but with no coherent approach that might justify the notion that this was a subject that was actually worth studying in its own right." Masterman's methodology gives both teachers and students an opportunity to explore, understand, and participate in the global village that McLuhan aptly named, as well as a consistent way to communicate the important ideas that underpin the discipline.

Unfortunately, a lack of teacher education in media and information literacy is endemic and contributes to a diffuse understanding that does not allow for the consistency in program development that can be measured, replicated and adapted to suit local and regional contexts. However, thanks to the steadfast support of global organizations such as UNESCO, media and information literacy continues to gain recognition and legitimacy worldwide and countries around the world have made MIL a priority. In Great Britain, the UK regulatory agency, Ofcom, has conducted research and advocated for media literacy (Ofcom, 2014) and Finland adopted a national strategy for encouraging media literacy (Ministry of Education and Culture, 2013). Ontario, Canada, the first jurisdiction in the world to mandate media literacy curricula, includes media literacy in Language Arts and English curriculum from grades 1 – grade 12 and continues to develop supportive curricular resources (Wilson & Duncan, 2008). The European Union calls for every member country to report annually on media literacy programs and activities (Livingstone & Wang, 2013, p. 166). Australia continues to embed MIL into its education system (Quin, 2011). UNESCO has advanced media and information literacy education throughout the world through several resources and initiatives that provide support for teachers and policy makers (Wilson & Grizzle, 2011).

We can take inspiration from new global developments in media and information literacy, and continue to build on the strength of the foundations that were laid by McLuhan, Masterman and Duncan many years ago. Media and information literacy skills for the post-2015 development agenda should be seen as the central tools through which to contextualize, acquire and apply content knowledge. These skills are based on heuristics that are 'constants' used in deconstructing and constructing communication. Content knowledge is 'variable', with an infinite number of subjects. Having media and information literacy skills, especially being able to use a consistent process of inquiry that is internalized, enhances the ability to communicate and to share ideas through a common vocabulary that transcends subject areas as well as geographic boundaries. Thus, there are no 'silos' with this method for teaching and learning because the media and information literacy skills are cross-curricular and common to all. It is through a process of inquiry that students interrogate, acquire and master content knowledge, but both media and information literacy skills and content knowledge rest on a continuum that can always be expanded and deepened (Jolls, 2014).

The integrated nature of media and information literacy skills supports the needs of a globally networked society, where problem-solving must span many domains using integrated approaches. Environmental disasters, terrorism, human trafficking, pandemics – all are ultimately human rights issues that present complex problems, calling for citizens to have a sophisticated ability to access, analyze, evaluate, communicate and create using the information and technologies that are available. Media and information literacy empowers citizens and leaders with an analytic approach and the type of critical thinking that transcends boundaries of all types – physical and geographic, cultural and conceptual – while increasing the capacity for citizens to participate actively in the global village.

Yet solutions to these global problems rest ultimately with each individual and with preparing each citizen to use the media and information literacy skills they need for life in a global media culture. As Masterman (2010) said:

> My own objectives were to liberate pupils from the expertise of the teacher, and to challenge the dominant hierarchical transmission of knowledge which takes place in most classrooms. In media studies, information is transmitted laterally, to both students and teachers alike. The teacher's role is not to advocate a particular view but to promote reflection upon media texts, and to develop the kind of questioning and analytical skills which will help students to clarify their own views.

Such connected learning has – and always will – pave the path to the future.

References

Aspen Institute. (2014). *Learner at the Center of a Networked World.* Retrieved from http://www.medialit.org/voices-media-literacy-international-pioneers-speak

Duncan, B. (2010). *Voices of Media Literacy.* Retrieved from http://www.medialit.org/reading-room/voices-media-literacy-international-pioneers-speak-barry-duncan-interview-transcript

Duncan, B. (2011). *Voices of Media Literacy: International Pioneers Speak.* Retrieved from http://www.medialit.org/voices-media-literacy-international-pioneers-speak

Jolls, T. (2014). "The Global Media Literacy Imperative." *The Russian-American Education Forum: An Online Forum, Volume 6, Issue 1.* Retrieved from http://www.rus-ameeduforum.com/content/en/?&iid=18

Jolls, T. & Wilson, C. (2014). "The Core Concepts: Fundamental to Media Literacy Yesterday, Today and Tomorrow." *Journal of Media Literacy Education.* Retrieved from http://digitalcommons.uri.edu/jmle/vol6/iss2/6

Livingstone, S. & Wang, Y-H. (2013). "On The Difficulties Of Promoting Media Literacy." In B. De Abreau & P. Mihailidis (Eds.), *Media Literacy in Action: Theoretical and Pedagogical Perspectives.* Retrieved from http://books.google.com/books?id=JoBiAgAAQBAJ&pg=PA166&lpg=PA166&dq=european+union+requirements+for+media+literacy&source=bl&ots=t-Bm4GNmqY&sig=3ludF6eqUKWbcv8yl3frXrj68-lg&hl=en&sa=X&ei=_hzsUt3YAc6oQSAuoGgAQ&ved=0CHwQ6AEwCQ#v=onepage&q=european%20union%20requirements%20for%20media%20literacy&f=false Routledge: New York.

Lotto, J. & Barrington, L. (2006). *Are They Really Ready to Work?* Retrieved from http://www.p21.org/storage/documents/FINAL_REPORT_PDF09-29-06.pdf

Masterman, L. (1980). *Teaching About Television.* United Kingdom: Palgrave Macmillan.

Masterman, L. (1985). *Teaching The Media.* Abingdon, Oxon, England: Comedia Publishing Group.

Masterman, L. (1989). *Media Awareness Education: Eighteen Basic Principles.* Retrieved from http://medialit.org/reading-room/media-awareness-education-eighteen-basic-principles

Masterman, L. (2010). *Voices of Media Literacy.* Retrieved from http://www.medialit.org/reading-room/voices-media-literacy-international-pioneers-speak-len-masterman-interview-transcript

McLuhan, M. (1964, reprint 1994). *Understanding Media: The Extensions of Man.* United States of America: MIT Press.

McLuhan, M. & Fiore, Q. (1967). *The Medium is the Massage.* Bantam Books.

McLuhan, M. (1969). "Playboy Magazine Interview." *Playboy Magazine.* March.

Ministry of Education and Culture, Finland. (2013). *Good Media Literacy: National Policy Guidelines.* Retrieved from http://www.minedu.fi/OPM/Julkaisut/2013/Hyva_media-lukutaito.html?lang=en.

Ofcom. (2014). *Media Literacy Research Index.* Retrieved from http://stakeholders.ofcom.org.uk/market-data-research/media-literacy-pubs/

Quin, R. (2011). *Voices of Media Literacy.* Retrieved from http://www.medialit.org/reading-room/voices-media-literacy-international-pioneers-speak-robyn-quin-interview-transcript

Thoman, L. (1993). *Skills and Strategies for Media Education.* Retrieved from http://www.medialit.org/reading-room/skills-strategies-media-education)

UNESCO. (2014). *Media and Information Literacy.* Retrieved from http://www.unesco.org/new/en/communication-and-information/media-development/media-literacy/mil-as-composite-concept/

UNESCO. (2015). *Position Paper on Education Post-2015.* Retrieved from http://unesdoc.unesco.org/images/0022/002273/227336E.pdf

Wilson, C. & Duncan, B. (2008). *Implementing Mandates in Media Education: The Ontario Experience.* Retrieved from http://www.revista.comunicar.com/pdf/comunicar32-en.pdf

Wilson C. & Grizzle, A. (2011). *UNESCO Media and Information Literacy Curriculum for Teachers.* Retrieved from http://www.unesco.org/new/en/communication-and-information/resources/publications-and-communication-materials/publications/full-list/media-and-information-literacy-curriculum-for-teachers/

Information and Communication Technologies (ICT) Literacy for Sustainable Development

Anubhuti Yadav

The digital divide is a huge concern in India. This divide emerges from the power, wealth, the dominance of English, absence of culturally relevant content, non availability of enabling infrastructure and digital literacy. According to Digital India, a flagship programme of the Government of India to transform India into a digitally empowered society and knowledge economy, this digital divide can be bridged by connecting all gram panchayats through high speed broadband and by ensuring mobile access in all the villages by 2018. Though the role of "digital" in transforming India into a knowledge economy is widely accepted, the concern over reaching the unreached and bridging the divide has been immense. Many initiatives have been taken in the past to bridge this divide and a number of projects and schemes were rolled out. The intent of the projects and schemes were good but their implementation has been unsuccessful because of the lack of coordination/collaboration amongst projects and their implementation agencies. The Digital India project, coordinated by DIETY, the Department of Electronics and Information Technology, Ministry of Communications and Information Technology, Government of India, attempts to address this problem by bringing all new and old e-projects under one umbrella with the objective to facilitate citizen engagement, provide access to Internet and phones, and build infrastructure. The whole idea is to have synchronised implementation. Mere infrastructure development is not a solution to bridge the digital divide. The readiness and preparedness of citizens is very important to bridge digital divide. This preparedness can be achieved through digital literacy. This article explores how important digital literacy is to bridge the digital divide and the role the digital literacy campaign can play in nation building. The article will also explore the initiatives taken by the Indian Government to make India digital literate.

Keywords: digital literacy, ICT curriculum, national digital literacy mission, digital divide

Introduction

According to Census 2011, there has been a rise in literacy rates from 64.8 per cent in 2001 to 73 per cent in 2011 in India. This shows the continuous and concerted efforts by the government, civil society and private sector to improve the quality of education in the country and is the result of numerous reforms in the field of education since Independence. But with the rapid advancements in new technologies, there are new challenges, possibilities and opportunities facing the Indian education system. The challenges include motivating teachers and students to embrace technology based education, making infrastructure – both hardware and software – available, making teachers and students digital literate so that they harness the potential of new technology, developing content in regional languages and providing the last mile connectivity. The opportunities and possibilities of new technologies include making education accessible to all, a shift from textbook centric education, reducing rigidity in the education system which is otherwise quite inflexible especially in the context of examination and handling the issue of lack of teachers/lecturers in schools and colleges. New technologies hold a potential to change the age old process of education.

To give new direction to the Indian Education System, the Government of India has initiated discussion on educational issues by creating a group "New Education Policy on MyGov Platform".

MyGov (2015)

http://mygov.in/new-education-policy-group.html

The objective of this Group is to formulate a new Education Policy for the country through an inclusive, participatory and holistic approach. The National Policy on Education was framed in 1986 and modified in 1992. Since then several changes have taken place that calls for a revision of the Policy. The Government of India would like to bring out a National Education Policy to meet the changing dynamics of the population's requirement with regards to quality education, innovation and research, aiming to make India a knowledge superpower by equipping its students with the necessary skills and knowledge and to eliminate the shortage of manpower in science, technology, academics and industry. For this purpose, 33 themes have been identified for discussions under this Group. The themes are divided separately for the School Education (13 themes) and Higher Education (20 themes) sectors. The group consists of Tasks and Discussions. Tasks are both online and on-ground. Discussions enable participants to share their thoughts and ideas.

Since new technologies hold a strong potential to overcome challenges of the Indian Education system and strengthen the system, both in school education and higher education, the New Education Policy group identified three themes for discussion that is related to ICT literacy:

- Promotion of ICTs in school education and adult education

- Promoting Open and Distance Learning and Online courses

- Opportunities for technology enabled learning

This process of formulation of a new education policy has started when India is going through a digital revolution. The New Education Policy should take into account various initiatives that have been launched under the Digital India Programme. (The Digital India Programme has been launched by the Department of Electronics and Information Technology, Ministry of Communications and Information Technology, Government of India). A lot of prominence is given to education in this programme as the mission of the programme is to prepare India for a knowledge future.

In India the policy framework, financial support and guidelines to ensure a national standard of education are provided by the Government of India through the Ministry of Human Resource Development (MHRD). The Ministry of Communications and Information Technology (MCIT) is also responsible for and engaged in designing and implementing various projects related to digital literacy. Various projects and initiatives to integrate ICT in education are in place, ranging from making hardware and software available to providing incentive to teachers for innovatively using ICT in education, from developing repositories of open educational resources to offering national platform for Massive Open Online course. The MHRD that operates through two departments (the Department of School Education and Literacy and the Department of Higher Education) has taken lot of initiatives both at school level and higher education level. There have been continuous efforts to integrate ICT in education in India and make India digital literate.

ICT Literacy Across the World

The need for ICT integration in education has been emphasized at many international forums in the last decade. During the 26th G8 summit held in Nago, Okinawa, Japan, in 2000 the focus was on Information and Communication Technologies (ICT). It was noted that ICT has become an engine of growth for the global economy and has the potential to contribute significantly to sustainable economic development, to enhance public welfare, to strengthen democracy, to increase transparency in governance, to nourish cultural diversity, and to foster international peace and stability. It was also emphasized during the conference that there was great need to develop human resources who are skilled enough to respond to the demands of the information age and to nurture ICT literacy and skills through education, training, and lifelong learning (Japan International Cooperation Agency, 2002).

The Organization for Economic Co-operation and Development (OECD) also emphasizes the economic importance and impact of ICT in developed countries and points out the need for these countries to develop a workforce with the skills to use ICT to increase productivity, as well as the need for young people to develop ICT skills in preparation for adult life. OECD countries are making substantial investments in ICT in order to improve the quality of teaching and learning. According to the OECD report *Measuring the information economy* 2002, economies increasingly depend on technological knowledge and skills, and ICT skills are particularly important. The use of computers at an early age helps students to learn ICT skills which can then be used as a tool in the education process.

The World Bank is also playing an important role in assisting countries in taking advantage of the opportunities in information and communications technologies (ICTs) to contribute to education goals and poverty reduction strategies. Support for ICT in education includes assistance for equipment and facilities; teacher training and support; capacity building; educational content; distance learning; digital literacy; policy development; monitoring and evaluation; and media outreach (World Bank, 2003).

A World Bank report (2003) cites the potential that ICT has to improve efficient delivery of resources to the poor, to bring markets within reach of rural communities, to improve government services, and to transfer knowledge needed to meet the Millennium Development Goals (Kozma, 2005).

At the World Summit on the Information Society, the United Nations (2005) noted the potential of ICT to expand access to quality education, to boost literacy, and to provide universal primary education in developing countries.

Based on the discussion which were held on various international platforms, countries the world over came up with different policies and schemes to integrate ICT in the education sector.

Initiatives to Promote Digital Literacy in India

The National Policy of ICT in Education

The National Policy of ICT in Education was formulated in India in 2008.

> *With the convergence of technologies, it has become imperative to take a comprehensive look at all possible information and communication technologies for improving school education in the country. The comprehensive choice of ICT for holistic development of education can be built only on a sound policy. The initiative of ICT Policy in School Education is inspired by the tremendous potential of ICT for enhancing outreach and improving quality of education.*

(National Policy on ICT in Education)

This policy endeavours to provide guidelines to assist states in optimizing the use of ICT in school education within a national policy framework. The policy aims to promote universal equitable, open and free access to a state-of-the-art ICT, and ICT-enabled tools and resources to all students and teachers; develop local and localized quality content; enable students and teachers to partner in the development and critical use of shared digital resources; develop professional networks of teachers, resource persons and schools to catalyze and support resource sharing, a critical understanding of ICT, its benefits, dangers and limitations.

ICT Curricula for Students and Teachers

National Policy on ICT in Education also proposed a model curriculum for ICT in education for teachers and students. The curriculum has been developed by the National Council for Educational Research and Training (NCERT), an autonomous body under the Ministry of Human Resource Development, Government of India. This ICT curriculum is a major shift from what the country had seen till now as a computer literacy programme. Through such computer literacy programmes not only do we portray ICT as more difficult than it actually is, but also hinder intellectual development and creativity. Also, using computers and Internet as mere information delivery devices grossly underutilizes their power and capabilities (ICT Curriculum).

The ICT Curriculum therefore anchors itself to the National Curriculum Framework 2005. The aim of the curriculum is to involve the teacher in a critical appraisal of the availability and appropriateness of technological solutions to address educational problems. For the student, emphasis is on the creative use of the medium and widening of one's horizons.

The curriculum proposes six thematic areas in which ICTs can be explored.

The six themes in the curriculum are:

- Connecting with the world
- Connecting with each other
- Interacting with ICT
- Creating with ICT
- Possibilities in Education
- Reaching out and bridging the divide

The main idea behind the curriculum is on learning to compute which includes learning to create using a variety of hardware and software tools. ICT literacy, defined as the knowledge and ability to wield tools and devices, shall be an incidental outcome of this learning (http://ictcurriculum.gov.in). The ICT curricula for the students and teachers hold a strong potential to promote digital literacy. However, there is a need to conduct research on how the curricula have been implemented. This would not only provide mid courses correction, if required but would also provide inputs on how the knowledge gained by the teachers and students through ICT curriculum was applied.

Open Educational Resources (OER) Movement in India

Under the National Mission on Education through Information and Communication Technology (NMEICT) an Open Licensing Policy was also formulated. This decision has its root in the National Knowledge Commission recommendation to the Government of India. The NKC was constituted in 2005 under the chairmanship of Mr. Sam Pitroda (an internationally respected telecom inventor, entrepreneur and policy maker) to prepare the blueprint for reforms of knowledge related institution and infrastructure which would enable India to meet the challenges of future. The NKC recommended the creation of a national educational foundation to develop a web based repository of high quality educational resources as OER through a collaborative process. It said,

> An enabling legal framework that would allow unrestricted access without compromising intellectual authorship must be devised for this purpose.

On the basis of NKC recommendations in the last ten years many institutions in India have embraced this idea of having open educational repositories to address the challenge of quality and equity. But initiatives such as the National Science Digital Library (NSDL), the Open Source Courseware Animations Repository (OSCAR), the National Programme on Technology Enhanced Learning (NPTEL), the Virtual Academy for the Semi-Arid Tropics (VASAT) and the Indira Gandhi National Open University (IGNOU) were limited to higher education. The National Policy on ICT in School Education proposed a web based digital repository and the responsibility to build this repository was given to the Central Institute of Educational Technology (CIET), NCERT. The National Repository of Open Educational Resources (NROER) was developed in collaboration with the Homi Bhabha Centre for Science Education, Mumbai. NROER is a comprehensive digital repository of resources that can be used by teachers in the teaching learning process.

According to the Open Licensing Policy, all educational educational materials shall be released under an appropriate open licensing regime. The current preference is CC-BY-SA (Creative Commons-Attribution-Share Alike). This license will permit users to share (copy and distribute) the material in any medium or format; and adapt (remix, transform, and build upon) the material for any purpose, even commercially. The user shall provide attribution to the original creator and also mandatorily, distribute any adaptation and or enhancement under the same license. All the knowledge resources developed under the NMEICT have to follow open licencing policy guidelines. Even though the policy is in place, the adherence to this policy is an issue. Many projects still do not mention the licence under which they are releasing the content. Also the adoption of different Creative Common licenses for different projects under NMEICT is a matter of debate. The rationale of using CC-BY-SA-NC (Creative Commons-Attribution-Share Alike-Non Commercial) for projects such as the National Programme for Technology Enhanced Learning (NPTEL), and the National Institute of Open Schooling (NIOS), and, CC-BY-SA for projects such as NROER, is not clear. Also, there is a great need to create awareness about these knowledge portals amongst teachers and students. Portals and repositories that offer open educational resources can play a huge role in bridging the digital divide by offering content that is contextual and also by allowing its content to be translated into different regional languages. The dominance of the English language (viewed as a major reason for the digital divide) can be reduced by creating portals that offer content in regional languages and also by releasing content under the Creative Commons licence so that the resources can be edited, remixed and translated according to the needs of different groups.

National Digital Literacy Mission

ICT intervention at the school level is the need of the hour as it can play a significant role in solving many problems that the Indian Education system is facing. At the same time digital literacy should not be treated as something that is possible within the formal set up of education system. The vision of Digital India can be possible with the Digital Empowerment of all citizens. This includes universal digital literacy, universally accessible digital resources, availability of digital resources/services in Indian languages, collaborative digital platforms for participative governance. IT mass literacy scheme has been formulated keeping in view "National Policy on IT 2012" which includes an objective of making one person IT literate in every household. As per the recommendation of the Standing Finance Committee, the name 'National Digital Literacy Mission' was adopted for the scheme. A digital literate person according to the scheme is one who:

- Knows the basics (terminology, navigation and functionality) of digital devices
- Uses digital devices for accessing, creating, managing and sharing information
- Uses the Internet to browse in an effective and responsible manner
- Uses technology to communicate effectively
- Appreciates the role of digital technology in everyday life, in social life and at work
- Uses technology to communicate effectively with government and other stakeholders (G2C, C2G and G2G)

Though the policies take into consideration the key issues of promoting digital literacy, developing content in regional languages and connecting gram panchayats through high speed broadband, and ensuring mobile access to bridge digital divide, there is still a need to have a synergy between what ICT can do and what the requirements are. The National Policy on ICT in Education does look at ICT intervention in a holistic manner and aims at making available infrastructure (hardware and software), connectivity, power supply and computer labs. It also aims at the digitization of available educational audio, video and print resources, development of e-content in multiple languages, teacher related interventions which includes capacity enhancement of all teachers in ICT and introduction of a scheme for national ICT awards as a means of motivation. The challenge now lies in the implementation: making ICT infrastructure available; development of e-content in multiple formats and multiple languages; training of teachers, teacher educators, policy makers in the use of ICT. To make this happen, various organizations have to join hands and pool the resources which are available in abundance in our country. The effort has to be made to map these resources to the school curriculum as well as higher education. Also, teachers after being trained in ICT have to start contributing to the creation of content and offer an individualized learning environment to their students.

Most of the time, ICT literacy or digital literacy programmes are introduced and implemented only when the required infrastructure and content is available. ICT literacy can also be introduced even with the limited infrastructure and content. This literacy would then generate demand for ICT infrastructure and content which can play a huge role in bridging the digital divide.

References

International Telecommunication Union. World Summit on the Information Society-Outcome Document, Available at http://www.itu.int/wsis/outcome/booklet.pdf

India. Ministry of Human Resource Development, Department of School Education and Literacy (2012), National Policy on ICT in School Education. Available at http://mhrd.gov.in/sites/upload_files/mhrd/files/upload_document/revised_policy%20document%20ofICT.pdf

National Council of Educational Research and Training (2005). National Curriculum Frame Work 2005. Available at http://www.ncert.nic.in/rightside/links/pdf/framework/english/nf2005.pdf

Organization for Economic Co-operation and Development (OECD) 2002. Measuring the Information Economy 2002. Available at http://www.oecd.org/sti/ieconomy/1835738.pdf

UNESCO (2014). A complete Analysis of ICT integration and e–readiness in schools across Asia.

World Development Report 2003: Sustainable Development in a Dynamic World--Transforming Institutions, Growth, and Quality of Life. Available at https://openknowledge.worldbank.org/handle/10986/5985

ICT curriculum, http://ictcurriculum.gov.in

National Mission on Education through Information and Communication Technology, http://www.sakshat.ac.in/

National Programme on Technology Enhanced Learning, http://nptel.ac.in/

National Repository of Open Educational Resources, http://nroer.gov.in/

Open source Courseware Animation Repository, http://oscar.iitb.ac.in/

http://mhrd.gov.in/sites/upload_files/mhrd/files/document-reports/NPE-1968.pdf

Media and Information Literacy: New Opportunities for New Challenges

Jordi Torrent

Contemporary societies are being digitalized in the widest and deepest sense, from big data connected to the personal profiles associated to digital footprints of individuals to the digital control of information and mis-information. Schools are adapting to these changes by eliminating humanistic studies and introducing technology education, but too often leaving behind the development of critical thinking skills adapted to the new societal paradigm. The future participants to democratic societies are dis-served by these shortcomings in the educational curricula.

Keywords: big data, computational thinking, censorship, coding, smart phones

> *The real issue in art and technology is not to make another scientific toy, but how to humanize technology and the electronic medium.*
>
> Nam June Paik

This 1970 thought of the late artist Nam June Paik, often identified as the father of "electronic-video art", is very much at the forefront of the challenges that education faces vis-à-vis the information and communication technologies (ICTs) relevant to our times. When I went to school in my early childhood, I was first taught how to read and write, and later I was invited to question what I was reading (What does the author mean by this? From whose point of view is the story told? What do you think of this character's reaction? Where is this character coming from? etc.). Language, Arts and Literature were venues for the development of critical thinking skills, for the enrichment of the child's personal and social modes on behavior, it facilitated the questioning of the child's and teenager's own emotions. Unfortunately, humanistic education is declining and the "technology education" courses that are substituting it are seldom, if ever, bringing about this kind of questioning. We teach (to the lucky ones with access to in-class technology[1]) how to use ICTs, but not how to read, analyze and question the messages arriving to us through these.

We teach how to use the software, the machine, perhaps even we ask the students to read the consumer's guidelines coming with the software they are using. And we are pleased with this; we call this "technology education." Point for many, there is not much more to teach. Somehow, we don't discuss in class why the information (or the hierarchical order of) provided by the Internet search engines are different depending of who is searching or from which country one is searching. Location and "personal profile" do count, but we don't call the attention of our children and teenagers to this. We don't mention as well that anybody can buy a domain name, or how easy it is to be an impostor on the Internet, pretending to be an expert, even overtly lying about someone or some historical event. Search "Tiananmen Square" in Beijing and in London, or "Edward Snowden" in Moscow or in Washington. Let's compare the search results. These are obvious exercises, but most don't think of them as "technology education", or of "digital literacy." This is as if we were teaching to read and write but not to think and discuss about the reading, the text. It was just pure spellings, grammar and syntax. But no critical thinking skills applied to the text, to the significance of the content.

It is telling of our educational systems that while governments and corporations are immersed in a deep conversation-research about how to best use "big data" -for their own interests, economic or political- but the school does not engage in this conversation. The lucky students (the really lucky ones!) will produce an app for cell phones as part of their technology education, for their "digital literacy" classes. Leaving out of the classroom, of the true media and information literacy education class. Again: all about spellings and grammar, very little (if any) in developing critical thinking skills applied to media messages. This approach to education is a dis-service to the future participant citizens of our democratic societies.

Those Caught Talking Will Be Severely Punished

Now a little bit of data. In February of 2014, the United Nations Alliance of Civilizations (UNAOC) organized (in collaboration with the Sidi Mohamed Ben Abdellah University of Fez, Morocco) a series of teacher training workshops on MIL for public school educators in the Fez region. We asked the participants to engage their students in filling up a questionnaire aiming at collecting data of their students' media habits. 200 students (51% male 49% female) aged between 14 and 21 responded to the questionnaire. Here are some of the results[2]:

- 70% have a cellphone
- 50% watch between 1 and 2 hours of TV each day
- 40% spend 30 minutes or less a day doing homework
- 25% spend 3 or more hours each day surfing the Internet
- 61% share media (photos or/and videos) in social media platforms
- 20% do this daily
- 40% engages in reading a book once a month
- 8% responded that they never read a book

It is obvious that they all read every day (many several hours a day), just that the reading happens elsewhere; it takes place on the screenings of their cellphones, on the screens of the computers they use to navigate the Internet. And by doing so they are also creating their "digital footprint", feeding the big data cloud along the way. Their digital footprint will continue to grow at infinitum, informing as it does to governments and corporations of their habits, tastes, interactions with others, of their sleeping patterns as well. Stuffing their digital profiles with all the details (or almost) regarding their lives (private and public). But for the most part, the school does not discuss this, only the spelling and grammar.

Concepts such as "freedom of expression", "privacy" and "censorship" are challenged as well throughout the process of this digital profile creation that each of us is (willingly or not) participating in. At times, while observing the new framework of our contemporary digital world, One should think of that phrase that the prisoners of the Chinese Revolution were told in the late 1940s: Those caught talking will be severely punished[3]. Around the world there are now many who are, in one way or another, severally punished (or being threatened to) for exercising their rights regarding the expression of their thoughts and concerns. This is yet another challenge that we are facing and that we should be able to address and discuss in the classrooms of our democratic societies.

Another challenge is the tension between "public information" and the right to manage one's own digital footprint. This conflict has resulted in policies, such as the recent policy from the European Union requesting Google to code their search engines in a way that they will not provide certain information regarding certain individuals. Opening in this way, the doors wide open to further manipulate media and information. While we understand the right to oversee one's own digital footprint, this ruling might not be the most desirable for a world where open information for all should be the goal. It's a challenge that educators (let alone citizens) need to face and respond to.

Another challenge (clearly exposed in the files shared by Edward Snowden[4]) are the efforts produced by governments towards ruining individuals' or organizations' reputations on the Internet. Creating fake digital footprints, posting and filling lies and misinformation regarding the targeted individuals and organizations with possible personal and professional catastrophic results. If an individual is caught doing this, criminal charges might be raised against him/her. Nonetheless, governments are doing it. These tactics are not new, let's recall one of the pearls of Joseph Goebbels, Hitler's Minister of Propaganda, "The bigger the lie, the more it will be believed." This is yet another challenge that educators should open for discussion in their classrooms, particularly in History and Social Sciences curricula.

But each challenge is indeed a wide open opportunity for debate and, if needed, re-dress. Regarding the themes that we are discussing the opportunities lay at the hands of educators. But in order to do so, the educational systems have to include in their core curriculum these questions (MIL education) and readjust the current modes of teaching "literacy". Education should embrace computational literacy and thinking but, as Divina Frau-Meigs called our attention at the 2014 European Media Literacy Forum, there should be "no coding, without de-coding."[5]

Yes, humanizing technology is at the core of our educational challenges. And in doing this we must remind ourselves of this Isaac Asimov's comment: "The computer merely takes a finite amount of data and performs a finite number of operations upon them." The human mind is far richer and complex than the most sophisticated computer humans will ever built. This is perhaps an assumption that some could read as almost a "religious belief", at any rate I do believe that humans have the capacity to outdo any machine when it comes to critical thinking skills. And we can do this because, among other things, we have the sixth sense: intuition. These are the opportunities.

But teachers cannot humanize technology by themselves, cannot shift the paradigms of education by themselves. They need the support of policy makers who advocate for the creation of new educational frameworks where MIL education is mandatory. MIL is at the core of the curriculum across the board, from the training of future teachers all the way to Kindergarten through the last year of college. Indeed a world, where MIL life-long learning opportunities are disseminated across societies, from vehicles of mass entertainment to news media operators.

Notes

1   Just as an example of the existing disparity of access to ICTs in the public schools in some parts of the world, let's mention a 2010 UNESCO's study. Of the 33 countries studied in Latin America, only 15 had access to electricity in the school. Only 17 of them had fast Internet connection. And while in Paraguay, the ratio of student-computer was of 1-1, in the Dominican Republic was of 1 computer for 128 students.

2   Special thanks to Professors Abdelhamid Nfissi and Mohamed Faoubar for their support.

3   The Last Emperor (1987), film directed by Bernardo Bertolucci.

4   See Edward Snowden's file "The Art of Deception: Training for a New Generation of Online Covert Operations."

5   UNESCO, Paris, May 2014.

From Living Rooms to Classrooms: "Turn on the Lights" of Mobile Learning in MENA

Ibrahim Mostafa Saleh

Most Arab countries started their own e-learning and mobile learning initiatives in order to cope with global integration of latest educational technologies. The high mobile phone penetration among Arabs as well as the availability of good mobile infrastructure are all important factors that can enhance the shift to mobile learning. Moreover, several studies indicate positive attitudes and perceptions toward mobile learning at different Arab learning institutions. However, specific challenges may act as barriers to mobile learning in the Arab world. This research reviews some of the current mobile learning practices in the Middle East and North Africa (MENA) and provides an overview of challenges faced by Arab students, educators, and probably researchers.

Keywords: MENA, mobile learning, multiple literacies, access and personalization, media education, innovation and learning

Overview of MENA

The research argues that mobile technology learning is increasingly helping resolve limitations of media education in two areas: access and personalization. Mobile learning illustrates the power of mobile technology in addressing some of the specific challenges affecting the quality and effectiveness of media education for learners.

Media studies are currently undergoing changes characteristic of an active and diverse community of scholars. This research examines aspects of this debate among media scholars, by focusing on the situation in MENA. It argues that the debate "Down Under" mirrors global differences on the issues of "theory" and "practice" in media education, especially with the use of new media tools in the classroom such as mobile phones.

Mobile learning can help address several challenges with the existing media educational system in MENA. As players across the education landscape explore ways to improve education outcomes through mobile technology, they can find ways which can help overcome challenges affecting education systems. The mobile learning culture is facing a paradigm shift that is not only in lifelong learning, but also in formal education and corporate training. Mobile learning could play a pivotal role in educational practices in offering useful platforms for knowledge transfer and for achieving behaviour change in MENA.

The accelerating rate of mobile phone penetration is a fundamental factor in this development. The emerging technology of smart phones and tablet PCs will lead to a drop in their cost, and the widespread use of wireless broadband will also increase dependency on the mobile as a platform for many applications, especially in rural and marginalised areas.

The ubiquity of mobile phones is presenting educators with a new, low-cost tool for teaching that could certainly offer new solutions for delivering real results for low-income learners. Mobile learning is assumed to wreak havoc and unleash cyber bullying, although the hurdles resulting from poor infrastructure including unstable mains electricity, poor broadband connectivity, lack of suitable clean secure buildings, lack of technical capacity, lack of software licenses and lack of human capacity, remain endless.

The MENA region represents a market for educational content and connectivity. The availability of higher technology, in the form of handsets and network capacity, continues to increase, providing an attractive environment for a wealth of value-added services (March 2015).

The mobile learning community in MENA is now faced with broader challenges of scale, durability, equity, embedding and blending in addition to the earlier and more specific challenges of pedagogy and technology, but these developments take place in the context of societies where mobile devices, systems and technologies have a far wider impact than just mobile learning as it is currently conceived.

In 2011, the US Agency for International Development and Stanford University held *m4Ed4Dev* (*Mobile for Education for Development*), which explored the use of mobile devices for education in developing countries. Mobile devices, and their technologies and systems, are eroding established notions of time as a common structure that had previously underpinned social organisation and the consensual understanding of the world. Mobile devices, systems and technologies also have a direct and pervasive impact on knowledge itself, and how it is generated, transmitted, owned, valued and consumed in our societies.

Information and communication technology (ICT) has radically changed the ubiquitous connectivity and sharing of mobile social media, though a cultural shift is required for journalism educators to enable engagement and critical reflection on the use of mobile social media (Balsamo, 2011).

Mena at the Heart of Media Education and Literacy Debate

The revenues for mobile learning products in the Middle East reached $88.3 million in 2012. The growth rate is 18.4 percent and revenues will more than double to $205.4 million by 2017. The largest buyers in the region are consumers, followed by academic buyers. There is a significant "threat of product substitution" in the Middle East, with mobile learning gaining traction at the expense of e-learning (Adkins, 2013).

Big challenges from the heterogeneous nature of the economies, geography, politics, and cultures in MENA require the development of specific domestic context of solutions (Jaatun, Zhao & Rong, 2010). However, according to Weber (2011), there is a widespread shortage of qualified information and communication technology (ICT) professionals, training programmes, and trained e-learning educational staff in the MENA region.

The political transformation of MENA from 2010 to 2015 created a series of personal and professional challenges for those involved in higher education in media in the region. Such fluidity has led to rumblings of dissent related to recent political upheavals, and the whole societies and their related educational systems are at risk.

Most of the higher education institutions in the region have started to offer online courses, some quite recently. These institutions are experiencing a boom in online course enrollments. The majority of the students enrolling in these courses use tablets and smartphones to access the content.

The Arab Open University (AOU) has seven branches in the region: Kuwait, Saudi Arabia, Egypt, Jordan, Lebanon, Bahrain, and Oman. AOU has physical campuses and offer most of their courses online (in physical labs and over the Internet).

AOU is a pan-regional higher education institution that makes extensive use of mobile learning in their programs. They are a pioneer of mobile learning in the region launching a content library for Java-enabled phones in 2007. AOU has over 50,000 enrolled students across the region with enrollments rising by over 20 percent a year.

Most theories of pedagogy fail to capture the distinctiveness of mobile learning, because of the lack of embracing the outside classroom activities and is personally initiated and structured. In fact, mobile learning has empowered the students, and forced educators to re-conceptualize their roles and core tools. Besides, incorporating new technology must be engaged through abdicating their responsibilities as cultural stewards (Balsamo, 2011). Mobile learning is a powerful catalyst for rethinking the role of the media and the nature of teaching and learning that requires a radical cultural rethink of pedagogy.

Setting the Scene

Digital convergence and literacy are intertwined as a result of the rapid and widespread uptake of mobile phones across the region. Africa is positioned as the second-largest mobile market in the world after Asia (GSMA and A.T. Kearney, 2011). In 2015, the *Mobile Africa Report* confirmed that more people in Africa will have mobile-network access than electricity in their homes, with a predicted 'off-grid, on-Net' population of 138 million (Rao, 2011). The number of mobile users in the MENA region is expected to reach an annual growth rate of 77 percent (Samih, 2013). For example, the annual growth rate for mobile telephony in MENA has been 65 percent, more than twice the global average (Livingstone, 2011).

In every era of technology, education has been formed to some extent in its own image. That is not to argue for the technological determinism of education, but rather that there is a mutually productive convergence between main technological influences on a culture and the contemporary educational theories and practices. For this era of mobile technology even in MENA, we may come to conceive of education as conversation in context, enabled by continual interaction through and with personal and mobile technology.

The MENA region though still experiences debilitating crisis in education as a result of limited access, lack of highly qualified teachers, and low levels of literacy and basic education skills. Such hazards are more intense because of the unmatched orientation of using knowledge in economic development.

Studies have suggested the positive impact of delivering course content and receiving student assignments using electronic means (Dabner, 2012). There is absence of awareness of media literacy potentials that resulted from gaps in alternative delivery, and promising possibilities (Meyer & Wilson, 2011).

Yet younger learners are increasingly aware of the significance of mobile phones (Stald, 2008). But technology is not the solution in itself (Eid, 2014). Such dim reality has resulted from the absence of knowledge or because they address it separately instead of following a holistic approach.

Mobile Learning

Media educators have shown particular interest in mobile learning (m-learning) which currently is treated as fashion, but at the same time is considered by corporations and educational institutions to be very promising. But m-learning tools remain limited to some extent, and there is a long way until it is fully integrated with curriculum and the blended learning approach.

Mobile learning is uneven in MENA, though it could be used to empower marginalized groups (Li, 2010), by reaching individual people in deeply remote areas where there are no libraries, tutors, and/or schools.

According to Elgort (2005), mobile learning is influenced by organizational, socio-cultural, and intra and interpersonal factors. Mobile learning equips learners with multiple literacies and skills (Steel et al., 2007). Mastering of the multi-skilling is a requirement for different media formats and rethinking of the new producer-consumer relationship is mandatory.

The mobile learning community in MENA has an increasingly clear sense of its achievements and its direction, but looking beyond the immediate community reveals a far more complex and changing situation. In this research, one can only sketch parts of the evolving picture, guess how the MENA society, its conception of learning and the role of mobile technologies in supporting that conception will fit together and wonder at the place of our current work at a regional level. Nonetheless, the challenge for the mobile learning community is the balance between facing inwards, to develop its work, and facing outwards, to understand the context and importance of that work.

The article proposes that m-learning provides opportunities for more creativity in designing and delivering the course with further enhancement of the student experience, but it will be utilized in its full potential in the area in the next decade. This study highlights the need to change the teaching and learning culture to student-oriented for more effective and appropriate use of m-learning. It highlights the need for institutions to invest in faculty and staff training, and in technology as well as provides suggestions to other stakeholders on the need to incorporate m-learning in decision-making for further development in the region.

Concluding Remarks

Understanding the factors may contribute to the effective use of m-learning to help different stakeholders to incorporate suitable designs and implementation of m-learning. It is thus necessary to identify the practices in terms of instructional design and adapt them to reflect the number of changes that have taken place in education from the use of e-learning and m-learning in MENA. A transformation towards m-learning requires not only the use of the devices but also awareness and familiarity with new technologies.

In conclusion, the limited, albeit growing, number of mobile learning projects in the MENA region confirms that the formal integration of mobile learning in education systems is very much in its infancy. Such delay is affected by the economies of scale, and the available infrastructure and technology. The nature of the individualized ways in which users are using mobile technologies suggest that mobile learning is transforming traditional paradigms of learning, teaching and education delivery.

There is a tremendous need for educating media experts and educators to use and exploit new devices fruitfully and purposefully in their profession. There remains the need to develop policies that define the 'rights and responsibilities of various classes of stakeholders to participate effectively and influence the changing governance system.'

The research suggests that we need a critical framework for supporting and implementing mobile social media for pedagogical change within media education. Mobile learning also creates new modalities for peer learning and mentorship, and can facilitate more student-centered learning, in contrast to traditional pedagogical models based on the teacher transferring knowledge to learners.

References

Adkins, S.S. (2013). The 2012-2017 Middle East Mobile Learning Market: Four Major Catalysts Drive the Adoption of Mobile Learning across the Region, *Ambient Insight Regional Report*, (October 2013). http://www.ambientinsight.com/Resources/Documents/AmbientInsight-2012-2017-Middle-East-Mobile-Learning-Market-Abstract.pdf

Balsamo, A. (2011). *Designing culture: The technological imagination at work.* USA: Duke University Press.

Dabner, N. (2012). "Breaking Ground" in the use of social media: A case study of a university earthquake response to inform educational design with Facebook. *Internet and Higher Education*, 15(1), 69-78.

Eid, N. (2014). ARAIEQ: Working Together to Improve Education Quality in the MENA Region. *Telecentre Foundation*, (July 21, 2014). http://community.telecentre.org/profiles/blogs/araieq-working-together-to-improve-education-quality-in-the-mena

Elgort, I. (2005). E-learning adoption: Bridging the chasm, *Proceedings of ASCILITE 2005*, 181-185. http://www.ascilite.org.au/conferences/brisbane05/blogs/proceedings/20_Elgort.pdf

GSM Association (GSMA) and A.T. Kearney. (2011). *African Mobile Observatory 2011: Driving Economic and Social Development through Mobile Services.* London, UK, GSMA.

Jaatun, M. G., Zhao, G. & Rong, C. (Eds.). (2010, Dec.). Cloud computing. *First International Conference, CloudCom 2009*, Beijing, China, 2009, Proceedings (Vol. 5931). Springer.

Li, J. (2010). Study on the development of mobile learning promoted by cloud computing. In *IEEE 2010 2nd International Conference on Information Engineering and Computer Science* (ICIECS), 1-4.

Livingstone, S. (2011). Africa's Evolving Infosystems: A Pathway to Security and Stability, *The Africa Center for Strategic Studies*, (March 2011).

Meyer, K. A. & Wilson, J. L. (2011). The role of online learning in the disaster plans of flagship universities. *Online Journal of Distance Learning Administration*, 14(1). http://eric.ed.gov

Rao, M. (2011). *Mobile Africa Report 2011: Regional Hubs of Excellence and Innovation.* Mobile Monday. http://www.mobilemonday.net/reports/MobileAfrica_2011.pd

Samih, M. (2013). How i-learn. *Al-Ahram Weekly*, (May 9, 2013). http://weekly.ahram.org.eg/News/2494/25/How--i-learn.aspx

Stald, G. (2008). Mobile identity: Youth, identity, and mobile communication media. In D. Buckingham (Ed.), *Youth, identity, and digital media* (pp. 143 – 164). Cambridge: MIT Press.

Steel, J. Carmichael, B., Holmes, D. Kinse, M. & Sanders, K. (2007). Experiential learning and journalism education – Lessons learned in the practice of teaching journalism. *Education + Training*, 49(4), 325-333.

Weber, A. S. (2011). Cloud computing in education in the Middle East and North Africa (MENA) Region: Can barriers be overcome? In *Conference proceedings of eLearning and Software for Education* (No. 01, p. 565).

Media and Information Literacy in Higher Education in India

Harinder Pal Singh Kalra

India has a large and complex higher education system with 693 universities including central, state, deemed, and private universities. Digital infrastructures of universities are improving and so is affordability of Internet enabled devices among large populations of students. Under the framework of GAPMIL, a Media and Information Literacy University Network of India (MILUNI) has been established. MILUNI organized a national consultation meeting on media and information literacy (MIL) policy and strategy, as well as on MIL curriculum for higher education. MIL has been selected as one paper for developing e-content for the 'e-PG Pathshala' project. This project is a gateway for freely available e-content on post graduate courses and is being developed by INFLIBNET, an inter-university centre of the University Grants Commission. With the availability of e-content on media and information literacy a possibility in the near future, there is bright scope for MIL in higher education system in India, particularly in library and information science and journalism and mass communication departments as well as an inter-disciplinary course in choice-based credit system institutions.

Keywords: India, MILUNI, MIL education, higher education, GAPMIL, e-PG Pathshala, INFLIBNET

Higher Education System in India

The higher education system in India is a complex system with its origins after the 1857 uprising in British India. From three universities in 1857 to 693 universities at the end of 2014 the university system has flourished, and has become complex over these years. Today, the system consists of various types of universities namely central universities (set up through acts of Parliament and funded by Central Government), state universities (set up through state legislative assembly acts and funded by state governments), "deemed to be" universities (institutes set up in public and private sector that have been conferred university status), and private universities (set up under the state acts but funded privately). The breakup of universities as in November 2014 according to the University Grants Commission (UGC) is shown in Table 1.

Table 1. Universities in India with breakup according to types

Type of university	Number
Central universities	45
State universities	325
Deemed to be universities	128
Private universities	195
Total	**693**

Source: University Grants Commission (2014)

Further, the system consists of general universities, and specialist universities covering one or more subject areas such as agriculture (agricultural universities), medicine, law, science and technology, journalism and mass communication, etc. Then there are universities that offer most of their courses under a formal mode and a few courses in distance mode, and several open universities. Besides Indira Gandhi National Open University, there are several open universities, one each in a major state of the country. In the higher education sector, digital infrastructure in the public sector universities (central and state universities, and public sector "deemed to be" universities) has been growing since the turn of the century, although in some of these institutions, particularly the elite ones, digital infrastructures were quite well developed in the decade of 1990s. Most of the universities and many colleges in the country have some digital infrastructure, and many more are aspiring to set up computer laboratories and wi-fi zones within their campuses. The academic library sector (consisting of college and university libraries) is one of the most developed sectors of the library system in the country with many elite university libraries having world-class facilities. Though a few university libraries no better than traditional libraries of the 1970s can be found, those are exceptions rather than the rule. Parallel to the development of their parent institutions, most of the university and college libraries also began to transform themselves into hybrid or polymedia libraries with digital content besides print publications, and access to a large number of networked resources.

In the last few decades, India has witnessed a telecommunication revolution with the majority of its population now having access to mobile phones. The upper and lower middle class, comprising about 300 million people, now also has access to smart phones, laptops, tablets, and computers through which they access the Internet at work places, homes, or during travel. This is because of easy availability and affordability of the devices, and the ease with which Internet connectivity in urban, suburban, and rural areas is now being made available.

In summary, a college or university student from an urban or suburban area is most likely to have used the Internet more than once and is more likely than not to own a smart phone, tablet, laptop or a computer (maybe more than one device). The situation of students from rural areas is not as well as that of students from urban/suburban areas. In short, the Internet has permeated the higher education system both from the top end (institutions going in for digital connectivity) and the bottom end (students, teachers and researchers using the Internet). This transformation to a large digitally connected population of the country, with the higher education system as a microcosm of this transformation, serve as a background in which media and information literacy is discussed in this article.

UNESCO's Role in Media and Information Literacy

Media literacy and information literacy developed independently as two separate subjects but under the aegis of UNESCO (in particular its Communication and Information section) they have converged into media and information literacy (MIL). To promote MIL as a composite concept with semantic relationships between media literacy (ML) and information literacy (IL), UNESCO has been very active in identifying key areas which are common to both ML and IL. To develop global partnerships between various organizations, UNESCO organised a *Global Forum for Partnerships on Media and Information Literacy* in June 2013 at the *Conference on Promoting Media and Information Literacy as a Means to Cultural Diversity* held at Abuja (Nigeria). Close to 300 organizations from across the world responded. The Global Forum was an effort for a permanent mechanism aiming at

- articulating concrete partnerships to drive MIL development and impact globally;

- enabling the MIL community to speak as one voice on certain critical matters, particularly as it relates to policies;

- further deepening the strategy for MIL to be treated as a composite concept by providing a common platform for MIL related networks and associations globally (Global Alliance for Partnerships on Media and Information Literacy, 2015).

The permanent mechanism as an outcome of this Global Forum was the launch of Global Alliance for Partnerships on Media and Information Literacy (GAPMIL) in June 2013. One of the initiatives of GAPMIL, has been to develop regional and national networks on MIL, for example, the Asia-Pacific Chapter of GAPMIL and the Pan-African Alliance on Media and Information Literacy (PAMIL), which are at different stages of development.

Media and Information Literacy University Network of India

At the national level, in India, a Media and Information Literacy University Network of India (MILUNI) was established with the support from UNESCO in 2014. The Punjabi University, Patiala in the state of Punjab (a state university), and Uttarakhand Open University, Haldwani in the state of Uttarakhand (a state university) have joined it along with FORMedia (Foundation for Responsible Media), a non-governmental organization. The Indira Gandhi National Open University (IGNOU) is also making efforts to join this network. Soon after its formation, an activity that was organised in November 2014 by FORMedia was a three-day National Consultation Meeting on MIL policy and strategy in which participants from Punjabi University, Uttarakhand Open University, IGNOU as well as many others from the media sector and the library and information sectors participated. Though seven ministries of the Government of India were invited for the National Consultation meeting, no one from the government sector turned up for the meeting. The third day of this meeting was reserved for discussion on developing a curriculum suited for Indian needs. On the third day, various MIL curricula, including the course curriculum of Athabasca University and a course on MIL developed by Central University of Himachal Pradesh, were discussed; and the meeting ended with developing a balanced curriculum on ML and IL contents. The outcome of the National Consultation meeting was a position paper on MIL Policy and Strategy, which is being submitted to various government authorities.

MIL as a Paper in e-PG Pathshala

'e-PG Pathshala' (pathshala=classroom) is an online gateway to freely available e-content for post-graduate courses. It is an initiative of the Ministry of Human Resource Development, Government of India under its project on the National Mission on Education through ICT (NME-ICT). INFLIBNET Centre (Information and Library Network Centre), an inter-university centre of the UGC is the implementing agency for the e-PG Pathshala project. During the national consultation meeting under the MILUNI, INFLIBNET agreed to develop e-content on MIL in e-PG Pathshala and organised a meeting of experts in February 2015.

Under the e-PG Pathshala plan, a Paper Coordinator is appointed who then assigns lesson writing of various modules of that paper to different subject experts. In the case of paper on MIL, the Paper Coordinator has been identified. Modules to be covered in the paper on MIL were also discussed and will be fine-tuned by the Paper Coordinator. Details of e-PG Pathshala and e-content are available at the website http://epgp.inflibnet.ac.in.

As per the INFLIBNET planning, a full-fledged paper on MIL at post-graduate level will soon be available. The modules of MIL paper have been designed keeping in mind the requirements of post-graduate students and would-be researchers. Many universities in the country are following choice-based credit system (CBCS) while a few others are in the process of shifting to CBCS. The availability of an online course on MIL would give a boost to various efforts that are largely directed at either IL or ML. Information literacy efforts are largely being carried out by university and other libraries who offer such programmes for their students. Several departments on library and information science in Indian universities have IL contents at Bachelors' and Masters' levels. The Punjabi University, Patiala offers a course on IL at the PhD level.

Scope of MIL in Higher Education in India

MIL has immense potential for adoption as an interdisciplinary choice-based credit course, if it is promoted properly. Many universities are offering inter-disciplinary courses at post-graduate level. It is for the departments of journalism and mass communications, and library and information science in Indian universities to adopt MIL as a paper in their course contents, and promote it as an inter-disciplinary paper, particularly where CBCS is in place. MILUNI can play a leading role in promoting MIL as an inter-disciplinary paper. With close to 700 universities in the country, and more than half of them in the public sector, there is a huge potential for MIL to be taken up in the near future, particularly so as digital infrastructures of the universities are improving and e-learning is becoming easier. If any direct support from the government sector is provided to MIL education in the near future, then there are even better chances of MIL being taken up as a paper in the higher education sector in the country.

In the next few years, MIL education through these initiatives has the potential to go a long way towards 'providing quality education and lifelong learning', which is one of the twelve universal goals and national targets of the post-2015 development agenda of the United Nations (A New Global Partnership, 2013). Developments in MIL education at the national level in India would also go a long way in furthering the objectives of GAPMIL.

References

A New Global Partnership: Eradicate Poverty and Transform Economies through Sustainable Development: The Report of the High-Level Panel of Eminent Persons on the Post-2015 Development Agenda (2013). http://www.un.org/sg/management/pdf/HLP_P2015_Report.pdf

e-PG Pathshala (2015). http://epgp.inflibnet.ac.in/about.php

Global Alliance for Partnerships on Media and Information Literacy (GAPMIL) http://www.unesco.org/new/en/communication-and-information/media-development/media-literacy/global-alliance-for-partnerships-on-media-and-information-literacy/

University Grants Commission (2014). Total No. of Universities in the Country as on 26.11.2014. http://www.ugc.ac.in/oldpdf/alluniversity.pdf

Information Literacy Initiatives at the Faculty of Philosophy in Sarajevo

Senada Dizdar & Lejla Hajdarpašić

Implementation of information literacy programmes in higher education institutions includes a spectrum of challenges especially in those institutions that are heterogeneous in terms of providing study programmes in different disciplines. In that regard, this article provides an overview of information literacy initiatives at the Faculty of Philosophy in Sarajevo (University in Sarajevo) that has fifteen different departments and illustrates major challenges in structuring appropriate information literacy programmes. This article provides a summary of the departments' information literacy initiatives and offers some recommendations through a discussion of planned activities for the introduction of information literacy programmes at the Faculty of Philosophy in Sarajevo.

Keywords: information literacy, lifelong learning, Faculty of Philosophy, University of Sarajevo

Introduction

The Faculty of Philosophy was opened in 1950 at University of Sarajevo which is one of the largest and oldest higher education institutions in Bosnia and Herzegovina. During its long tradition of existence, the Faculty of Philosophy initiated great efforts towards improving the quality of the educational process and study opportunities in the field of social sciences and humanities. Today, the faculty has 15 departments[1] whose curricula are structured according to the requirements of the Bologna principles introduced at University of Sarajevo in 2003.

The Bologna process that started in 1999 with the aim of the harmonization of the European higher education context significantly changed previous concept of education in social sciences and humanities as well as in other sciences. During its introduction among other things, the implementation of information literacy (IL) programmes gained importance and was followed by creation of different IL models and standards that are essentially "the premise for the initiation and implementation of IL programs" (Špiranec & Banek Zorica, 2008, p. 79). Concerning the presence of IL programmes at University of Sarajevo (UNSA), the analysis of a survey, carried out in 2011, involving a sample of 23 regular members and 3 associate members of UNSA found that at UNSA "the content of information literacy is addressed within the course entitled Methodology of scientific research (f = 11), within the subject Informatics (f = 7), in the regular schooling (f = 5)" (Hajdarpašić, Muslić & Isović, 2012, p. 44). This was a preliminary study to assess implementation of IL programmes at this higher education institution[2]. The findings supported the justification for a separate course (elective or mandatory) entitled 'Information Literacy' in the curriculum of Faculties and Academies of UNSA. Such step would enable UNSA to, on an on-going basis, "raise awareness of the importance of the lifelong learning concept and its connection to information literacy, promote the importance and the role of information professionals in the implementation of information literacy programmes, raise awareness of the necessary inclusion of information literacy subject in the curricula of higher education institutions at the University of Sarajevo" (Hajdarpašić, Muslić & Isović, 2012, p.46).

In response to the changes and recommendations above, the Department of Comparative Literature and Librarianship, and the Department of Education, introduced two IL projects in order to raise awareness on the significance of IL in contemporary formal higher education environment and consequently to stimulate and help the processes of implementing IL programmes.

Overview of IL Initiatives

Insights into the present state of IL at UNSA consequent to the above mentioned survey prompted a spectrum of IL initiatives at UNSA[3], motivated its regular and associate members, and stimulated other proactive activities at the Faculty of Philosophy as well. In the academic year 2011/2012 the programme of pedagogical training of teachers (PON– Pedagoško obrazovanje nastavnika) managed by Department of Education (funded by Open Society Fund-Bosnia and Herzegovina) during its innovative redefinition included the content entitled 'Information Literacy' in its structure. In the same academic year a project entitled 'School Libraries as a Means to Develop a Democratic Society through Strengthening Information Literacy and Lifelong Learning' was launched.

Programme of Pedagogical Training of Teachers

Programme of Pedagogical Training of Teachers (PON) is designed in accordance to the latest international recommendations and standards related to pedagogical training of teachers. It is a systematically designed educational process for pre-trained teachers. "Persons participating in PON usually have previously completed college or specialized school and gain diploma for certain professional fields such as architecture, biology, economics, etc. Accordingly, PON participants have professional qualifications but do not have qualifications for teaching" (Dedić & Hajdarpašić, 2013, p. 80). During the PON redefinition in academic year 2011/2012 "supporting idea for innovating teachers education came from two European documents on education, one is the OECD DeSeCo Program (Definition and Selection of Competencies: Theoretical and Conceptual Foundations) which defines the key competencies for active participation in life, and the second is the list of ISSA (International Step by Step Association) pedagogical standards that define the quality of teaching practice" (Mavrak & Hajdarpašić, 2012, p. 167). Since both documents recognize information literacy as indisputably important competency for teachers, the course 'Information Literacy' was inevitably introduced into new education cycles and was conducted in cooperation with the information professionals from the Department of Comparative Literature and Librarianship.

Content structure was designed around the themes selected in line with the heterogeneous needs of participants and *inter alia* with the following anticipated learning outcomes: "understanding the changes in the educational process, learning and transfer of skills that underpin information literacy, mastering skills needed for the evaluation of information sources, mastering search strategy skills on both the visible and the invisible web, understanding the concept of the Internet as a new paradigm of social relations, raising awareness about the importance of promotion, creation and use of open educational resources, etc." (Mavrak & Hajdarpašić, 2012, p.172).

The inclusion of information literacy content in PON 2011/2012 was followed by extensive comparison of the expected learning outcomes with actual learning outcomes obtained from the analysis of the evaluation sheets that the participants of the first innovative PON cycle had filled. Since the analysis discovered that actual learning outcomes largely correspond to anticipated learning outcomes, in the next cycle of PON 2012/2013, the content information literacy was once again performed in similar arrangement. In the second cycle, it was once again revealed that there was a large correspondence between actual and anticipated learning outcomes. This confirmation was especially encouraging in terms of participants' plans regarding application of the acquired competencies. The process and findings continued in the 2013/2014 and 2014/2015 cycles as well.

School Libraries as a Means to Develop a Democratic Society

In order to further draw attention to IL as the key to development of both the society and economy, the Department of Comparative Literature and Librarianship in association with Department of Education launched in 2012, initiated another IL related project entitled 'School Libraries as a Means to Develop a Democratic Society through Strengthening Information Literacy and Lifelong Learning.' The objective of this Project (funded by U.S. Embassy in Sarajevo) was to promote, implement and strengthen information literacy in 39 high-school libraries across Canton Sarajevo. In order to achieve this objective, it was stated in the project documentation that the curriculum of the school librarian needs to be fortified with new competencies which would be relevant to information literacy. This in turn calls for the following aims to be met: (1) Research and analysis of the current situation in the libraries and library profession in high-schools of Canton Sarajevo, (2) Clearly delineating professional and generic competencies of a school librarian, (3) Implementation of the educational programme – information literacy for lifelong professional development of librarians in the context of their lifelong learning, (4) Developing information literacy competencies of the librarians in order to be able to: define the information needs, locate, assign value and use the given information, (5) Strengthening the pedagogical competencies of the librarian and their didactic and methodical skills in communication and education of other target groups (students, teachers, school management, etc.), (6) Increasing the awareness of the modern role of the library as an information centre of life-long learning (Libraries as a Means to Develop a Democratic Society through Strengthening Information Literacy and Lifelong Learning, S-BK800-13-GR-032).

During the project implementation and through organization of a round-table and series of workshops on different topics including information resources, information control, understanding economic, legal and social aspects of information, and its ethical and legal use, librarians were reminded that the newly emerging paradigm of learning and the reformative efforts call for including the information literacy in education. Accordingly, librarians were familiarized with all the latest guidelines, standards in the field of school librarianship and modern pedagogical principles and approaches so that they could knowledgeably implement IL programmes within their libraries and school communities. Special attention was given to the librarians' feedback during the project implementation. One of this feedback resulted in the creation of School Libraries Information Portal[4] that is still running. The librarians addressed their problems regarding insufficient and slow communication among the secondary school library community. The mentioned specialized portal was created in order to connect and inform librarians of primary and secondary schools of Bosnia and Herzegovina and all other interested parties about the latest activities, projects and innovative programmes in the field of school librarianship.

The objective of project 'Libraries as a Means to Develop a Democratic Society through Strengthening Information Literacy and Lifelong Learning' was to assist in transforming the school library into a place for preparing individuals for an active participation in a democratic society through strengthening IL as well as to discover potential librarian professionals and other needs in order to improve and where necessary redefine the departments curriculum in upcoming period. Analysis of the surveys of the participants of the workshops and round-tables, as well as post-meeting follow-up feedback showed that this project successfully reached its pre-set objectives. Some of the key results from the evaluation surveys are as follows: understanding the concept of information literacy and its role in lifelong learning, recognition of different librarian roles in the new school/community environment, increasing responsible development/use of information and IT competencies of librarians (skills related to information locating, understanding and use of information in order to encourage positive attitudes and value judgment in relation to information), popularization and broadening of ICT use in education and school work.

Lessons Learned, Future Plans and Conclusions

Experiences of four cycles of the PON and the school librarian oriented projects regarding implementation of IL contents demonstrated that through careful selection of IL themes, purposeful IL programmes can be structured for participants that are diverse in terms of their existing knowledge, interests and competencies. Among the participants that graduated in Bologna and pre-Bologna study systems, there is a strong evident need for strengthening their existing IL competencies. These and other useful findings are stimulating departments to start initiatives on the inclusion of a separate IL course in all departments' curricula. In this regard, these departments are planning to raise awareness that the implementation of a separate IL course in the departments' curricula should be focused on students at the Bachelor of Arts level and should be presented as a mandatory course. The design of such course and its administration take into consideration all relevant IL standards, models, and recommendations oriented towards higher education institutions. In addition, the course should be thoroughly examined and adapted in accordance to faculty needs as accentuated in the 'Guidelines on Information Literacy for Lifelong Learning (2006).' Since these improvements require major changes in the design of the departments' already complex curricula, strong management commitment is expected. In the context of an evidenced-based approach to IL implementation, it is emphasized that in recent times IL has become a subject of study in a few masters' papers and doctoral studies in the Department of Comparative Literature and Librarianship, and numerous studies and papers already discussed IL issues at UNSA, some promoting IL as a meta-competency of lifelong learning (Dizdar, 2012). These considerable research efforts should be interpreted as additional foundations, advantages and motives for the inclusion of IL courses in the curricula of all the departments.

References

Dedić, E. & Hajdarpašić, L. (2013). Informacijska pismenost: sadržaj programa obrazovanja nastavnika / ca. *Obrazovanje odraslih: Časopis za obrazovanje odraslih i kulturu*, (1) pp. 79-89.

Dizdar, S. *Informacijska pismenost – metakompetencija za cjeloživotno učenje*. Retrieved March 4, 2015, from the UNSA website: http://unsa.ba/s/index.php?option=com_content&task=view&id=1151&Itemid=348&lang=bosanski

Hajdarpašić, L., Muslić, F. & Isović, J. (2012). Information Literacy and Faculties / Academies of University of Sarajevo. *Zbornik radova IX Međunarodne naučne konferencije bibliotekara „Juni na Uni": Informacijska pismenost – cjeloživotno učenje* (pp. 49-57). Bihać: Kantonalna i univerzitetska biblioteka Bihać.

Lau, J. (2006). *Guidelines on Information Literacy for Lifelong Learning*. Retrieved March 4, 2015, from the IFLA website: http://www.ifla.org/files/assets/information-literacy/publications/ifla-guidelines-en.pdf

Mavrak, M. & Hajdarpašić, L. (2012). Informacijska pismenost i pedagoško obrazovanje nastavnika. *6 Savjetovanje o reformi visokog obrazovanja. Kontinuitet reforme visokog obrazovanja* (pp. 165-179). Sarajevo: Univerzitet u Sarajevu.

Špiranec, S. & Banek Zorica, M. (2008). *Informacijska pismenost: teorijski okvir i polazišta*. Zagreb: Zavod za informacijske studije Odsjeka za informacijske znanosti Filozofskog fakulteta Sveučilišta u Zagrebu.

Notes

1   Faculty of Philosophy has following departments: Department of English Language and Literature, Department of Bosnian, Croatian and Serbian languages, Department of Philosophy and Sociology, Department of German Language and Literature, Department for Romanic Studies, Department of Bosnian, Croatian and Serbian Literatures, Department of Comparative Literature and Librarianship, Department of Oriental Philology, Department of Education (Pedagogical Sciences), Department of Psychology, Department of Slavic Languages and Literatures, Department of History, with a History of Art Studies Program and Archeology Studies Program.

2   This analysis findings should not be inadequately interpreted i.e. they are somewhat justified with the unenviable social and economic opportunities, consequences of war conflicts, and other complexity of Bosnia and Herzegovina as a country in transition.

3   In respect to the findings provided by interpretation of the UNSA Questionnaire and in order to help the processes of IL programs implementation at UNSA in upcoming period UNSA, inter alia, throw its active and notable participation in Tempus Project entitled *Developing information literacy for lifelong learning and knowledge economy in Western Balkan countries* already in 2012 published the publication *Information Literacy: Guidelines for Innovative Network Modules Developing* (by authors Senada Dizdar, Lejla Turčilo, Baba Ešrefa Rašidović and Lejla Hajdarpašić). Second edition of this textbook was published in 2014 and once again was funded by aforementioned Tempus Project with pre-set objective to raise awareness on IL significance and provide preconditions for the inclusion of IL Programs in curriculums of UNSA academies and faculties.

4   See: http://ipzb.ff.unsa.ba/

Media Organizations, Information Providers, and Freedom of Expression

Measuring Media and Information Literacy: Implications for the Sustainable Development Goals

Alton Grizzle

In January 2015, the Leadership Council of the Sustainable Development Solution Network released a seminal draft report on proposed indicators and a monitoring framework for the Sustainable Development Goals (SDGs). As the world embarks on measuring and monitoring the SDGs, the level of information and media competencies of all citizens around the world must also be measured to help to stimulate their involvement in sustainable development. This article suggests that there is an urgent need for media and information literacy (MIL) or information and media literacy revolution (whichever juxtaposition is preferred by the reader). It describes MIL in the context of development. Drawing on existing research and frameworks it considers the what, why, and how of MIL measurement. It intersperses implications for the SDGs and ends with a focused section on further implications, recommendations and actions for further research.

Keywords: media and information literacy, development information, sustainable development goals, measurement, assessment, UNESCO

Introduction

Communicating development to citizens and their participation in the development processes necessitate that development is communicated in manner understandable to the public. Mr Ban Ki Moon, Secretary-General of the United Nations in his synthesis report, the *Road to Dignity by 2030* notes, "…making our economies inclusive and sustainable, our understanding of economic performance, and our metrics for gauging it, must be broader, deeper and more precise…to realize the sustainable development agenda, we also need measurable targets and technically rigorous indicators."[1] He goes on to say that if people are to be at the centre of development, development progress must go beyond Gross Domestic Product.

The seminal draft report on proposed indicators and a monitoring framework for the Sustainable Development Goals (SDGs) of the Leadership Council of the Sustainable Development Solution Network[2], a global initiative for the United Nations, has attracted much attention from the development community. The subtitle of the report reads, "Launching a data revolution for the SDGs". The world has been witness to the information age for over two decades. UNESCO's introduction of the concept of "Knowledge Societies[3]" at 2003 World Summit on Information Society (WSIS) would suggests that citizens of the world have been experiencing the knowledge age (the author's twist on this concept) for more than a decade now. This would indicate a certain progression towards the age of wisdom, the age of innovation, and the age of finding that there is a God or one may add finding that there is no God[4]. Then why the sudden turn again to "Big Data"? The astronomical advances in technology and exponential growth in digital storage capacities and speed have caused a sort of fixation and obsession with the massive amount of data that exist and is being collected. A "data revolution for the SDGs" means more data about development. Many experts, including a chapter in this 2015 MILID Yearbook have been calling for "data literacy". It is unequivocal that we need more new, precise and measureable data on development for 21st Century. Yet, an Internet search for the term "Development Information" yielded 2,450,000 pages[5]. The world is already standing under a Niagara Falls of development information and data[6]. With citizens at the centre of development, what competencies must they possess to have even a basic understanding of how the SDGs will be measured and monitored and how these relate to their lives? For the purposes of this article, by measuring media and information literacy the author means assessment and monitoring media and information literacy levels among citizens and the extent to which countries possess the necessary expertise or human resources, pedagogical material, access to information, media and technology, and policies to ensure media and information literacy for all[7].

Media and Information Literacy and Development

Before delving into how to measure media and information literacy (MIL), let us first consider what MIL is? MIL is a "Big Tent[8]", a composite concept that covers all competencies related to media literacy and information literacy buoyed and anchored by digital or technological literacy.

I offer a simple but not simplistic proof that "media literacy" = "information literacy" = "digital literacy" driven by a common denominator, technology.

The following simple mathematical equation would help:

If   M = X,

       I = Y

       L = Z and

       X, Y and Z are equal,

Then, M=I= L, taken together is MIL, media and information literacy with technology embedded.

The Table 1 below illustrates and illuminates the point well. In the table X = competencies of media literacy[9]; Y = competencies of information literacy[10] and Z = competencies for digital literacy[11].

Table 1. Broad media and information literacy competencies as described from various sources

	X (Media Literacy)	Y (Information Literacy)	Z (Digital Literacy/ ICT Literacy)	Comments on Broad Competencies
1.		Define information needs		
2.	Able to access and media, information and technology	Effectively access information from variety of sources	Access – knowledge about being able to collect or retrieve, get access to information	Symmetry exists
3.	Basic skills to use the Internet and computers	Knowing how to use computers, technology or the Internet to access information	Access – be able to open software, sort out and save information on computers, simple skills to use computers and software, download different types of information from the Internet, ability to orient oneself in the digital world and strategies to use the Internet	Symmetry exists
4.	Critically analyse media text	Critically evaluate and reflect on information, its nature, accuracy, balance, relevance, and technical infrastructure, social and cultural context etc.	Evaluate –be able to check, evaluate make judgment about, the quality relevance, objectivity, efficiency, usefulness, of information found or information searched for including on the Internet	Symmetry exists

	X (Media Literacy)	Y (Information Literacy)	Z (Digital Literacy/ICT Literacy)	Comments on Broad Competencies
5.	Distinguish between media content	Differentiate between different types of information	Integrate – interpreting and representing information or be able to compare and put together different types of information that relates to "multimodal texts". In other sense it is being able to summarize, compare and contrast information.	Symmetry exists
6.	Recognize importance to rely on information	Define information needs	Recognize the importance of information and communication technology (ICTs)	Symmetry exists
7.	Critically analyze media systems for ownership concentration, pluralism and regulations, rules and rights, authors' rights and users' rights etc.	Recognize and assess ethical, legal, social, economic, and political issues concerning information and technology	Critical evaluation of information sources	Symmetry exists
8.	Explore information and critical search for information	Design investigative methods and search strategies search for information from variety of sources	Same as Access above. In addition, Search – know about and how to get access to information	Symmetry exists
9.	Citizens participation activities such as intercultural dialogue, democracy, e-government	Seeking and using information for self-learning, lifelong learning, participatory citizenship and social responsibility	Communicate – "be able to communicate information and express oneself through different mediational means" (Erstad, 2010, p. 45)	Symmetry exists
10.	Cooperation and collaborative work and problem solving	Use information for problem solving and decision making	Cooperation and interaction through networked environment such as the Internet, social media, collaborative working tools, taking advantage of digital technology for learning and collaboration	Symmetry exists

	X (Media Literacy)	Y (Information Literacy)	Z (Digital Literacy/ ICT Literacy)	Comments on Broad Competencies
11.	Media production skills, creativity and user genera- ted content	Synthesize new idea to generate new knowledge, story or ideas or know how to create or cause to be created unavai- lable information	Create – ability to produce, sample, remix, adapt, create, design, invent, author, different forms of information as multi- modal text, including designing web pages. Ultimately to produce new information or new products based on specific tools or software	Symmetry exists
12.		Know how to orga- nize, preserve and store information	Manage or Classify – being able to organize information according to existing organizational schemes, classifica- tion or genre	Symmetry exists

Of course these competencies may vary from context to context or expert to expert. As Livingstone (2004) pointed out; "how media literacy is defined has consequences for the framing of the debate, the research agenda, and policy initiatives" (ibid, p.5; see also Fedorov, 2015, p. 11-16 for similar discussion). In functioning knowledge societies, there is consensus that citizens of all ages need information literacy competencies to cope with continuous social, econo- mic and cultural changes there is less agreement on which set of competencies priority should be placed (cf. Virkus, 2011). However a closer analysis of Table 1 reveals that there is more agreement than departures on what are the key com- petencies. Symmetry exists across almost all the competencies though prima- rily from different viewpoints and standpoints with diverging yet converging emphases. These ever converging emphases are often crowded out by "noise channels[12]" of communication on MIL. In sum, these "divconverging" emphases are information and information and library studies; media and media, com- munication and journalism studies; and finally the digital and information and technological studies (see Livingstone et al., 2009 for similar analysis).

It has been mentioned earlier that development information must be com- municated simply to all citizens to ensure their understanding and participa- tion. It now applies to MIL to address why it should be measured. The MIL competencies detailed above have been compared to basic literacy (numeracy, reading, writing etc.) by many experts (ibid; see Lau, 2009). Media and information literacy is literacy (Grizzle, 2014). The importance of literacy to development needs no further evidence in this the 21st Century. Figure 1 illustrates the connection between MIL and development. A basic triangle that everyone can identify with, "While media [and information] literacy is deemed crucial for the development and sustainability of a healthy democratic public sphere, it is often forgotten as a precondition when discussing democracy and development" (Martinsson, 2009, p. 3).

Figure 1. The Thrust of MIL

Sustainable development, good governance, intercultural and interreligious dialogue, freedom of expression, equality etc.

Media and other Information providers including those on the Internet

Media and information literate citizens

Source: Grizzle, Moore et al., (2013)

Measuring the SDGs

Now that the "what" of and "why" MIL should be measured have been established and before exploring "how", let us consider a snapshot of deliberations underway to measure the SDGs. As is the case with measuring any concept, phenomenon or object, measuring sustainable development also starts with the question of what to measure. At the time of writing this article, the international development community was finalizing agreement on 17 development goals[13]. They range from poverty, hunger, health, education, gender equality, environment, infrastructure, peace and inclusive societies to international partnerships for development.

In January 2015, the Leadership Council of the Sustainable Development Solution Network (SDSN) released a seminal draft report on proposed indicators and a monitoring framework for the SDGs. The stated purpose of the indicators is:

> …*management (to stay on course), and accountability (to hold all stake-holders to the SDGs). For management purposes, the indicators need to be accurate and frequent, reported at least once per year (p. 124).*

They will enable track of the SDGs at local, national, regional, and global levels. The target groups for use of these indicators are local and national governments, "civil society can use them for operational, monitoring, and advocacy purposes," and businesses. In short all stakeholders. The 17 SGDs are each described, furnished with an indicator(s) and linked to five other cardinals which are: rationale and definition of the indicators, disaggregation, comments and limitations, preliminary assessment of current data availability by Friends of the Chair and potential lead UN agency or agencies. An example 'verbatim example' of Goal 16: Promote peaceful and inclusive societies for sustainable development, provide access to justice for all and build effective, accountable and inclusive institutions at all levels – is provided below for illustration.

In the January 15, 2015 version of the report an extract of Goal 16 reads as follows:

> *Indicator 99: [Indicator on freedom of expression, peaceful assembly, association] – to be developed*
>
> *Rationale and definition: The ability to express oneself freely, to assemble peacefully, and to associate are enshrined in the Universal Declaration of Human Rights and form an important part of achieving peaceful and inclusive societies. Possible indicators for freedom of expression include measures of press freedom, such as censorship, perceptions of press independence, and intimidation, harassment or imprisonment of journalists.192 Indicators on freedom of peaceful assembly and association include measures of whether these freedoms are guaranteed in law and respected in practice.193*
>
> *Disaggregation: To be determined.*
>
> *Comments and limitations: To be determined.*
>
> *Preliminary assessment of current data availability by Friends of the Chair: To be determined.*
>
> *Potential lead agency or agencies: To be determined (p. 100).*

In the March 20, 2015 version the extract now reads as follows:

Indicator 93: Existence and implementation of a national law and/or constitutional guarantee on the right to information

Rationale and definition: This indicator helps assess whether a country has a legal or policy framework that protects and promotes access to information. Public access to information helps ensure institutional accountability and transparency. It is important to measure both the existence of such a framework and its implementation, as good laws may exist but they may not be enforced. This can be simply due to a lack of capacity, more systematic institutional resistance, or a culture of secrecy or corruption. 234 Furthermore, exceptions or contradictory laws, such as government secrecy regulations, can erode these guarantees.

Disaggregation: TBD.

Comments and limitations: It is also important that public access to information be timely, accessible, user-friendly and free of charge, though this is beyond the current scope of the indicator.

Preliminary assessment of current data availability by Friends of the Chair: TBD.

Primary data source: International monitoring (p. 179).

Whether the latter or former formulation holds in the final version of the indicators, media and information literate citizens would be aware that laws guaranteeing access to information and/or freedom of expression is a necessary but not sufficient step towards achieving open, inclusive, accountable and transparent sustainable development. All citizens require media and information literacy competencies to effectively and ethically capitalize on the opportunities and navigate the challenges attendant to free access to information and freedom of expressions (cf. Grizzle, Moore et al., 2013; see also Martinsson; Panos, 2007). The SDSN recommended that relevant SDG indicators be disaggregated according the following dimensions: sex and gender, age, income, disability, religion, race, ethnicity, familial descent or indigenous status, economic activity, spatial disaggregation (e.g. by metropolitan areas, urban and rural, or districts), and migrant status.

Measuring the SDGs will generate a huge amount of development information; most of which will be understood by experts. Some will find its way into academic research again mostly targeting the well-educated. Yet this information will be sampled and adapted by the media and other information providers, including those on the Internet, in the form of news, articles, talk shows, videos, animation, etc. At whatever level the development information will be assimilated, MIL or information and media literacy will be critical to enable all citizens to understand and critically analyze it (the development information) irrespective of how it is communicated. Furthermore, even at the stage of articulation of the SDGs and their indicators, despite the wide consultation, achieving media and information literacy for all would enable even wider consultation and involvement of the masses in determining priorities and setting targets. At the moment of writing, the media, ICTs and freedom of expression are largely marginalized in the proposed SDGs despite mounting evidence of their centrality to development[14] (see also Banda, 2014[15]).

The next section tackles how to measure MIL.

Measuring Media and Information Literacy

There is consensus among MIL experts that more research needs to be done to affirm the impact of MIL on societies (Frau-Meigs, 2006; Buckingham, 1998; Casey et al., 2008; Dovy & Kennedy, 2006 as cited in Grizzle & Calvo, 2013).

Kamerer (2013) noted, "While media literacy education advocates have published abundantly, there are relatively few data-based studies…" (ibid, p.15). In the main, empirical studies are related to media and information literacy techniques such as interpersonal interventions; assessing the effectiveness and impact of MIL school programmes as well as non-formal initiatives; MIL and health such as drug or alcohol abuse and eating habits; and research habits or information seeking behaviour of students and citizens in general (cf. ibid; see also Pariera, 2012; Singh & Horton, 2013 in Carlsson & Culver, 2013).

Hobbs and Frost (2003) undertook a long term study on media literacy in secondary schools in the United States of America. The research was carried out over a one year period, in a quasi-experimental design, to assess the acquisition of media literacy by a group of grade eleven students at the Concord High School. Along with the quasi-experimental design, other methods such as interviews with students and teachers and classroom observations were used. Data were collected on the entire population of 293 students in this treatment school and random sample of 89 students from the control school. The treatment group was exposed to a year-long programme in media literacy programme which focused on specific competencies. Students who were exposed to the media literacy programme and received pre-test and post-test were compared to those who did not do the media literacy course but also received pre-test and post-test. The researchers found that, for reading and comprehension, the group that did the media literacy course scored higher than those of the control group. Statistically significant differences were shown between the two groups' ability to listen and identify the main ideas of television news broadcast. In sum, the "results indicate that media-literacy instruction improves students' ability to understand and summarise information they learned from reading, listening and viewing" (ibid p. 344; see also Kamerer, 2013).

Hobbs and Frost adapted the model used by Quin, McMahon and Quin (1996) which was the first school-based long-term research on media literacy education. The study was conducted in Australia and involved a sample of 1500 students (Kamerer, 2013, p. 16).

In a short term research, over six months, Cheung (2011) carried out a study of the impact of media education on students' media analysis skills. He employed what he calls a "multi-method, multi-source data collection strategy." Evidence from different methods were then triangulated. This consisted of both qualitative and quantitative methods such as, document analysis, interviews, classroom observation, and "diary writing in the form of reflection sheets" (ibid p. 58). The sample was made up of three groups of schools, School A, B, and C – each group had similar characteristics. 151, 153 and 164 secondary school students were selected from each group of schools, respectively. Cheung administered a questionnaire as the pre-test and post-test. He used ten 40 minute media education lessons over a three month period. The lessons covered media messages from advertisement songs, television games shows, movies, and comics. The research findings revealed significantly higher overall scores for students in School A and B after the media education lessons in comparison to scores before the intervention. An interesting detail of the findings showed that "female students scored significantly higher and demonstrated significantly greater improvement in overall skills than male students", where media messages bore personal relevance to them as females (ibid p. 65).

It is necessary to consider empirical studies about information literacy in line with the proposed analysis for assessment to move from two separated fields, media literacy and information literacy, to a new convergent field, media and information literacy.

In a study of information literacy on the web, Pariera (2012) set out to ascertain, in the main, whether participants depended more on *textual or visual cues* to determine credibility of health information on the web. The perceptions as to whether or not the website was credible were compared between those websites with appealing designs of high quality, and those with perceived poor design quality (ibid p. 37). Websites were specifically designed for the purposes of the study. The sample consisted of 75 undergraduate students pursuing a course in psychology at a private US university. The research divided the sample into two different experimental groups – *low credibility group (LCG) and high credibility group (HCG)* – and carried analysis between and within the groups. In general, based on certain characteristics, the LCG was considered as *below average information seekers* and the HCG as a*bove average information seekers*. Participants in each group were shown a website of *low design quality* and one of *high design quality*. Both groups were exposed to the same websites. In addition to design, high credibility *textual cues* such as author name, author credentials and affiliation, date of publication, references, and no advertisements (ibid p. 41) were featured. The research showed that "participants in the low credibility group ranked both websites as equally credible, despite the difference in design quality. Participants in the high credibility group, however, ranked the high design website as more credible… overall, when viewing a website with traditional high credibility cues, a good design will bolster the credibility rating but cannot compensate for a lack of credibility cues. This indicates that textual cues (or lack of them) are more important than visual cues" (ibid p. 44).

Kamerer (2013) noted that one of the most frequent applications of media literacy to research is in relation to how "the media form images of health and body image" (ibid p. 16). He cited many media literacy scholars in health education research. Irving, Dupen and Berel (1998, referred to in Kamerer, 2013) gave short one-off training to high school girls on how attractiveness is represented by media. The study showed that students who were exposed to the study "were less likely to internalize a thin beauty standard" and showed lower perceived realism of the types of beauty images portrayed by the media (ibid p.16; see also Wade, Davidson & O'Dea, 2003; Watson & Vaughn, 2006; Austin & Johnston, 1997 for similar studies relating to media literacy and health) [cf. Grizzle, 2014].

Comparing and Contrasting Media and Information Assessment Frameworks

Two of the leading international development organizations working on MIL, UNESCO and the European Commission, have developed or commissioned the development of MIL assessment frameworks and studies.

Table 2. Comparison of two MIL frameworks based on eight key dimensions

Critical Dimensions of the Frameworks	UNESCO MIL Assessment Framework[16]	European Commission Study and Assessment Criteria for Media Literacy[17] (ML)
	This assessment framework is being piloted. UNESCO's General Conference requested need to "develop the critical abilities of media and information users by increasing media and information literacy".	This assessment framework has been tested and some results provided. It has developed and applied under European Commission Directive.[18]
Context	• Global in scope. • An overall focus on development. • Literacy in the context of 21 Century and sustainable development. • Lifelong learning and citizens participation in sustainable development. • Knowledge society including digital and knowledge divide, managing risks and opportunities. • Rights based approach, fundamental freedoms such as freedom of expression and access to information.	• European/regional scope. • An overall focus on business and society, economy and globalization. • Advances in technology and social networks and the effects of these and traditional mass media on the European economy and citizens, citizens' participation in democracies and safe and appropriate use of media and ICTs. • Competitive audiovisual and content/online information services industry and inclusive knowledge society/economy; protection of minors in context of this competiveness. • Lifelong learning.
Purpose/Objectives	• Provide evidence-based information to improve governments capacity to design and implement MIL. • Provide tools that can be used for assessments of competencies among citizens including students, young people, teachers and other professionals. • Promote self-assessment by national governments of national. • Enable the effectiveness of the work of educational institutions, media and other information providers.	• Promote critical thinking and skills and awareness with a more general objective of free speech, right to information and intercultural dialogue. • Provide the Commission with criteria to measure M. • Provide an actual assessment of the 27 EU counties. • Evaluation social and economic impact of various ML levels and policies. • Offer recommendations for EU level to support further country/community level actions.

Critical Dimensions of the Frameworks	UNESCO MIL Assessment Framework[16]	European Commission Study and Assessment Criteria for Media Literacy[17] (ML)
Interdisciplinary approach	It employs an explicitly stated interdisciplinary approach to MIL conceptualization and assessment. Firstly, it adopts a definition of basic literacy which must be broader than reading, writing and arithmetic. Secondly, it espouses media and information literacy as a composite concept through integration of competencies related information, libraries, media and technology, including the Internet and social media.	It does not consider an explicit interdisciplinary concept of MIL in its context/rationale. However "interdisciplinarity[19]" is evident in the broad competencies and indicators (what the UNESCO framework calls, 'performance criteria') as described below. ML is taken to cover traditional media, technology/digital skills as well as some information competencies but with no specific reference to libraries or information literacy.
Type of learning domains	Competencies covers knowledge, skills and attitude related to MIL – cognitive, psychomotor, and affective.	Competencies covers knowledge, skills and attitude related to MIL – cognitive, psychomotor, and affective.
Broad assessment levels	Employed a two-tiered approach; **Tier One** – *MIL Country Readiness* and **Tier 2** – *MIL Competencies.*	Identifies two dimensions of ML to be assessed: the **first dimensions** *Individual Competencies* and the **second**, *Environmental Factors.*
Broad Assessment Categories/Competencies/Components of the Frameworks at each level	**At the Tier One** level main categories of indicators for **country readiness** assessment are: 1) Is MIL integrated in education? 2) Do national MIL policies and strategies exist? 3) Are media and quality information readily available to public? 4) Overlapping with category 3, assesses whether citizens actually access and use information, media and technology, and 5) 'muti-stakeholderism', is there a vibrant civil society involvement of civil society in MIL? **At the Tier Two** level broad **MIL competencies** consist:1) Access and Retrieval, 2) Understanding and Evaluation, and 3) Creation and Utilization – of information and media content. • All competencies are considered of equal weight and importance.	The dimension **Environmental factors** is equivalent to country readiness in the UNESCO framework and consists of: 1) media availability/penetration (including cinema), 2) availability of media education[20] 3) media literacy policies, 4) media industry and their role in promoting ML.. The dimension **Individual Competencies** (is equivalent to MIL Competencies in the UNESCO framework)is divided into social competencies and personal competencies and covers: 1) Communicative Abilities, 2) Critical Understanding and 3) Use and Skills. • Environment factors and individual competencies were weighted according to importance/value.

Critical Dimensions of the Frameworks	UNESCO MIL Assessment Framework[16]	European Commission Study and Assessment Criteria for Media Literacy[17] (ML)
Assessment Process/ Methodology/Use of the Frameworks	• The process entail simple and complex steps such as establishing national committee and teams, prepare plan, adapt tools, collect, process, analyze and dissemination of data. Use of statistical modeling and Computer Assisted Testing. • Outcome of assessment at the **Tier One level** can be that country readiness is Favourable, Favouable/Balance or Unfavourable; At the **Tier Two level** the MIL proficiency level of an individual can be Basic, Intermediate or Advanced.	• No detailed step by step process for use of this MIL assessment framework was given but was implicit in certain aspects of the methodology used to carry out the pilot assessments and centered on the use of various tools created. • Outcome of the assessment for both dimensions can be that the individual and environment is a at a Basic, Media and Advanced level in respect to ML competencies and development/stimuli, respectively. Use of statistical model.
Tools/Instruments provided	**At the Tier One** level three questionnaires are provided, one each for national context, teaching institutions, and individual. **At the Tier Two** level comprehensive **MIL competency** matrix is provided with 113 performance criteria covering the three broad competencies described above. In addition, a questionnaire for paper-pencil based test of teachers is being prepared.	Questionnaire for experts in connection with **Environmental Factors;** 22 indictors are used for this dimensions. An assessment tool, connected to **both dimensions** that can be used to select certain indicators and weight them according to relevance to illustrate the overall assessment of ML at the national level. 36 indicators are used to assess **Individual Competencies.**

There are similarities but noticeable and important difference in perspectives across all critical dimensions of the two frameworks. While further discussion on this comparison is warranted, the scope of this article does not permit more in depth analysis. The author will publish this analysis in a future paper. Other broad-based and multiple nations MIL assessments have been carried out in Europe drawing on both frameworks described above. The European Cooperation in Science and Technology (COST) Network and ANR TRANSLIT[21] and the European Media Education Research Study[22] (EMEDUS). Both studies involved MIL or ML assessment in European countries. The former focused on MIL Policies in 29 countries, investigating cardinals such as conceptualization of MIL (linking media literacy, information literacy, computer literacy and digital literacy), policy frameworks, training, resources, funding and evaluation. The latter focused more on media literacy curricula and education policies in 27 Europe countries. Fedorov (2015) undertook a comprehensive research of media literacy environment or country readiness in Russia, based on his own analytical frameworks. UNESCO has also supported preliminary assessment of MIL levels among teachers[23] in the Caribbean, Africa and Asia. Finally, UNESCO supported MIL assessment among university students[24] in 12 Asian countries.

Conclusion and Implications for the Sustainable Development Goals

According to the World Bank "open development is about making [development] information and data freely available and searchable, encouraging feedback, information-sharing, and accountability[25]…"The United Nations have made significant strides to get better at citizens' engagement in development. A good example is the Massive Open Online Course (MOOC) on Citizens' Engagement[26] launched by the World Bank. This article has proposed that citizens engagement in development and open development in connection with the SDGs are mediated by media and information providers including those on the Internet as well their level of media and information literacy. It is on this basis that UNESCO, as part of its comprehensive MIL programme has set up a MOOC on MIL[27]. Measuring MIL has ramifications for measuring and monitoring the SDGs implementation. If we recall the SDG 16 referenced above, *Promote peaceful and inclusive societies for sustainable development, provide access to justice for all and build effective, accountable and inclusive institutions at all levels*, and its proposed indicators for instance right to information laws – it is necessary to accept that effective measurement of this SDG should go beyond the mere existence of access to information laws to measures citizens' capacity to use these laws and their actual use of these laws.

A similar analysis can be carried for Goal 5, Gender Equality, and related targets.

UNESCO already developed and is monitoring these and other cardinals, which can make important contribution to monitoring the SDGs. In no specific order, these include (cf. Banda, 2015[28]):

- *Media and Information Literacy Indicators*
- *Gender-Sensitive Indicators for Media*
- *UNESCO Media Development Indicators*
- *World Trends in Freedom of Expression and Media Development:*
- *UNESCO Journalist Safety Indicators*

The challenge before civil society actors is not to be blinded by the debate of media and the information industry, online and offline, as businesses versus development. That media and the information industry are businesses is irrefutable. That media and the information industry are also indispensable to sustainable development is still to be grasped by the masses. Hence, their apparent absence from the SDGs. Measuring and stimulating MIL among citizens can help to change this mind set.

More research is needed on MIL in societies and its impact on development. To this end UNESCO and UNAOC have set up the International University Network on MIL. UNESCO is taking step further and has joined forces with Nordicom to undertake a feasibility study to establish an International MIL Institute.

The author has learned from Tiffany Shlain via a Youtube video.[29] The Internet is a vast resource with one trillion of web pages and 100 trillion links. If we consider neurons as web pages and communication between neurons (synopsis) as links – one will find that an adult brain has 300 trillion links. But listen to this, brain of a child has a quadrillion links, 10 times the links on the Internet. Focus on impact of media and technology on citizens must be balanced with equal focus on how women and men of all ages can shape information, media and technology for sustainable development. This is what media and information literacy is about. It is about shaping minds that are more powerful than the media and the entire Internet. We need to shape minds that will create change – sustainable change! Then we can literally change and shape development. In the video Tiffany Shlain noted, "Attention is the brain's greatest resource. Let us pay attention to what we are paying attention to so that we can set the foundation for worldwide empathy, innovation and human expression."

Recommendations

- UNESCO calls on all UN agencies/programmes/funds, governments, and all development partners globally to collaborate with us to organise a Joint Development Cooperation/Donor Framework Meeting on Media and Information Literacy for Open and Inclusive Development in 2016. This will be a revolutionary step towards getting better at citizens engagements in the first year of the Post 2015 Development Agenda;

- All governments should articulate national MIL policies and strategies leading to national MIL targets and assessment/measurement of MIL;

- Organizations that will be monitoring the Sustainable Development indicators should integrate sub-indicators such as MIL indicators, media development indicators, and gender-sensitive indicators for media where these are relevant;

- More research should be undertaken on citizens' response to media and information literacy competencies in relation to, inter alia, personal, social, economic, political and cultural/interreligious challenges and opportunities;

- All governments should take steps to integrate MIL into formal, informal and non-formal education systems to ensure MIL for all. Media and information literacy is literacy.

References

Abu-Fadil, M. (2007). Media Literacy A Tool to Combat Stereotypes and Promote Inter-cultural Understanding. United Nations Literacy Decade. Research paper prepared for the UNESCO Regional Conferences in Support of Global Literacy Literacy, Doha, 12-14 March, 2007.

Austin, E.W. & Johnson, K.K. (1997). Effects of general and alcohol-specific media literacy training on children's decision making about alcohol. *Journal of Health Communication, 2, pp. 17-42.*

Banda, F. (2015). Why free, independent and pluralistic media deserve to be at the heart of a post-2015 development agenda. Executive Summary of the Discussion Brief: "Free, independent and pluralistic media in the post-2015 development agenda: a discussion brief". UNESCO, Paris.

Buckingham, D. (1998). Children and television: a critical overview of the research. In R. Dickenson, R. Harindranath & O. Linné (Eds), *Approaches to audiences. Reader of the MA in Media and Communications (by Distance Learning),* Department of Media & Communication, University of Leicester, United Kingdom, London: Arnold, pp. 131-145.

Carlsson, U. (Ed.) (2006). *Regulation, Awareness, Empowerment: Young people and harmful media content in the digital age.* Gothenburg: Nordicom, The International Clearing-house on Children, Youth and Media.

Carlsson, U. & Culver S.H. (Eds) (2013). *MILID Yearbook 2013. Media and Information Literacy and Intercultural Dialogue.* Gothenburg: Nordicom, The International Clearinghouse on Children, Youth and Media.

Casey B., Casey N., Calvert B., French L. & Lewis J. (2008). *Television Studies: The Key Concepts.* London: Routledge.

Catts, R. (2005a). Information Literacies and Lifelong Learning: Keynote Address. Motesplats Infor Framtiden. Swedish Library Association Annual Conference, Boras, Sweden, October.

Celot, P. & Pérez Tornero, J. M. (2010*). Study on Assessment Criteria for Media Literacy-Final Report.* European Association of Viewers Interest, Brussels.

Chen, H L. & Williams, J.P. (2009). "Pedagogical Design for an Online Information Literacy Course: College Students' Learning Experience with Multi-modal Objects". Library and Librarians' Publication. Paper 1. http://surface.syr.edu/sul/1

Cheung, C. K. (2011). A study of the impact of media education on students' media analysis skills – an interim report. In C. von Feilitzen, U. Carlsson & C. Bucht (Eds), *New Questions, New Insights and New Approaches: Contribution to the Research Forum at the World Summit on Media for Children and Youth2010,* pp. 57-67. Gothenburg: Nordicom, The International Clearinghouse on Children, Youth and Media.

Dovey J. & Kennedy H. W. (2006). *Game Cultures: Computer Games as new Media*. Maidenhead: Open University Press.

Dupuis, J., Coutu, J. & Laneuville O. (2013). Application of linear mixed-effect models for the analysis of exam scores: Online video associated with higher scores for undergraduate students with lower grades. *Computers & Education*, 66, pp. 64–73.

Erstad, O. (2010). Educating the digital generation: exploring media literacy for the 21st century. *Digital kompetanse – Nordic journal of digital literacy*

Erstad, O. (2010). Paths Towards Digital Competencies. Naïve Participation or Civic Engagement? In Carlsson, U. (Ed.): *Children and Youth in the Digital Media Culture*, Gothenburg: Nordicom, The International Clearinghouse on Children, Youth and Media.

Fedorov, A. (2015) Media Literacy Education. Moscow: *ICO "Information for All"*, p. 577.

Frau-Meigs, D. (2011). Attaching media education to human rights by socializing young people to ethics online – competencies and e-strategies. In C. von Feilitzen, U. Carlsson & C. Bucht (Eds), *Yearbook 2011. New Questions, New Insights and New Approaches: Contribution to the Research Forum at the World Summit on Media for Children and Youth 2010*. Gothenburg: Nordicom, The International Clearinghouse on Children, Youth and Media, pp. 173-187.

Frau-Meigs, D. & Istraž, M. (2008). Media literacy and human rights: education for sustainable societies (pp. 51-82), *PRIOPČENJE SA SKUPA UDK*: 316.77:342.7 Primljeno: svibanj 2008.

Frau-Meigs D. & Torrent J. (2009). *Mapping media education policies in the world: visions, programmes and challenges*. UN-Alliance of Civilization, New York and GrupoComunicar, Spain.

Gene, B., Durval, C. & Anthony, C. (n.d.). *Data, Information, Knowledge and Wisdom*. [online] Available at: http://www.systemswiki.org/index.php?title=Data,_Information,_Knowledge_and_Wisdom [Accessed 11 May 2015].

Goodman, S. & Cocca, C. (2013). *Youth voices for change: building political efficacy and civic engagement through digital media literacy*. http://www.jodml.org/2013/02/01/youth-voices-for-change/

Grizzle, A. (2014). Enlisting media and information literacy for gender equality and women's empowerment. In Montiel, V. A. (2014): *Media and Gender: A Scholarly Agenda for the Global Alliance on Media and Gender*. UNESCO, Paris

Grizzle, A. & Calvo, M.C.T., (Eds) (2013). *Media and Information Literacy – Policy and Strategy Guidelines*. France: UNESCO

Hobbs, R. (1998). The seven great debates in the media literacy movement. *Journal of Communication*, 48, pp. 16–32.

Hobbs, R., Cohn-Geltner, H. & Landis, J. (2011). Views on the news – media literacy empowerment competencies in the elementary grades. In C. von Feilitzen, U. Carlsson & C. Bucht (Eds), *Yearbook 2011. New Questions, New Insights and New Approaches: Contribution to the Research Forum at the World Summit on Media for Children and Youth 2010*. Gothenburg: Nordicom, The International Clearinghouse on Children, Youth and Media, pp. 43-55

Hobbs, R. & Frost, R. (2003). Measuring the acquisition of media-literacy skills. *Reading Research Quarterly* 38(3), pp. 330-355.

Hodge, B. & Tripp, D. (1998). Ten theses on children and television. In R. Dickenson, R. Harindranath & O. Linné (Eds). *Approaches to audiences. Reader of the MA in Media and Communications (by Distance Learning)*, Department of Media & Communication, University of Leicester, United Kingdom, London: Arnold, pp. 146 – 150.

Horton, Jr., F.W. (2007). *Understanding information literacy. A primer*. Paris, France: UNESCO.

Horton, Jr., F.W. (2013). *Overview of information literacy. Resources worldwide*. Paris, France: UNESCO.

Kamerer, D. (2013). Media Literacy. *Communication Research Trends*, Centre for the Study of Communication and Culture, 32(1). ISSN: 0144-4646.

Lau, J. (2009). Information Skills: Conceptual Convergence between Information and Communication Sciences. In Frau-Meigs, D. & Torrent, J. (2009). *Mapping Media Education Policies in the World*. UN-Alliance of Civilizations, New York and Gupo Communicar, Spain.

Law-Wilson, L. et al. (2013). Enhancing Research Capacity for Global Health: Evaluation of a Distance-Based Program for International Study Coordinators. *Journal of Continuing Education in the Health Professions* 33(1)

Lee Alice Y.L. & So York K. C. (2013). "Information literacy and media literacy: Subset, intersection, or parallel relationship?". Paper presented in the 63rd Annual Conference of the International Communication Association (ICA), June 17-21, 2013. London.

Livingstone, S. (2004). Media Literacy and the Challenge of New Information and Communication Technologies. *Communication Review,* 7, pp. 3-14, 2004. Taylor and Francis Inc. ISSN/ 1071-4421 print. DOI: 10:1080/1071440490280152

Livingstone, S. (2010). How can we make media literacy easier for each citizen to access? In *"Media Literacy for all", IHECS and European Parliament*, Brussels, 2nd and 3rd December, 2010.

Livingstone, S., Couvering van, E. & Thumin, N. (2008). Converging traditions of research on media and information literacies: disciplinary, critical and methodological issues. In Coiro, J. et al., (Eds) *Handbook of research on new literacies*. New York, USA: Routledge

Marchis, J., Ciascai, L. & Costa, V. (2008). Intercultural and Media Education in Teaching Practice. An example of good practice. *Acta Didactic Napocensia* 1(2).

Martinsson, J. (2009). *The Role of Media Literacy in the Governance Reform Agenda*. World Bank, Washington DC.

Moeller, S. D. (2009). *Media Literacy: Understanding the News*. Washington, USA: Center for International Media Assistance, National Endowment for Democracy (NED).

Moeller S. D. (2009). *Media Literacy: Citizen Journalists*. Washington, USA: Center for International Media Assistance, National Endowment for Democracy (NED).

New London Group (1996). Pedagogy of multiliteracies: designing social futures. *Harvard Educational Review*, p. 66.

Panos (2007). *At the Heart of Change: The Role of Communication for Sustainable Development*. London.

Pariera, K.L. (2012). Information literacy on the web: How college students use visual and textual clues to assess credibility on health websites. *Communication in Information Literacy*, 6(1).

Pérez Tornero, J. M. & Varis, T. (2010). *Media literacy and new humanism*. Moscow Institute for Information Technologies in Education.

Pérez Tornero, J. M. & Pi, M. (2011). A new horizon – media literacy assessment and children in Europe. In C. von Feilitzen, U. Carlsson & C. Bucht (Eds), *Yearbook 2011. New Questions, New Insights and New Approaches: Contribution to the Research Forum at the World Summit on Media for Children and Youth2010*. Gothenburg: Nordicom, The International Clearinghouse on Children, Youth and Media, pp. 69-81.

Quin, R., McMahon, B. & Quin, R. (1996). *Teaching viewing and visual texts*. Carlton, Vic.: Curriculum Corporation.

Scharrer, E. (2009). Measuring the Effects of a Media Literacy Program on Conflict and Violence. ML Conflict and Violence, *The National Association for Media Literacy Education's Journal of Media Literacy Education* 1, pp. 12-27.

Scoullos, M. J. (Ed.) (1998). Environment and society: Education and public awareness for sustainability. Proceedings of the Thessaloniki International Conference organised by UNESCO and the Government of Greece, 8-12 December 1997.

Shultz, L. & Kajner, T. (2013). *Engaged scholarship: the politics of engagement and disengagement. Comparative and international education* (Sense Publishers); v. 26. Sense Publishers

Torras, M.C. & Sætre, T.P. (2009). Information literacy education, a process approach: Professionalizing the pedagogical role of academic libraries. Oxford: Chandos.

Tufte, T. & Enghel F. (Eds) (2009). *Yearbook 2009. Youth Engaging with the World – Media, Communication and Social Change.* Gothenburg: Nordicom, The International Clearinghouse on Children, Youth and Media.

Virkus, S. (2011). Information Literacy as an Important Competency for the 21st Century: Conceptual Approaches. *Journal of the Bangladesh Association of Young Researchers* 03/2012; 1(2). DOI: 10.3329/jbayr.v1i2.10028

Wade, T., Davidson, S. & O'Dea, J. (2003). A preliminary controlled evaluation of a school-based media literacy program and self-esteem program for reducing eating disorder risk factors. *International Journal of Eating Disorders*, 33(4), pp. 371-383.

Watson, R. & Vaughn, L. (2006). Limiting the Effects of the Media on Body Image: Does the Length of a Media Literacy Intervention Make a Difference? *International Journal of Eating Disorders*, 14(5), pp. 385-400.

UN Reports:

Secretary-General, (2014).*The Road to Dignity by 2030: Ending Poverty, Transforming All Lives and Protecting the Planet.* [online] New York: United Nations. Available at: http://www.un.org/disabilities/documents/reports/SG_Synthesis_Report_Road_to_Dignity_by_2030.pdf [Accessed 11 May 2015].

Secretary-General of the United Nations, the Leadership Council of the Sustainable Development Solutions Network, (2015). *Indicators and a Monitoring Framework for Sustainable Development Goals: Launching a data revolution for the SDGs.* [online] United Nations Sustainable Development Solutions Network (UNSDSN). Available at: http://unsdsn.org/wp-content/uploads/2015/01/150116-Indicators-and-a-Monitoring-Framework-for-SDGs-working-draft-for-consultation.pdf [Accessed 11 May 2015].

Why free, independent and pluralistic media deserve to be at the heart of a post-2015 development agenda .Executive Summary of the Discussion Brief: "Free, independent and pluralistic media in the post-2015 development agenda: a discussion brief", Available at: http://www.unesco.org/new/fileadmin/MULTIMEDIA/HQ/CI/CI/pdf/news/post_2015_agenda_brief.pdf [Accessed 11 May 2015]

Towards Knowledge Societies, Background Paper: From Information Society to Knowledge Societies.(2003). [online] Geneva: UNESCO. Available at: http://portal.unesco.org/ci/fr/file_download.php/89b1186916abc49f328d765ba3e7c86aUNESCO+background+paper+-+From+the+Information+Society+To+Knowledge+Societies.pdf [Accessed 11 May 2015].

Search bars:

Google Search, https://www.google.com/#q=%22Development+Information%22 [Accessed 15 May 2015].

Bing Search, http://www.bing.com/search?q=%22Development+Information%22&qs=n&form=QBRE&pq=%22development+information%22&sc=1-25&sp=-1&sk=&cvid=39636b740d52482da9a264a717a135ad[Accessed 15 May 2015].

Yahoo Search, https://search.yahoo.com/search;_ylc=X3oDMTFiN25laTRvBF9TAzIwMjM1MzgwNzUEaXRjAzEEc2VjA3NyY2hfcWEEc2xrA3NyY2h3ZWI-?p=%22Development+Information%22&fr=yfp-t-594 [Accessed 15 May 2015].

DuckDuckGo Search, https://duckduckgo.com/?q=%22Development+Information%22[Accessed 15 May 2015].

Websites:

2015 NAMLE Conference, (2014). *Global MIL Week.* Available at: http://namleconference.org/milweek [Accessed 11 May 2015].

Anon, (2015). Available at: http://www.worldbank.org/open/ [Accessed 15 May 2015].

Coursera, (2015). *Coursera – Free Online Courses From Top Universities.* Available at: https://www.coursera.org/course/engagecitizen [Accessed 15 May 2015].

European Commission Audiovisual Media Services Directive, Article 12, Available at: http://europa.eu/rapid/press-release_IP-10-803_en.htm [Accessed 15 May 2015].

Elab.lms.athabascau.ca, (2015). *e-Lab Courses.* Available at: http://elab.lms.athabascau.ca/ [Accessed 15 May 2015].

International ICT Literacy Panel, (2002). Digital *Transformation: A Framework for ICT Literacy.* ETS. Available at: https://www.ets.org/Media/Research/pdf/ICTREPORT.pdf [Accessed 15 May 2015].

Matheory.info, (2015).*The Mathematical Theory of Information: Chapter 1, About Information.* Available at: http://www.matheory.info/chapter1.html [Accessed 15 May 2015].

Sustainabledevelopment.un.org, (2015). *Proposal for Sustainable Development Goals.* Sustainable Development Knowledge Platform. Available at: https://sustainabledevelopment.un.org/sdgsproposal [Accessed 11 May 2015].

YouTube, (2015). BRAIN *POWER: From Neurons to Networks.* Available at: https://www.youtube.com/watch?v=zLp-edwiGUU [Accessed 22 May 2015].

This article is connected to a research on citizens' response to media and information literacy competencies in relation to personal, social, economic, political and cultural challenges and opportunities on and offline after having acquired MIL related competencies through different kinds of on-line courses.

Notes

1   Road to Dignity by 2030, p. 37,www.un.org/.../reports/SG_Synthesis_Report_Road_ to_Dignity_by_2030.pdf Accessed on 11 May 2015.

2   Indicators and a Monitoring Framework for Sustainable Development Goals: Launching a data revolution for the SDGs, http://unsdsn.org/resources/publications/ indicators/Accessed on 11 May 2015.

3   Towards Knowledge Societies, Background Paper: From Information Society to Knowledge Societies (December 2003), www.unesco.org/.../HQ/CI/CI/pdf/wsis_ geneva_prep_background_paper.pdfAccessed on 11 May 2015.

4   See http://www.systemswiki.org/index.php?title=Data,_Information,_Knowledge_ and_WisdomAccessed on 11 May 2015.

5   Google Search, https://www.google.com/#q=%22Development+Information%22Acce ssed on 15 May 2015. For diversity I did two other searches on Bing, http://www.bing.com/search?q=%22Development+Information%22&qs=n&form= QBRE&pq=%22development+information%22&sc=1-25&sp=-1&sk=&cvid=3963 6b740d52482da9a264a717a135ad; Yahoo, https://search.yahoo.com/search;_ylc= X3oDMTFiN25laTRvBF9TAzIwMjM1MzgwNzUEaXRjAzEEc2VjA3NyY2h- fcWEEc2xrA3NyY2h3ZWI-?p=%22Development+Information%22&fr=yfp-t-594; and DuckDuckGo, https://duckduckgo.com/?q=%22Development+Information%22 which yielded the following results respectively, 1, 880,000, 2, 270,000, and no figure given. Accessed on 11 May 2015.

6   This statement was inspired by an anecdote about the need for media and information literacy given by Janis Karklins, Former Assistant Director-General for Communica- tion and Information, UNESCO.

7   Inspired by Sonia Livingstones' use of the phrase 'media literacy for all'.

8   MIL was first called a "Big Tent" Sherri Hope, Director of the Media and Information Literacy Centre at Temple University in a concept note for the Global ML Week 2015.

9   These are actual competencies of media literacy taken from authoritative sources namely, Celot, P. and Pérez Tornero, J. M. (2010) *Study on Assessment Criteria for Media Literacy-Final Report*. European Association of Viewers Interest, Brussels; Fedorov, A., *Media Literacy Education*. Moscow: ICO "Information for All". 2015. p. 577.

10 These are actual competencies of information literacy taken from authoritative sour- ces namely, Horton, Jr., F. W. (2008). *Understanding Information Literacy: A primer.* UNESCO, Paris France; Information Literacy Competency Standards for Journa- lism and students and Professionals. Association of College and Research Libraries (ACRL).Approved by ACRL Board of Directors, 2011, USA. The publication is based on ACRL Information Literacy Competency Standards. Virkus, S., Information Literacy as an Important Competency for the 21st Century: Conceptual Approaches. In *Journal of the Bangladesh Association of Young Researchers* 03/2012; 1(2). DOI: 10.3329/jbayr.v1i2.10028

11 These are actual competencies of digital literacy taken from authoritative sources namely, Erstad, O., (2010) 'Paths Towards Digital Competencies. Naïve Participation or Civic Engagement?' In Carlsson, U. (Ed.), *Children and Youth in the Digital Media Culture*, Gothenburg: Nordicom, The International Clearinghouse on Children Youth and Media. See also Digital Transformation: A Framework for ICT Literacy. A Report of the International ICT Literacy Panel. Educational Testing Service, www.ets.org/.../ ictreport.pdf. Accessed on 15 May 2015.

12   Reflection of the Mathematical Theory of Information as applied by Shannon in his communication model to explain noisy communication channels or interference http://www.matheory.info/chapter1.html Accessed on 15 May 2015.

13   They are listed in the introduction of this MILID Yearbook 2015 but can also be found at https://sustainabledevelopment.un.org/sdgsproposal Accessed on 11 May 2015.

14   Cross referenced from unpublished remarks, Remarks for the side event hosted by the Article 19 at CSW 2015, Fackson Banda 9 February, UN, New York, USA.

15   Why free, independent and pluralistic media deserve to be at the heart of a post-2015 development agenda Executive Summary of the Discussion Brief: "Free, independent and pluralistic media in the post-2015 development agenda: a discussion brief", Available at: http://www.unesco.org/new/fileadmin/MULTIMEDIA/HQ/CI/CI/pdf/news/post_2015_agenda_brief.pdf Accessed on 11 May 2015.

16   See Catts, R. and Lau, J. et al. (2013). UNESCO Global Media and Information Literacy Assessment Framework. UNESCO, France.

17   Celot, P. and Pérez Tornero, J. M. (2010) Study on Assessment Criteria for Media Literacy-Final *Report. European Association of Viewers Interest, Brussels.*

18   European Commission Audiovisual Media Services Directive, Article 12, http://europa.eu/rapid/press-release_IP-10-803_en.htm Accessed on 15 May 2015.

19   Word coined by author of this article – Measuring MIL: Implications for the SDGs.

20   A term used the European Commission and others interchangeable with media literacy. UNESCO abandon use of this term because it is often confused with higher level education, media studies or media and communication studies. UNESCO has coined the composite concept, media and information literacy.

21   See Frau-Meigs, Flores et al., 2014, http://www.translit.fr/ Accessed on 15 May 2015.

22   See Tornero et al., 2014, http://eumedus.com/Accessed on 15 May 2015.

23   For a summary of the report from four Caribbean countries, see Shelley-Robinson, 2013 in *Media and Information Literacy and Intercultural Dialogue, MILID Yearbook 2013,* Edited by U. Carlsson & S. H. Culver, Gothenburg: Nordicom, The International Clearinghouse on Children, Youth and Media. The reports for Africa and Southern Asia are unpublished.

24   Singh & Horton, 2013 in *Media and Information Literacy and Intercultural Dialogue, MILID Yearbook 2013,* Edited by U. Carlsson & S. H. Culver, Gothenburg: Nordicom, The International Clearinghouse on Children, Youth and Media.

25   See official website of World Back on Open Development, http://www.worldbank.org/open/ Accessed on 15 May 2015.

26   See https://www.coursera.org/course/engagecitizenAccessed on 15 May 2015.

27   See http://elab.lms.athabascau.ca/Accessed on 15 May 2015.

28   Unpublished remarks, Remarks for the side event hosted by the Article 19at CSW 2015, F. Banda 9 February, UN, New York, USA

29   Listen to Tiffany at https://www.youtube.com/watch?v=zLp-edwiGUU Accessed on 15 May 2015.

Data Literacy: An Emerging Responsibility for Libraries

Tibor Koltay

In the natural sciences, the social sciences and the arts and humanities, the importance of research data has grown to an extent, never seen before. There is also a heightened attention towards data in businesses and in everyday civil life. These developments require a new form of media and information literacy, called data literacy, which has a strong enabling potential and – similarly to media and information literacy – demands a critical stance from users. It focuses on data quality and data citation and it is also closely connected to data sharing, data management and data curation. Data literacy skills are vital for researchers, whose work requires them to become efficient users of research data. These skills are also of prime interest for (potential) data management professionals, who intend to acquire skills and abilities that are required for fulfilling their role as effective and efficient supporters of research, among others, by providing data literacy education, which has the potential to foster sustainable development, first of all as it advocates openness.

Keywords: data-intensive research, data sharing, data citation, data literacy, library and media literacy

Introduction

Today's information environment requires that we strengthen and deepen the knowledge concerning media and information literacy on a global level. There is also a need for stimulating research and practices within this field by using and promoting a holistic perspective. Such holistic approach should characterize data literacy that – by emphasizing open access to data, mainly through open licenses, such as Creative Commons ones – may act as a catalyser in the process leading towards sustainability of scientific research and shaping the role of the library in supporting these aims.

Definition and the Importance of Data

Data can be defined as "any information that can be stored in digital form, including text, numbers, images, video or movies, audio, software, algorithms, equations, animations, models, simulations, etc." (NSB, 2005: 9). Research data is the output from any systematic investigation that involves a process of observation, experiment or the testing of a hypothesis (Pryor, 2012). Data also originates from works of art and literature, as well as from artefacts of cultural heritage (Nielsen & Hjørland, 2012). In the digital environment, text can also become data, and numerical results can be visualized in ways, never seen before (ACRL, 2013). These are only a few examples of tremendous changes that show a potential to widen the circle of sources and means of interpretation that can be used for advancing sustainable development.

An important though not exclusive facet of the data-rich world is *big data* that is enabled by the capacity of computers to search, aggregate and cross-reference large data sets, so it is not only big, but fast, unstructured, and overwhelming (Boyd & Crawford, 2012; Smith, 2013).

The highly developed information and communication technology infrastructure of today has also triggered enormous interest in research data that is present in the natural sciences, the social sciences, as well as the arts and humanities (Boyd & Crawford, 2012).

Data-intensive research has the potential to foster sustainable development by recognizing and advocating the need for openness in sharing data among researchers. Beyond the world of research, data also begins to dominate different kinds of businesses. In everyday life, access to data helps people in seeing different issues more holistically, thus make informed decisions, which can be based on data collected about regional, national, and global trends across domains, including unemployment, poverty, or carbon footprint easily and conveniently (Dechman & Syms, 2014). Open data is not restricted to research, but is one of the prerequisites of open government (Black, 2012).

Libraries are not only required, but are willing to maintain a sustainable ecosystem for data, among others by implementing data management services and imparting data literacy skills.

The Nature of Data Literacy

The heightened interest in data generates a need for data literacy, the main characteristic of which is a critical approach towards data, first of all by differentiating between data of low and of high quality.

Though there are several different approaches towards data literacy and there is a variety of names for this concept, it can be regarded as an important new form and a novel subset of media and information literacy. It empowers individuals to access, interpret, critically assess, manage, handle and ethically use data (Calzada Prado & Marzal, 2013) and enables us to transform data into information and into actionable knowledge. Data literacy skills include knowing how to identify, collect, organize, analyze, summarize, and prioritize data. Developing hypotheses, identifying problems, interpreting data, and determining, planning, implementing, as well as monitoring courses of action also pertain to the required abilities (Mandinach & Gummer, 2013).

Data quality is a major constituent of data literacy. It includes the ability to trace data back to its origin and justification. Another important aspect of quality is trust, which is utterly complex in itself by including the lineage, version and error rate of data and the fact that data is understood and acceptable (Buckland, 2011). It also depends on subjective judgements on authenticity, acceptability or applicability of the data; and is also influenced by the given subject discipline, the reputation of those responsible for the creation of the data, and the biases of the persons who are evaluating the data (Giarlo, 2013). Authenticity measures the extent to which the data is judged to represent the proper ways of conducting scientific research. In order to evaluate authenticity, the data must be understandable. The presence of sufficient context in the form of documentation and metadata allows the evaluation of the understandability of data. To achieve this, data has to be usable. To make data usable, it has to be discoverable and accessible; and be in a usable file format. The individuals, judging data quality need to have at their disposal an appropriate tool to access the data. Data quality can also be assessed according to its integrity, which assumes that the data can be proven having been recorded exactly as intended and remaining the same as it was at the time of recording (Giarlo, 2013).

Data formats, discovery and acquisition, data analysis and visualisation, as well as preservation are the main fields, where core competencies of data literacy can be used. These fields are supplemented by ethical questions and metadata creation (Carlson et al., 2011). The spectre of data-related activities is wide and it includes data sharing, data management, data curation and data citation. Data management is usually understood as a broad concept that comprises a wide array of activities, not restricted to data analysis and modelling, maintenance, security management, quality management and providing metadata. Data management is not entirely identical with data *curation*, which is more closely related to long-term preservation and reuse. Notwithstanding, practically all of these activities have to be taken into account when thinking about data literacy.

Researchers, Librarians, Everyday People and Data Literacy

Data literacy is conceived for those, who will use the data and will need education about how to understand and interpret it (ACRL, 2013). Acquiring data literacy skills is thus an issue for researchers, who need to become data literate science workers. As Haendel et al. (2012) put it, creating a culture of semantic researchers requires that we accompany their scientific training with education in data literacy in order to establish a new cultural standard, especially because researchers often do not realize that their own scholarly communications constitute a primary source of data. Data literacy is also vital for data management professionals, and those aspiring to be, who intend to acquire skills and abilities that are required for fulfilling their role as effective and efficient supporters of research. Many of these professionals come out of the library profession.

The main motive in teaching data literacy to everyday people is the societal need in fostering the critical appraisal of data among them.

Media and Information Literacy and Data Literacy

Data literate persons have to know, how to select and synthesize data and combine it with other information sources and prior knowledge. They have to recognize source data value, types and formats; determine when data is needed; access data sources appropriate to the information needed. With these qualities, the close relationship between media and information literacy and data literacy stands out (Calzada Prado & Marzal, 2013). Data literacy is not different from other literacies in the sense that it accentuates the need for being critical first of all because data triggers numerous hopes of higher intelligence and better knowledge (Boyd & Crawford, 2012).

The Importance of Data Sharing

Data literacy also should include answers to the question about *openness*. As said before, openness could contribute to sustainable development by the simple fact that data may be accessible to a wider circle of researchers and potentially to the public. This can happen to an extent, never seen before.

In the case of research, it is often researchers themselves, who argue that, by promoting open data, science can be scrutinized and thus made more accountable. The spirit of open science requires data sharing that means the release of research data for use by others (Borgman, 2012).

Sharing research data may be a condition of gaining access to the data of others, and may be the prerequisite of receiving funding, as set forth by different funding agencies with a varying degree of rigour. On the other hand, researchers can have a number of reasons not to share their data. For instance, documenting data is extremely labour intensive. However, the main reason is the lack of interest, caused by the well-known fact that in most fields of scholarship the rewards come not from data management, but from publication (Borgman, 2010). Besides of this, there are other, legitimate boundaries to openness. Some of them are set by commercial interest, others by the protection of privacy, safety and security (Royal Society, 2012). The latter barriers are often present when deciding about sharing or not sharing civil data.

The Role of Data Citation

To be accessible, data has to be cited in a standardized way. Otherwise, its openness and its input to sustainable development will not prevail. This is one of the reasons, why data literate persons should pay attention to citing data (ACRL, 2013). This especially important in research setting, as it allows the identification, retrieval, replication, and verification of underlying published studies (Carlson et al., 2011). At present, there are no standard formats to cite data, which could provide motivation for researchers to share and publish their data by the potential of becoming a tool of reward and acknowledgment, but works are underway (Mooney & Newton, 2012).

Conclusion

Traditionally, libraries have not been involved in teaching people to read. However, reading data requires skills that librarians may need to teach to their users (Seadle, 2012).

It is not by accident that data-related issues have been identified by the ACRL Research Planning and Review Committee as one of the top trends in academic libraries (ACRL, 2014). Among other measures, libraries can react to the need in data management and data literacy by creating posts that reflect this need. Even though not exclusively, these professionals can be named *data librarians*. Libraries and the underlying discipline of librarianship, i.e. library and information science have begun to take non-textual resources into consideration in a serious way more than ever before. Despite these developments, future studies have to examine the relationship between data literacy and media and information literacy.

Data literacy is an answer to the development of developed information and communication technologies, the role of which is still not fully understood, but are supposed to play a central role in advancing sustainable development (Mohamed, Murray & Mohamed, 2010). However, with its different sets of variables and desired outcomes, sustainability changes with culture and with time. We should think of sustainability as a process rather than a specific goal (Gorman, 2003) and in this process, data literacy might prove to be a crucial step.

References

ACRL (2013). Intersections of scholarly communication and information literacy: Creating strategic collaborations for a changing academic environment. Chicago, IL: Association of College and Research Libraries. Retrieved from http://acrl.ala.org/intersections/

ACRL (2014). ACRL Research Planning and Review Committee. Top ten trends in academic libraries. A review of the trends and issues affecting academic libraries in higher education. *College & Research Libraries News, 75*(6), 294-302.

Black, A. (2012). Open data movement. Where it's been and where it appears to be going. *Public Management*, July, Retrieved from http://newamerica.net/sites/newamerica.net/files/articles/Alissa%20Black_Open%20Data%20Movement.pdf

Borgman, Ch. (2010). Research Data: Who will share what, with whom, when, and why? *China-North America Library Conference*, Beijing, Retrieved from http://works.bepress.com/borgman/238

Borgman, Ch. (2012). The conundrum of sharing research data, *Journal of the American Society for Information Science and Technology, 63*(6), 1059-1078.

Boyd, D. & Crawford, K. (2012). Critical questions for big data: Provocations for a cultural, technological, and scholarly phenomenon. *Information, Communication & Society, 15*(5), 662-679.

Buckland, M. (2011). Data management as bibliography. *Bulletin of the American Society for Information Science and Technology, 37*(6), 34-37.

Calzada Prado, J. & Marzal, M. Á. (2013). Incorporating Data Literacy into Information Literacy Programs: Core Competencies and Contents. *Libri, 63*(2), 123-134.

Carlson, J. et al. (2011). Determining data information literacy needs: A study of students and research faculty. *Portal: Libraries and the Academy, 11*(2), 629-657.

Dechman, M. K. & Syms, L. R. (2014). Working Together to Maximize the Utilization of Open Data Across Social Science and Professional Disciplines. *Behavioral & Social Sciences Librarian*, 33(4), 188-207

Giarlo, M. (2013). Academic Libraries as Quality Hubs. *Journal of Librarianship and Scholarly Communication, 1*(3), 1-10.

Gorman, G. E. (2003). Sustainable development and information literacy: IFLA priorities in Asia and Oceania. *IFLA Journal, 29*(4), 288-294

Haendel, M. A. et al. (2012). Dealing with Data: A Case Study on Information and Data Management Literacy. *PLoS Biology, 10*(5), e1001339

Mandinach, E. B. & Gummer, E. S. (2013). A systemic view of implementing data literacy in educator preparation. *Educational Researcher, 42*(1), 30-37.

Mohamed, M., Murray, A. & Mohamed, M. (2010). The role of information and communication technology (ICT) in mobilization of sustainable development knowledge: a quantitative evaluation. *Journal of Knowledge Management, 14*(5), 744-758.

Mooney, H. & Newton, M. P. (2012). The anatomy of a data citation: Discovery, reuse, and credit. *Journal of Librarianship and Scholarly Communication, 1*(1), 1-14.

Nielsen, H. J. & Hjørland, B. (2014). Curating research data: The potential roles of libraries and information professionals. *Journal of Documentation, 70*(2), 221-240.

NSB (2005). National Science Board. *Long-Lived Digital Data Collections: Enabling Research and Education in the 21st Century*. Arlington, VA: National Science Foundation.

Pryor, G. (2012). Why manage research data? In G. Pryor (Ed.), *Managing Research Data* (pp. 1-16). London: Facet.

Royal Society (2012). *Science as an Open Enterprise,* London: Royal Society Science Policy Centre.

Seadle, M. (2012). Library Hi Tech and information science. *Library Hi Tech*, *30*(2), 205-209.

Smith, S. (2013). Is Data the New Media? *EContent*, *36*(2), 14-19.

MIL Policies in Europe 2004-2014: The Uniqueness of a Policy and its Connection to UNESCO

*José Manuel Pérez Tornero, Tomás Durán Becerra
& Santiago Tejedor Calvo*

Since 2004 the European Union (EU) has been committed to the development of media literacy (ML). Examples of this fact can be seen in the Safer Internet, eLearning, MEDIA and Creative Europe programmes -within which different studies have been conducted- and the enactment of different public policies in the field, such as the AVMS (2010) as well as the European Commission (2007; 2009) and the European Parliament's (2006) recommendations on ML implementation. These processes have been influenced and guided by different international organizations such as UNESCO and the Council of Europe. In this regard, the EU has pursued one of the most active ML public policies in the world. The 2014 Paris MIL Forum -sponsored by the EC and UNESCO- was the occasion to visualize the EU's progress. This article describes and analyses, in an objective and systematic manner, what this development means to the creation of innovative ML public policies and educative processes. The result is an interpretative analysis that showcases the principal outcomes of the EU's programmes and actions in the field. In addition, this article examines how recommendations and conclusions from different EU-funded research projects on digital, media and audiovisual literacy have been executed, and describes the European approach in the hope of making it a reference for the development of ML in other regions of the world.

Keywords: media literacy, MIL public policies, eLearning

Introduction

Since 2004[1] the European Union has demonstrated its commitment to the development of media literacy which has produced public policies and private initiatives in the areas of legislation, education, the media itself and economics. In all cases the objective has been to acquire new skills related to the environment of new digital media. In few areas of the world has there been such movement in the field of ML, with respect to public and private policies, in such an integrated, systematic and organised fashion as has taken place in the European Union over the last ten years.

Why is this the case? What are the pillars of this organisation? What are the characteristics of this movement, its mechanisms and its modus operandi? These are the questions that this report will try to answer. In it we hope to describe the unique process carried out in the designing and execution of policies that have been developed since 2004, paying special attention to the concatenation of initiatives realized over the last decade.

A New Conceptual Framework

With the name of media literacy, the European Commission (EC) adopted a broad and inclusive term whose definition would include the necessary skills citizens would need to develop in order to use all media (digital or not) critically, understand its content and specific/technical languages and thus develop – through the acquisition of such competences – active and democratic citizenship.

It must be said that this framework is the same used by UNESCO, also recently created, which, however, adopted a slightly different name: media and information literacy (MIL). Within this framework different approaches are used and incorporated, approaches that have been circulating for some time now, both in academic circles and in public policies: "audio-visual literacy", "digital", "media", "information", "film", "media education".

UNESCO, as with the EC, understands the conceptual framework of MIL to be the processes of acquisition of skills and competencies that promote the understanding and use of traditional media of mass communication as well as new media; this is a direct result of the digital age (UNESCO, 2011a).

In accordance with the approach adopted by UNESCO, promoting the critical consumption of the media, and encouraging the development of an autonomous awareness of the media, leads to the improvement not only of the individual circumstances of its consumption, but also to the creation of a truly committed and active citizenry (Carlsson et al., 2008). All this demonstrates that the last ten years have witnessed a unique conceptual agreement between important international organisations such as the European Commission and UNESCO, albeit with slight variations.

From the Seville Seminar to
the Consolidation of the Media Approach

The concurring positions between the EC and UNESCO had a foundation in shared landmarks. These shared conceptual frameworks were reached through a process of conceptual development and through shifting paradigms that should now be described, albeit briefly.

UNESCO was the first to initiate a series of historical milestones in Europe that constitute the development of what is now known as MIL. These milestones are the Grünwald Conference, 1982; the Toulouse Conference, 1990; the Vienna Conference, 1999; the Seville Seminar, 2002. In addition, its development involved a large number of European experts[2] as well as different governments within the EU.

But it was precisely after the Seville Seminar on Media Education in 2002[3] (which concentrated on media-education) when the landmark policies of UNESCO and the European Commission began to intertwine. In fact, since then, the EC has become an active agent in the construction and introduction of the new paradigm of media literacy[4].

Between 2004 and 2010 the European Commission displayed leadership in European policies and managed to inspire the entire European movement, which also had an influence internationally. It did so in a systematic way. Namely by:

• Trying to integrate and promote all existing initiatives on the subject.

• Combining studies and research with recommendations for action and even legislation.

• Introducing economic incentives and influencing political will through subsidies, contracts and political consensus.

All this has led to an unprecedented movement in Europe and has stimulated action both in the public and private sectors.

For their part, the European Commission has been working on digital literacy since the early 1990s. In 1991 it launched the MEDIA Programme aimed at promoting the European audiovisual industry. This soon led to the realisation that there was a need to develop new capabilities which also included audiences and the public in general. In a similar vein, other programmes developed by the EC emphasised the need to empower citizens. The program launched in 1999, Safer Internet, is an example of this. In fact, many of the concepts, policies and actions developed in these two programmes were gradually integrated into the new paradigm of media literacy.

The historical landmarks for the emergence of this paradigm can be summarised as follows:

1. The promotion of digital literacy included in the policy on the Information Society adopted at the European Council in Lisbon (2000).

2. The transition from digital to media that occurred after the Seminar of Seville (2002), which can be found in the study: Promoting Digital Literacy (Pérez Tornero, 2004); its consequences being the most significant milestone.

3. The consolidation of the "media approach," which is based on the study commissioned by the EC in the *Study on the current trends and approaches on Media Literacy in Europe* (Pérez Tornero, 2007). It was in this study, where the term "media literacy," which includes all media, became popular.

This work understands that media literacy corresponds to a process that involves and integrates literacy skills combined with an understanding of the use of any kind of media. However, beyond its conceptual nature, what the cited study initiated was the possibility to define a comprehensive policy strategy for the development of MIL in Europe, a policy which should involve all stakeholders in the field: political, legislative and regulatory institutions, families, schools and teachers, the media and cultural industry as well as associations in coordinated, integrated and arranged actions (Pérez Tornero & Varis, 2010).

Legislative Development

This study led the EU to develop over the last decade certain legislative instruments which consolidate public policy related to media literacy. This development includes an aspect of conceptualization which was driven by the EC and the European Parliament between 2006 and 2007, culminating with the enactment of the European Directive on Audiovisual Services of 2010.

In the *Communiqué* from the EC to the European Parliament, the Council of Europe, the European Economic and Social Committee and the Committee of the Regions –COM(2007)833–, the EC formally established, via statute, an initial definition of media literacy. This *communiqué* sought to develop what was established in the strategy of Lisbon (2000), relating media literacy to the digital environment.

Similarly, the Council of Europe (the maximum governing body of the EU) launched in May 2008 a message of support to the EC *Communiqué* of 2007, in which it gives its blessing to the statement by the EC indicating that industry should encourage and include actions for the development of media literacy at EU level. It establishes that the EU should promote the development of actions to encourage media literacy and the active participation of European citizens, creating opportunities for economic, social and democratic development (European Council, 2008).

In this report the Council of Europe[5], where it makes reference to these developments, already emphasizes that the Audiovisual Media Services Directive of 2007 "calls for the 'development of media literacy in all sections of society' and for close monitoring of progress in media literacy. It sets out a reporting obligation for the Commission to measure levels of media literacy in all the Member States. Criteria for the assessment of levels of media literacy are therefore needed".

In 2009 the EC recommended that EU countries and the media industry should work together to increase the awareness of people as to the many forms and types of media messages present in the European communicative environment (advertising, movies and/or online content).

As a result, among the Council's conclusions on media literacy in the digital environment adopted at the meeting of the Board of Education, Youth and Culture on 27 November 2009, the commitment to ML was reiterated. The EC recommendation of 20 August 2009 –C(2009)6464–, was also welcomed which again urged governments to include ML in their national curricula.

In 2010 the directive of the European Parliament (AVMS) –Directive 2010/13/EU– established the compulsory need to measure and promote the development of ML in all Member States as of the year 2011. The directive also issued the need to develop and establish a tool to measure these levels.

A System of Indicators

The legislative policy was soon accompanied by measures of executive order.

The *Study on Assessment Criteria for Media Literacy Levels* (2009) identified seven different areas that are important for the measurement of media literacy. These seven areas were proposed by the *European Charter for Media Literacy*[6] as the measurement model. They are:

1. the efficient use of technologies

2. the capacity to access information and make informed choices and decisions

3. the need to understand how media content is produced

4. critical analysis of techniques, language and content related to the media

5. the use of the media to express and communicate ideas

6. the need to identify and avoid harmful media content and services

7. the efficient use of the media in order to exercise democratic and civil rights (Pérez Tornero, 2007:12-13).

These seven areas can be divided into media availability and media literacy context, on the one hand, and use, critical understanding and communication skills, on the other, which take place within the measuring scheme proposed (Pérez Tornero, 2009). This pioneering study was completed by a subsequent study conducted by EAVI and the Danish Technological Institute (DTI) in 2011 in which the criteria laid down initially were refined.

The *Study on Assessment Criteria for Media Literacy Levels* laid the foundation for the first reliable ML assessment system in Europe and enabled the EC to fulfil its obligation of reporting on levels of ML in Europe. The conceptual model illustrated in a pyramid chart – developed in this study – has been used specifically as a measuring tool for ML in Europe by different research groups and institutions involved in the development of this discipline.

Members of the EC expert panel on media literacy have developed individual pilot projects using these indicators in several European countries. The Spanish project DINAMIC (Developing Indicators of Media Literacy for Individuals, Corporations and Citizens) is an example of state investment in this area.

From European Indicators to UNESCO Indicators

Study on Assessment Criteria for Media Literacy Levels helped to inspire work done in parallel on MIL by UNESCO. The first expression in this regard appeared in a document published in 2011 titled, *Towards Media and Information Literacy Indicators*, in which UNESCO began to develop the concepts for their study in an attempt to systematize the various indicators that lead to measuring national levels of MIL.

In this document, UNESCO makes it clear when summarizing the advances proposed in the research conducted by the EC (Pérez Tornero, 2009), that "it is (and will be) through their critical assessment in the application of the tool [to be developed for the EC to assess MIL levels] that this expert knowledge and insight in each territory is (and will be) able to measure appropriately media literacy levels (EAVI, 2009)" (…) "It is important to note that if this is true for one (relatively small) continent it is all the more likely to be true across the globe" (UNESCO, 2011b: 17).

The pilot document proposed in 2008 for measuring indicators of information literacy (Lau & Catts, 2008), gives an initial systematization of competences to take into consideration when developing a scenario of information and digital literacy. On the other hand, the document published in 2013 by UNESCO establishes values, indications, competencies and variables for the actual assessment of MIL levels.

In accordance with UNESCO, "defining and measuring a country's MIL readiness and available competencies at national levels should be regarded as a key component of national information and media development policies. This kind of assessment should also be linked to educational plans and can contribute to employment, productivity, innovation, participation and empowerment" (UNESCO, 2013: 37-38).

In developing the guidelines for measuring levels of MIL, the EC and UNESCO worked simultaneously and in parallel on a theoretical-conceptual framework (UNESCO, 2013) which coincided with the findings submitted to the EC in 2009 (Pérez Tornero, 2009), which demonstrate the correlation between contextual factors and communication skills. Consensus shows that MIL development is better when there is a public policy in place that encourages these skills. This correlation, as outlined in the document UNESCO 2013, is set forth in the following table:

European and UNESCO MIL Assessment Frameworks			
UNESCO (2013: 47)		**Pérez Tornero[7] (SC. Coord.) (2009: 34-50)**	
Tier One: MIL Country Readiness	**Tier Two: MIL competencies**	**Environmental Factors (for ML)**	**Personal Competences**
1. MIL education, 2. MIL policy, 3. MIL supply, 4. MIL access and use, and 5. Civil society.	1. Access and retrieval; 2. Understanding and evaluation; 3. Creation and sharing.	Media literacy context: 1. Media education (presence in curriculum; teacher training 2. Media literacy policy (regulation) 3. Media industry 4. Civil society Media availability: (mobile phone; Internet; television; radio; newspapers; cinema)	Use: 1. Computer and Internet skills 2. Balanced use of media 3. Advanced Internet use Critical Understanding: 1. Understanding media content and its functioning 2. Knowledge of media and regulation 3. User behaviour
MIL competency		**Communicative skills**	
Cognitive elements: attitudes (rights, principles, values and attitudes), knowledge and skills. Which "together play an important role in the MIL Assessment Framework, as they do in the learning and teaching processes, and in relation to employment, for participation and empowerment in societal life" (2013: 47).		Social relations; Citizen participation; Content creation. "Social relationships demonstrate the potential for individual and group relationships via the media. (…) the media manages social groups and dictates the type of frequency of contact (…) [cooperation or conflict] among them" (2009: 44).	

Source: Authors' own elaboration, Information from UNESCO (2013) and Pérez Tornero (SC.Coord) (2009)

ML Takes Off in Europe

Since 2004 a series of initiatives related to media literacy, which highlight the vitality of a movement, has taken place, namely: the launch of the European Charter for Media Education; the celebration of EUROMEDUC –a major effort to bring together experts and European institutions in the sector conducted in 2004 and 2009; the MEDEA Conference in Brussels; events created within the framework of the EC MEDIA Programme (2007-2013); Creative Europe (2014-2020) and the Prix MEDIA. For their part, the Education, Audio-visual and Culture Executive Agency (EACEA) has been active in financing educational activities and programs such as Creative Europe.

In 2014, the EC then implemented EMEDUS: European Media Literacy Education Study Project, which aimed at consolidating and stabilizing the European movement for media literacy. This project had a double objective: 1) the description of how media literacy was developing in the European education system and 2) the creation of a European Observatory on Media Literacy. Specifically, the Observatory was created to serve as continuity to the policies and programs developed by the EC.

Along with the Observatory, the EMEDUS Project –in conjunction with other European projects such as Translit (Frau-Meigs et al., 2014)– convened the First European Forum on Media and Information Literacy in Paris in May 2014. It is significant that this first European Forum on MIL was organised with the help and sponsorship of the EC and UNESCO.

On the other hand, the FilmEd Project (Showing films and other audio-visual content in European Schools – Obstacles and best practices) analysed and studied the development of a specific field of media literacy – film literacy. It contributes to research that coincides in recommending the creation of opportunities to exchange knowledge and experiences in MIL. It was proposed as a continuation of the study of the British Film Institute (BFI), "Film Literacy in Europe 2012".

2014 is also the year of the emergence of the European Digital Agenda, one of the seven pillars supporting the EU 2020 Strategy, which aims to create a suitable space for the development of daily tasks and economic, social, educational (and any online activities) in the EU. Like other initiatives and programs described, the Agenda responds to legislative and academic developments that have taken place on the continent, and constitutes the promotion of an environment conducive to the emergence of media literate citizens.

European policies, with their uniqueness and specific strategies, have launched media literacy in Europe, which is now in the process of consolidation. Above all, it is clear that the European model is unique and can be used as a reference in other contexts.

A European Policy Model for ML

In view of the evolution of European policies on media literacy it is possible to trace the defining features of what may be called the European model in this field.

Firstly, the active role of the European Commission must receive a mention as an intergovernmental institution as it has led the process in MIL, proposed objectives and established milestones. It has also managed to bring together and involve experts and institutions to participate in the task of promoting MIL. Its modus operandi has been the following:

1. The creation of expert groups which, through the exchange of experiences, defined the conceptual framework, established objectives and proposed studies and research.

2. The execution of studies and research proposals from the panel of experts. These studies were put to public tender although private and public institutions, as well as individual private interest groups, could participate.

3. Legislative and/or concerted action with Member States. As far as possible, the EC presented before Parliament *communiqués* that collected the recommendations of the studies commissioned or consensus reached among experts.

4. Activity to create incentive. In this context the EC, through public tenders, provided subsidies for the implementation of initiatives to coincide with strong policies, involving different actors from the system.

5. Evaluation. Finally, the EC established criteria and indicators, as well as other evaluation systems, which served as feedback for the projects developed.

Secondly, the overall involvement of stakeholders in the system. EC policies have always tried to integrate all participants in the system. This was characterized by the establishment of formal and informal platforms depending on the various participants at the European level. This has been carried out using the following scheme:

1. The creation of large participation platforms.

2. The commitment to consensus and reciprocity.

3. The acceptance of common objectives.

Thirdly, we must highlight the emphasis placed by the EU on human capacities, both creative and critical, with respect to the use of the media. Until 2004 the topic of media education had been guided by the principle of active resistance and critical media content while digital literacy was oriented towards the practical and instrumental use of technologies (or, in any case, to its safe use). But since 2004 media literacy in Europe has balanced critical and protective principles with creative skills. The development of these capabilities will lead to, according to the EC, a substantial improvement of the media in terms of transparency, pluralism and communication security.

Fourthly, we must recognize that the majority of EU countries have already opened the possibility, or have actually included MIL, in their compulsory school curricula (EMEDUS, 2014).

The promotion of media literacy, according to the European model, includes in its objectives the consideration of such literacy as a new right to add to the right to education, the right to information and the right to freedom of expression (Gavara & Pérez Tornero, 2012). This has been transferred to some laws – especially from the Directive on audio-visual services – but has also, in some cases, included the direct involvement of regulatory authorities in promoting audio-visual media education. Media literacy has become the third pillar of the rights of communication of our time. This opens a new European horizon for the development of communication within the European Union.

Finally, all these characteristics have made the European model of media literacy an effective policy capable of promoting development in Europe in this area that had not been previously achieved; hence its impact and relationship to other policies such as those of UNESCO, which have recently begun to spread across the entire planet.[8.]

References

Buckingham, D. (2010). The Future of Media Literacy in the Digital Age: Same Challenges for Policy and Practice. *Media Education Journal*, 47, 3-10.

Burn, A. & Reid, M. (2012). Screening Literacy: Reflecting on Models of Film Education in Europe. *Nordic Journal of Digital Literacy*, 314.

Carlsson, U., Tayie, S., Jacquinot-Delaunay, G., Pérez Tornero, J. M. (2008). *Empowerment through Media Education. An Intercultural Dialogue*. Göteborg: International Clearinghouse on Children, Youth and Media – Nordicom – Göteborg University.

Catts, R. & Lau, J. (2008). *Towards Information Literacy Indicators*. Paris, UNESCO.

Council of Europe. (2008). Council conclusions of 22 May 2008 on a European approach to media literacy in the digital environment. http://eur-lex.europa.eu/legal-content/EN/TXT/PDF/?uri=CELEX:52008XG0606(01)&from=EN

Creative Europe Programme 2014-2020. http://ec.europa.eu/programmes/creative-europe/opportunities/documents/ce-presentation_en.pdf

Digital Agenda for Europe. (26/02/2015). http://ec.europa.eu/digital-agenda/en/digital-agenda-europe-2020-strategy

DINAMIC (unpublished). Developing Media Literacy individual, corporate and citizen indicators. Autonomous University of Barcelona.

EAVI – European Association for Viewers' Interests & DTI – Danish Technological Institute (2011). Testing and Refining Criteria to Assess Media Literacy Levels in Europe. Commissioned by the European Commission Directorate-General for Information Society and Media. Media Literacy Unit.

European Commission and European Parliament. (2007). Directive 2007/65/EC of the European Parliament and of the Council of 11 December 2007 amending Council Directive 89/552/EEC on the coordination of certain provisions laid down by law, regulation or administrative action in Member States concerning the pursuit of television broadcasting activities. http://eur-lex.europa.eu/legal-content/EN/TXT/PDF/?uri=CELEX:32007L0065&from=ES

European Commission. (2007). COM(2007) 833 final. Communication from the Commission to the European Parliament, the Council, the European Economic and Social Committee and the Committee of the Regions. http://eur-lex.europa.eu/legal-content/EN/TXT/PDF/?uri=CELEX:52007DC0833&from=ES

European Commission. (2009). Commission Recommendation on media literacy in the digital environment for a more competitive audiovisual and content industry and an inclusive knowledge society. http://ec.europa.eu/culture/media/media-content/media-literacy/c_2009_6464_en.pdf

European Parliament. (2010). Directive 2010/13/EU of the European Parliament and of the Council of 10 March 2010 on the coordination of certain provisions laid down by law, regulation or administrative action in Member States concerning the provision of audiovisual media services (Audiovisual Media Services Directive). http://eur-lex.europa.eu/legal-content/EN/TXT/PDF/?uri=CELEX:32010L0013&from=EN

Frau-Meigs, D. (2012). Transliteracy as the New Research Horizon for Media and Information Literacy. *Medijske studije*, 3(6), 14-26.

Frau-Meigs, D.; Flores, J.; Tort, F. & Velez, I. (2014). Translit. Presentation at the European Median and Information Literacy Forum. Paris. UNESCO. http://ppemi.ens-cachan.fr/lib/exe/fetch.php/colloque140528/presentation_unesco_session_6.pdf

Gavara, J. C. & Pérez Tornero, J. M. (2012). La alfabetización mediática y la Ley General de comunicación audiovisual en España (Vol. 4). Editorial UOC.

Grunwald Declaration on Media Education. (1982). http://www.unesco.org/education/pdf/MEDIA_E.PDF

Pérez Tornero, J. M. (2004). Promoting Digital Literacy. http://www.gabinetecomunica-cionyeducacion.com/files/adjuntos/comprender%20DL.pdf

Pérez Tornero, J. M. (2007). Study on the current trends and approaches on Media Literacy in Europe. http://ec.europa.eu/culture/library/studies/literacy-trends-report_en.pdf

Pérez Tornero, J. M. (Sc. Coord) & Celot, P. (Ed.), (2009). *Study on assessment criteria for media literacy levels. Final report*. http://ec.europa.eu/culture/library/studies/litera-cy-criteria-report_en.pdf

Pérez Tornero, J. M. & Varis, T. (2010). *Media literacy and new humanism*. UNESCO Institute for Information Technologies in Education.

Pérez Tornero, J. M. (Coord.) (2014). *EMEDUS – European Media Literacy Education Study. Research on Existing Media Education Policies*. Barcelona, Gabinete de Comunicación y Educación. UAB.

Pérez Tornero, J. M. (Coord.) (2015). *FilmEd -Showing films and other audio-visual content in European School – Obstacles and best practices*. European Commission, Brussels. ISBN: 978-92-79-45353-3 DOI: 10.2759/168063

Programa MEDIA. (2006). (1718/2006/CE). http://www.programasue.info/documen-tos/2006-L327-12.pdf

Recommendations addressed to the United Nations Educational Scientific and Cultural Organisation UNESCO Adopted by the Vienna Conference ''Educating for the Media and the Digital Age''. (1999). 18-20 April. http://www.mediamanual.at/en/pdf/recom-mendations.pdf

Safer Internet Programme. http://www.saferinternet.org/

The Seville Recommendations, Youth Media Education Seminar. (2002). Seville, February. http://portal.unesco.org/ci/en/files/5680/10346121330Seville_Recommendations.rtf/Seville%2BRecommendations.rtf

Thoman, E. (1990). New Directions in Media Education, Toulouse Colloquy. Center for Media and Values, Los Angeles, CA. www.mediagram.ru/netcat_files/106/104/h_7fe56ea22e436049bf54427065a06679

UNESCO. (2011a). Alfabetización mediática e Informacional. Currículo para Profesores. http://unesdoc.unesco.org/images/0021/002160/216099S.pdf

UNESCO. (2011b). Towards Media and Information Literacy Indicators. Background Document of the Expert Meeting Prepared by Susan Moeller, Ammu Joseph, Jesús Lau, Toni Carbo 4 – 6 November 2010 Bangkok, Thailand. Paris, UNESCO.

UNESCO. (2013). Global Media and Information Literacy Assessment Framework: Country Readiness and Competencies. Prepared by UNESCO. Paris. http://unesdoc.unesco.org/images/0022/002246/224655e.pdf

UNESCO. (2014). Paris Declaration on Media and Information Literacy in the Digital Era. Paris, UNESCO. http://www.unesco.org/new/fileadmin/MULTIMEDIA/HQ/CI/CI/pdf/In_Focus/paris_mil_declaration_final.pdf

Verniers, P (ed.). (2009). *Media literacy in Europe Controversies, challenges and perspectives*. EUROMEDUC. Brussels. http://www.euromeduc.eu/IMG/pdf/Euromeduc_ENG.pdf

Zachetti, M. (2007). Media Literacy: A European approach. *Medienimpulse* Heft 61.

Notes

1   2004 was the year in which *Promoting Digital Literacy* (Pérez Tornero, 2004) was published and in 2014 the European Media Literacy Forum was held which completed a cycle in which Europe changed its policies from digital literacy to the more complete concept of media literacy.

2   It would be difficult to cite everyone but the following deserve mention: Evelyne Bevort, Suzan Krugsay, Cary Bazalgette, Manuel Pinto, Vitor Reia-Batista, Divina Frau-Meigs, José Manuel Pérez Tornero, Lluís Artigas, Hara Paddy, David Buckingham, Sonia Livingstone, Len Masterman.

3   Seville Seminar was conducted by José Manuel Pérez Tornero, Divina Frau-Meigs, Valentín Gómez Oliver and representative of UNESCO Lluís Artigas.

4   As an example, the MENTOR Project, financed by the EC, created a curriculum for media education for teacher trainers in the Euro-Mediterranean area.

5   Council conclusions of 22 May 2008 on a European approach to media literacy in the digital environment (2008/C 140/08).

6   This initiative stems from the efforts of the British Film Institute (BFI) and the UK film Council in 2005 which organised two seminars (EUROMEDUC) up to 2009. Although the initiative is still active, they have not organised any seminars since. Initial countries participating in this charter were Austria, Belgium, France, Germany, Portugal, Spain, Sweden and the UK.

7   *Study on Assessment Criteria for Media Literacy Levels* was coordinated by J.M. Pérez Tornero (scientific coordinator) and P. Celot (Project coordinator and editor).

8   Proof of this is the establishment of MIL observatories in Latin America and Europe, the Arab and European forums and the forum of Mexico City, as well as the expansion of the Chairs of UNESCO- UNAOC MILID UNITWIN.

Information Freedom and GAPMIL in Asia-Pacific Region: Challenges and Suggested Action Plan

Kyoko Murakami

This article examines the nature of the media and information literacy (MIL) conditions and its challenges concerning information freedom in Asia and Pacific regions, and addresses the Global Alliance for Partnerships on Media and Information Literacy suggested Action Plan in Asia-Pacific region. The questions that this article explores are: what challenges has MIL faced in Asia and Pacific countries and regions?; and how can culturally diverse national/ regional/international groups be strengthened and connected?

Keywords: Global Alliance for Partnerships on Media and Information Literacy (GAPMIL), Asia-Pacific, information freedom, media freedom, media and information literacy

Introduction

An emergence of new forms of communication technologies, particularly advancement of the Internet has created unprecedented opportunities and potentialities for media and information users around the world. All citizens in the digital age need to acquire media and information competencies and skills to explore their personal abilities since the vital communication technologies have completely transformed our conventional structure of knowledge, media messages and distribution of ideas. At the same time, we should recognize that media messages, knowledge and ideas are culturally, politically and religiously constructed by their very nature. Cultural understanding, tolerance, and dialogues are indispensable to survive the flood of information that is culturally embedded in the virtual world.

Reflecting communication technologies' potential challenges based on cultural, moral, political and religious intolerance in the world, there is the temptation for protectionism; however, it is generally agreed that empowerment through media and information literacy is one of the most important and urgent agendas for both citizens and governments to promote and enhance various types of media and information related opportunities. Simultaneously the importance of freedom of expression and rights to access information and knowledge to maintain a democratic society cannot be overemphasized, particularly in relation to freedom of the press and safety of journalists.

To promote international cooperation the Global Alliance for Partnerships on Media and Information Literacy (GAPMIL) was established by a joint initiative of the United Nations Educational, Scientific and Cultural Organization (UNESCO) and other global stakeholders during a pioneering initiative of the Global Forum for Partnerships on Media and Information Literacy in June 2013 in Abuja, Nigeria, in conjunction with the International Conference on MIL and Intercultural Dialogue. According to UNESCO' website, GAPMIL is:

> a more focused and permanent mechanism aiming at: articulating concrete partnerships to drive MIL development and impact globally; enabling the MIL community to speak as one voice on certain critical matters, particularly as it relates to policies; further deepening the strategy for MIL to be treated as a composite concept by providing a common platform for MIL related networks and associations globally.[1]

To promote GAPMIL and the concept of MIL in the Asia-Pacific region, this article examines general characteristics of the Asia-Pacific region and challenges that MIL has faced concerns about media and information freedom in Asia-Pacific regions, and proposes a suggested action plan for Asia-Pacific region.

Characteristics of the Asia-Pacific Region

Where is the Asia-Pacific region? It is a good question on which to start. Although there are some official/unofficial geopolitical regional groups that were divided by UNESCO and/or the United Nations[2], it has always been involved in a certain degree of discrepancies among the concerned parties depending on their political, cultural and historical context. Regarding GAPMIL regions, UNESCO indicates that there are 195 member states and 9 associate members that organize five regional groups; Africa, Arab States, Asia and the Pacific, Europe and North America and Latin America and the Caribbean[3]. Concerning a large landscape of the Asia-Pacific region, there are at least five sub-regions that are distinct from other sub-regions, namely: East Asia, South East Asia, South Asia, Central Asia and Oceania. Though UNESCO and the UN define the region according to political, legislative, cultural, historical context and international dynamics, the regional definition and individual identity for the region may vary depending on its cultural and historical background.

The large population in Asia-Pacific is another interesting characteristic. According to the United Nations' Population Division at the Department of Economic and Social Affairs (2013), for instance, the world population reached over 7 billion on March, 2012, and is continuously growing. Among five regional groups, Asia-Pacific, particularly Asia, is the most populous region. There are 4.3 billion inhabitants accounting for 60% of the world population in Asia. It is because two of the most populated countries in the world, China and India, together constitute approximately 37% of the world population. Concerning world population and the number of Internet users in the world, the Asia-Pacific region has a great potential for growing the number of Internet users.

Figure 1. Individuals using the Internet & individuals using the Internet per 100 inhabitants

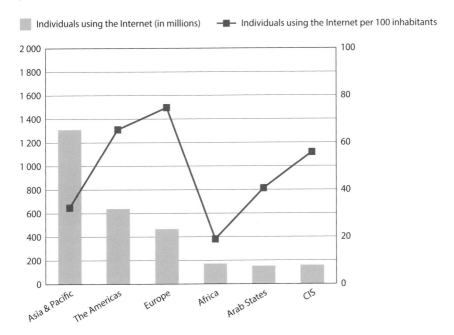

Source: International Telecommunication Union (ITU) World Telecommunication/ICT Indicators database. Retrieved from http://www.itu.int/en/ITU-D/Statistics/Pages/stat/default.aspx

CIS means Commonwealth of Independent States, former Soviet Republics. For country classification, see http://www.itu.int/en/ITU-D/Statistics/Pages/definitions/regions.aspx

According to the International Telecommunication Union (ITU), the United Nations' specialized agency for the information and communication technologies (ICTs), the number of global Internet users shows significant growth. Approximately forty percent (78% in developed countries and 32% in developing countries) of the world population, approximately 3 billion people use the Internet globally by accessing the Internet at home, by computer or mobile device in 2014. In other words, about 4 billion people in the world do not use the Internet yet, and more than two third of those users are in Asian countries (see Figure 1). Concerning the market potential for the growth of Internet users, the Asia-Pacific region is a positive prospect.

Information Freedom and Some Challenges in the Asia-Pacific Region

Having consultative status with the United Nations and UNESCO, the Reporters Without Borders', 2015 World Press Freedom Index examines 180 countries and regions to classify information performance into 5 levels relating to a variety of criteria such as pluralism, media independence, environment and self-censorship, legislative framework, transparency, infrastructure and abuses. These criteria reflect freedom of expression for both global citizens and journalists[4]. Covering 87 questions comparing different years, the Reporters rank the countries with 0 being the best, to 100 the worst for the target countries. This index provides a good starting point concerning the global media environment and independence in the Asia-Pacific region.

This article computes the mean of the following 5-point scale (5: Good situation, 4: Satisfactory situation, 3: Noticeable problems, 2: Difficult situation, 1: Very serious situation) based on the rank by the Index. Table 1 discloses that there are significant differences concerning the situation of media and information freedom by the five regions[5]. The mean score of the 2015 World Press Freedom Index is 2.9 among a maximum value of 5. The highest score is the Europe and North America region, and the mean score of 48 countries in the region is 3.8, while the Arab states' mean score of 19 countries is 1.9, the lowest score among 5 regions. Asia and the Pacific region is the second lowest region, the mean score of 37 countries is 2.4. The second highest region is Latin America and the Caribbean, 3.2 among 26 countries, and Africa is 2.7 among 48 countries.

Table 1. Mean of the 5-point scale

Region	Number of Countries	Mean
Africa	48	2.7
Arab States	19	1.9
Asia & Pacific	37	2.4
Europe & North America	50	3.8
Latin America & Caribbean	26	3.2
Total/World	**180**	**2.9**

Figure 2. Percentage of 5-point scale computed by regions and world mean

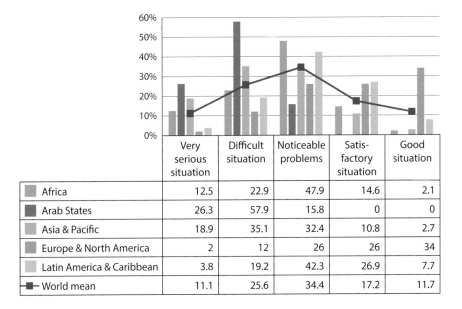

	Very serious situation	Difficult situation	Noticeable problems	Satis-factory situation	Good situation
Africa	12.5	22.9	47.9	14.6	2.1
Arab States	26.3	57.9	15.8	0	0
Asia & Pacific	18.9	35.1	32.4	10.8	2.7
Europe & North America	2	12	26	26	34
Latin America & Caribbean	3.8	19.2	42.3	26.9	7.7
World mean	11.1	25.6	34.4	17.2	11.7

The Figure 2 data table shows the percentage of the 5-point scale by region and world mean. When the study looks more closely at some of the important features of the 2015 Freedom of Information Index, there are three interesting indications. First, there are significant imbalances between the regions that obtain a higher score on the Index and those that obtain a lower score. Europe and North America, for instance, occupy the highest score of the 2015 Index; with 60 percent of the countries in either a "Good situation" or a "Satisfactory situation" out of the 5-point scale. However, the region that obtains the lowest score, the Arab states, counts neither higher scales of "Good" nor "Satisfactory." Rather, 84 percent of the Arab states are categorized into either "Difficult situation" or "Very serious situation." The Asia-Pacific region indicates a similar trend; 13.5% of the countries in the Asia-Pacific region are either "Good" or "Satisfactory," whereas 54% are "Difficult situation" or "Very serious situation." More specifically, 17 countries (34%) in Europe and North America are classified as "Good;" however, only one country, New Zealand, obtains "Good" status in the Asia-Pacific region.

Second and more important is relevancy between development stage of the countries and regions and the Index score. Although Europe and North America are defined by the United Nations as "more developed regions", these regions enjoy the highest mean score of the information freedom Index; however, such freedom is not always for the rich countries. Africa is a good example. According to the Population Division of the United Nations, Africa is categorized as a less developed region, similar to Asia (except Japan), Latin America, the Caribbean plus Melanesia, Micronesia and Polynesia and 34 out of 49 are considered as the least developed countries (United Nations, 2013, Notes). However, Africa's mean score of the Index implies that less developed countries could have stronger media freedom than their counterparts. Media and individuals' pluralism and independence would be the key to promote a better environment of media and information freedom.

Third and the most important of all is relevancy between regions, as well as consideration of countries that are classified as either "Difficult situation" or "Very serious situation" and the population of the region. Asia-Pacific is the most populous region, and many populous countries in Asia-Pacific are categorized as either "Difficult" or "Very Serious" in the 2015 Index because of their political use of media and information control. Although the Index is just an indicator of information freedom, it implies both positive and negative perspectives. The Asia-Pacific region seems to have much room for further improvement, but such improvement likely entails a great deal of difficulty. In order to promote the concept of MIL, the next section will show three suggested GAP-MIL action plans for the Asia-Pacific region.

Proposed Action Plan in Asia-Pacific Region

Three actions are proposed in order to foster and advance MIL in the Asia-Pacific region. The first suggested action is to recognize and partner with important national and regional MIL stakeholder groups and individuals in Asia-Pacific. To do so, it is important to identify leading national and regional stakeholders including consultations with media, library and information, national government units, foundations, MIL training institutions, etc. which promote the concept of MIL, and build the network nationally and regionally. Since Asia-Pacific region is very broad, the level of MIL recognition and involvement may vary. It is very important to find stakeholders and/or individuals whose countries and region's reflect that MIL is still in a developing stage.

The second suggested action is raising awareness by establishing links with GAPMIL, UNESCO-UNAoC University Network on MIL and Intercultural Dialogue (MILID), and/or other relevant MIL related organizations. Once leading national and regional stakeholders are identified, it would be better to plan and implement promotional activities in connection with the existing MILID Week, a global MIL Week, and the UN International Days such as the International Literacy Day, World Press Freedom Day, and World Information Society Day. Establishing partnerships in cooperation with the wider international community could accelerate the recognition of MIL in Asia-Pacific and promote MIL competencies among participants of the network internationally, nationally and regionally.

The third suggested action is to identify both global and local MIL and/or MIL related programs. It is essential to encourage and support other Chapter members to develop relevance in local projects, particularly in countries and regions where MIL is still a developing concept. It will promote national and regional cooperation and collaboration for education on MIL related programs and activities, and to create national/regional spaces for sharing any information and knowledge, research, and new projects.

Promoting MIL education is a set of competencies for active and democratic participation, including ethical use of information, cultural understanding/development, lifelong learning, decision-making and increased social participation, and access to methods of self-expression and information in the Asia-Pacific region. Since the Asia-Pacific region includes much complexity, building academic leadership as well as a solid grass-roots movement including academics, NPO, NGO, civil society, and educators rather than political leadership is strongly encouraged at this moment.

References

Frau-Meigs D. & Torrent J. (2009). *Mapping Media Education Policies in the World*: Visions, Programmes and Challenges. The United Nations-Alliance of Civilization in co-operation with UNESCO.

Grizzle A. & Calvo, M.C.T. (2013). *Media and information literacy: policy and strategy guidelines*. Paris, France: UNESCO. Retrieved from http://unesdoc.unesco.org/images/0022/002256/225606e.pdf

Reporters Without Borders. (2015). *2015 World Press Freedom Index*. Retrieved from http://index.rsf.org/

United Nations, Department of Economic and Social Affairs, Population Division (2013). *World Population Prospects: The 2012 Revision*, DVD. Retrieved from http://esa.un.org/unpd/wpp/unpp/panel_population.htm.

Notes

1   UNESCO, Global Alliance for Partnerships on Media and Information Literacy: About GAPMIL Retrieved from http://www.unesco.org/new/en/communication-and-information/media-development/media-literacy/global-alliance-for-partnerships-on-media-and-information-literacy/about-gapmil/

2   United Nations Statistics Division- Standard Country and Area Codes Classifications (M49). Retrieved from http://unstats.un.org/unsd/methods/m49/m49regin.htm

3   Worldwide United Nations Educational, Scientific and Cultural Organization. Retrieved from http://www.unesco.org/new/en/unesco/worldwide/

4   The Reporters Without Borders World Press Freedom Index. Retrieved from http://index.rsf.org/

5   Ibid. The Index details are retrieved from http://index.rsf.org/#!/index-details The index used the following regional definitions; Americas, Africa, North Africa and Middle East, Asia-Pacific, Eastern Europe and Central Asia, European Union and Balkans. However, the study adopted UNESCO's regional definitions and converted the data.

MIL Empowerment for an Enhanced Democracy: An India Perspective

Neelima Mathur

The Indian media continues to be one of the most free in the world and keeps political democracy on its toes. Even so, due to various factors, the character of Indian media has got coloured and changed. By and large, grass root public interest has been put on the back-burner.

In this context, media and information literacy (MIL) has immense and immediate validity and necessity. Citizens across India are deeply questioning the role and performance of media. A growing populace is talking about regulation, even after accepting and fully believing in Freedom of Expression. There is an overall impression for initiating wide-scale social debate between citizens, media and government for a Media Code of Conduct.

Citizens also wish to actively participate in the democratic space of the Internet through social media. Recent MIL trainings by FORMEDIA (The Foundation for Responsible Media) have shown the structured thoughts citizens have about how to use MIL skills for direct professional work or issues linked to the Post-2015 Sustainable Development Goals (SDGs).

This article reflects the import of the findings from pilot MIL training initiatives conducted by FORMEDIA in India.

Keywords: MIL in India, KAICIID MIL India religious training, Uttarakhand Open University MIL Pilots, MIL and development stakeholders, media in India

The world is facing up to the fact that we did not achieve the Millennium Development Goals (MDGs). We are setting a new agenda for the same. While there is a lot of re-thinking and new thinking, there is the fear that we may still not fully comprehend the missing links. Nearly eight years ago, in 2007, DFID (the Department of International Development of the United Kingdom that administers overseas aid) supported a study by PANOS London. It was entitled 'At the Heart of Change – The Role of Communication in Sustainable Development'. The opening parts of the Executive Summary cannot be overstated enough:

161

Development efforts are not fulfilling the promises made in the Millennium Development Goals (MDGs), to reduce poverty and improve poor people's lives. Why not? One fundamental reason is that policymakers and development experts do not recognise the essential role that information and communication play in development. Sustainable development demands that people participate in the debates and decisions that affect their lives. They need to be able to receive information, but also to make their voices heard. The poor are often excluded from these processes by geography and lack of resources or skills; and many groups – including women – are also kept silent by social structures and cultural traditions.

Towards the end of the Executive Summary, the report made strong recommendations for achieving the MDGs:

Reaching the MDGs in 2015 will require huge investments of political will and financial resources by governments in both the developed and the developing world; but it will also require a belated recognition that communication is central to all aspects of sustainable development. What needs to be done to realise the potential of communication in maximising development outcomes?

- *Build more open, transparent information and communication systems and political cultures...*

- *Treat information, communication and the media as public goods and invest accordingly...*

- *Take a holistic view of communication processes and integrate communication into development planning and implementation...*

- *Invest in media development...*

Indian Media Landscape

In this context, let us briefly reflect on the media landscape of India. It is oft forgotten that India is a sub-continent and it is easily termed a country like any other. In fact, it is akin to Europe – with 29 states and 7 union territories with every possible type of geographical terrain. It has 18 official languages and innumerable dialects. While every region has its regional media in all forms, the dominant languages are Hindi (that covers a huge northern-central belt) and English. This is important to note in reference to television. At prime time, right across the nation, it quite easily leaves out – not just in terms of language but also culturally – a huge part of the country and its populace, from what is easily termed 'mainstream'.

Again, especially in context that it has become the dominant media, the character of television has shifted from news to views. The audience is constantly besieged with views – both of the channel via anchors and the panellists, who represent different interests. The power structure of this kind of programming makes audiences vulnerable and their own voice or the first voice of grass root people remains either unheard or gets unwittingly submerged in the daily *blitzkrieg*. So, while undoubtedly, there is a throbbing media in India that keeps political democracy on its toes, this characteristic of television is impacting society all round.

Ripe Ground for MIL

The interesting fact is how the increasing use of social media now comes into the picture. Citizens may not have formed enough movements or campaigns on social media yet but it has become a platform for exchanging, questioning, commenting about what comes on/in mainstream media – particularly if it is individual or issue-based 'news'.

It is also increasingly becoming a space for sharing 'relevant' information albeit in personalised contexts – information that is increasingly not displayed prominently or at all even in print media. Just as an example: There may be an agricultural fair where almost-extinct varieties of rice were displayed. Someone buys a bit to take home, cooks it and displays it with pictures and minimal information on Facebook. Soon enough, there is a trail of posts about extinct varieties, where one could buy them, equivalent forms of rice in other parts of India, the issue of genetically modified seeds, etc.

In today's media landscape in India, the media is not taking these personal interests and choices of people into account. The citizens are not taking to this very kindly anymore, as we will see further down.

Here is where we come to the relevance of media and information literacy (MIL) and how the citizens of India are poised for empowerment. There is enough material and a formidable galaxy of experts in India regarding media literacy and information literacy as separate components. The GAPMIL vision of combining the two is a comparatively new one. In association with UNESCO and the MIL University Network of India (MILUNI), FORMEDIA has had the honour of being engaged in the first steps for MIL in India.

Between November 2014 and February 2015, FORMEDIA conducted three face-to-face entry-level MIL trainings for a) religious leaders b) for Master of Education (M. Ed) scholars who will become school teachers c) development stakeholders and university academics. Each training has been a learning and the lessons learnt are being briefly shared here.

India is a society where the secular concept is held dear. Various religions thrive in a spirit that is largely accommodative. Communal or ethnic flashes are not uncommon and are known to get out of control. The pioneering training of religious leaders was conducted under a programme offered by KAICIID (King

Abdullah Bin Abdulaziz International Centre for Interreligious and Intercultural Dialogue, an inter-governmental organisation headquartered in Austria) in partnership with All Religion Dialogue in India. It was entitled "Media Wise: Empowering Responsible Religious Leaders in the Digital Age" on Media and Information Literacy.

Some excerpts from FORMEDIA'S executive summary report submitted to KAICIID are interesting to note.

The group of participants was a suitable mixed one and quite equally balanced between Hindus (different strands) and Muslims (different strands). Christians, though a strong presence in India, were somewhat under-represented. Sikh, Jain, Buddhist and Zorastrian (Parsi) representation was missing. This point is being mentioned for a specific reason.

In the absence of sufficient other religious representation, such a group can easily slip into the traditional Hindu-Muslim finger-pointing in India. In such a training, it is already a tall task to keep religious leaders away from 'religious' talk and keep them focussed on media & information issues. When the majority of participants are from just two communities, the escalation points can creep in rapidly…

A major issue was language. A large number of participants were not comfortable with English and the Trainer had to make a quick mental switch to a bi-lingual training. This situation can prove disastrous if the Trainer is not comfortable with the major Indian language, Hindi. It is a very important point that must be noted for future trainings in India. Specially, since MIL has several concepts and words that do not get easily translated and need to be explained very well in the local language…

It was interesting to note that almost no session was considered irrelevant and the participants remained engaged. The ones that garnered most interest were by and large linked to social media/new media, specifically in relation to how the religious leaders can/should function in that space. In fact, more than five participants have requested for an intensive follow-up training in utilisation of social media for their area of work.

The executive summary report to KAICIID further states the overall impact:

- *The group developed a better understanding of what is information and how it is accessed through different media platforms*
- *The concept of Freedom of Expression as a right and the importance of self-regulation versus regulatory bodies for the Press became clearer to them*
- *They partially understood the constraints under which journalists work (A visit to a newsroom is a demonstrable need for this to be fully understood)*
- *The 5Ws &1H (means what, why, when, where, by whom, and how) plus the straight and inverted triangle for news reports and features was an eye-opener for most*

- *The analysis of text and photographs and related issues of representation were discussed animatedly*
- *They developed an understanding of the difference between traditional media and new media and the value of the latter in today's world*
- *The session on youth and challenges/risks in cyber world was of great interest*
- *The issues of copyright, defamation, privacy in the cyber world were discussed at great length*
- *Negotiating of meaning by audiences seemed like absolutely new territory and the group was very engaged in this topic*
- *The Trainer's give-aways of new terminology was of much interest and picked up quickly. Namely, how in the world of new media, there is 'nanoisation' of information, 'tribalisation' of information flow and 'iconisation' of every aspect of human life that is impacting how information is conveyed, to whom and how diversity may be under threat.*

Uttarkhand Open University Trainings

Having successfully tested a pilot curriculum based on the UNESCO MIL Training of Trainers (TOT) Manual, FORMEDIA was equipped to pilot test a similar entry-level basic and extended curriculum for the Uttarakhand Open University (UOU), in the marginalised state of Uttarakhand in northern India.

The basic curriculum was conducted over approximately six hours for about 50 M. Ed Scholars, who potentially will be school teachers. Over 50% of the group comprised of women. The extended curriculum was conducted over approximately 18 hours for 19 participants. In this group, the development stakeholders included representatives from sectors as diverse as women's empowerment, disaster management, health, academy of administration, teaching. The UOU academics, who contribute to the university's Open and Distance Learning (ODL) programmes, came from different departments like history, sociology, social work, psychology.

The over-all impact of the training was similar to the MIL religious training as stated above. The important additional aspect was the keen debate on Freedom of Expression, Freedom of the Press and whether there is a need for regulation. It can be encapsulated in what one of the M. Ed scholars said. In India, the four pillars of society are perceived as the political system, the judiciary, the executive administration and the media. The M. Ed scholars, supported by many others, strongly felt: There is an inherent mechanism of checks-and-balances for three pillars of society, namely the politicians, the judiciary and the executive. There is none for the media. He felt this was unfair and questioned why it should remain so. He further emphasised the dire need to develop a code of conduct for the media. He felt the time has come for a wide-scale social debate in which the media, government and citizens should participate. He was quite clear that this code should not in any way jeopardise Freedom of Expression but that it is equally clear that the media is in no way showing the will or intent to self-regulate itself.

The important point to note is that in all three trainings:

- Participants were grateful for a better understanding of 'media'
- They wished to utilise this better understanding in an empowered way
- They unanimously expressed the desire for further training targeted on social media
- They wished for more examples of case studies for analysis and more activities to better understand the whys and wherefores of media
- Note: in the three-day trainings, there was exhaustive activity but clearly, the participants find this not just interesting but empowering and wish for much more time to be allocated for it. The overall impression is that they would like to leave the training with a sense of satisfaction that they can 'do it' on social media.

The experience of these three trainings brings us back to the core of 'At the Heart of Change', namely and to repeat:

- *Build more open, transparent information and communication systems and political cultures…*
- *Treat information, communication and the media as public goods and invest accordingly…*
- *Take a holistic view of communication processes and integrate communication into development planning and implementation…*
- *Invest in media development…*

The above four points are, in essence, the basis for a MIL policy and strategy.

Freedom of Expression in a World of Social Media

Historically, India has a very active and free press and from the time of the Independence movement until now, has performed its role with courage, especially with exposing corruption in recent years. Equally, anomalies, including those of cross-media ownership, have crept in and changed the identity and character of media.

Sometimes, the government has tended to react with knee-jerk reactions, which have not always been welcomed. Some examples may not be out of place. In the late sixties, there was a storm of controversy around the films of French film-maker Louis Malle ('Calcutta' and a television series 'Phantom India') broadcast on BBC. For several years, BBC was banned from filming in India. While there can be unending debate on the right or wrong of the controversy, no one was referring to an earlier comparative example of 'The Lovers' by the same film-maker. It had been banned in several states of the United States in the late 50s. It also led to a landmark judgement of the country's Supreme Court on the definition of obscenity.

Several years later, in the mid-70s, BBC correspondent, Mark Tully, was barred from entering India, a country he had been reporting for years. This was during the infamous Emergency when Indian journalists (among others) were also put behind bars. Later, Mark Tully settled in India permanently and continues to reside there.

Even as this article goes to the editors, there is a burning issue around a film, 'India's Daughter' that has been broadcast on BBC. There are contrarian views whether it is right for the government to ban this film. The real point, though, is that unlike in the time of Louis Malle or Mark Tully, we now have cross-continental new media. Banned within the country or not, it is a bit hard to keep the film off from the citizens. It goes off Google and pops up somewhere else.

People cannot be stopped from being engaged with burning issues, rightly or wrongly. Government-owned public institutions like public broadcasters and documentary funders do not address and provide platforms for anything that could be or become controversial. The seething undercurrents erupt in parallel genres that carry the narratives anyway, which get seen worldwide anyway.

MIL – a Must Need

Keeping all this in mind and knowing the huge burden of achieving the new Sustainable Development Goals (SDGs), it will be interesting to see how MIL-linked policies evolve in India. The first voice of all those who still live under the proverbial one-dollar-a-day is not being heard enough. Those who want to showcase that voice are finding new power in social media. Can we risk the informally empowered but unskilled citizen to run amok on social media? Or do we want to catch the bull by its horns, empower citizens with competencies and ensure democracy is enhanced and not disintegrated into a cacophony of voices in cyber space leading to social instability…

References

At the Heart of Change – The Role of Communication in Sustainable Development (2007). London: Panos London. http://panos.org.uk/wp-content/files/2011/01/heart_of_change_weby2wvJO.pdf

Pilot Curriculum Media Wise: Empowering Responsible Religious Leadership in the Digital Age Media and Information for Religious Leaders (2014). Vienna: King Abdullah Bin Abdulaziz International Centre for Interreligious and Intercultural Dialogue. https://www.kaiciid.org/node/1791

Impact of Social Media on Political Participation of Egyptian Youth

Sally S. Tayie

This study aims at examining the role played by social media in empowering and encouraging the Egyptian youth for political participation. Previous studies found that traditional media have not been influential enough to drive youth's political participation. On the other hand, recent studies found that social media have a significant role in this respect. The current study investigates the possible roles of the social media in the transition to democracy in Egypt; questioning the ability of social media to act as a platform where citizens are represented and empowered enough to transform virtual online discussions to real life actions. The study was carried out on a purposive sample of 400 young Egyptians aged 18-30 based on the statistics of social media users in Egypt. A sample of opinion leaders and elites in the field was also studied. The research follows a triangulation by combining two research methodologies; survey as a quantitative method and in-depth interviews as a qualitative one. The theoretical framework is Uses and Gratifications Theory. According to the findings of the study, social media became most prominent among youth in Egypt after January 25th Revolution. The study also found that most Egyptian youth use social media on a daily basis. Egyptian youth consider social media as a platform through which they manage to share their common concerns and possibly turn it into collective real-life actions; which reflects their interest in becoming more politically involved.

Keywords: social media, political participation, Egyptian youth, democracy, new media, traditional media and non-traditional media

Introduction

With the emergence of social media, a new definition of networking and socializing has been introduced. Social networks initially facilitated communication among friends and families. However, social media have remarkably changed and so has their role. Throughout the past few years, social media has impacted young people's political participation. Political participation is very important in any modern society; it is the enabler for people to introduce real changes and express themselves.

It is important to understand the reason such platforms have a strong impact. Generations of young people need to unite on common causes in order to be able to have attitudinal or behavioral changes toward their countries or regimes. This is exactly what social media have done: they helped youth "develop a consciousness of their common interests and form group solidarity to harness their collective power" (Herrera, 2012). According to Klatch (1999) significant changes in the lives of generations occur most strongly in cases where a "social trauma" exists, such as during economic crises or times of political and social revolutions. According to Feldman (2010) the new media can act as important resources to youth for empowerment:

"Generations shift from being a passive cohort…into a politically active and self-conscious cohort…when they are able to exploit resources (political/educational/economic) to innovate in cultural, intellectual or political spheres" (Herrera, 2012).

According to scholars and researchers, including Callum Rymer and Douglas Kellner, the Internet, and new media in general, present the possibility and have the power to lead to a public sphere that can be described as democratic in the postmodern era. This comes as a result of new media providing citizens with an interactive platform on which they can become a vital part of a debate that is based on solid information and that is not based on hierarchical knowledge coming from specific sources. On the other hand, some observers indicate that having a "virtual sphere" is not applicable; despite the mentioned advantages of providing citizens with a platform to express themselves, "technology alone cannot foster democracy" and this goes back to the idea that the Internet and new media help enhance "political communication" but does not introduce effective changes to its "internal structure" (Singer, 2006, p. 266).

Today's young generation is regarded as a media-savvy one that manages to master the idea of "online to offline organizing" for purposes that directly have to do with a country's political life. Revolts that took place in what is dubbed the 'Arab Spring' are good examples; also movements that took place in New York City (Occupy Wall Street) and in Spain (Los Indigados movement). The name 'Arab Spring' came from the belief that such uprisings could result in a democratic transition in countries that has long suffered from dictatorships.

Applying this to Egypt, the term "Facebook revolution" has been widely circulated in the media on a global level to describe the Egyptian revolution; mainly triggered by the Facebook page "We Are All Khaled Saeed". The page was initiated after Khaled Saeed, a young Egyptian, was killed by police officers. It was developed in order to spread awareness and encourage people to rage on "police brutality". The page has always been action-oriented as it encouraged its members "to get up from behind their computer screens and go out into the streets…to attend the public funeral of Khaled Said" (Herrera, 2012). By time the page started calling people to take to the streets and revolt against the tyranny of the 30-year-old autocratic regime, torture and social injustice on January 25th its members were already increasing massively. Such events highlight the true impact of social media on youth in general.

Statement of the Research Problem

With the turn of the twenty-first century, in many developing countries, social media have transformed the function of the media from being a mouthpiece of the state, to media and sites for participation of citizens and ordinary people. People themselves have become contributors to the content of the new media.

In light of the rapid and wide spread of social media and the increased number of users, as well as the political turmoil in the Arab area which led to mass uprisings described by the international media as the "Arab Spring", social networks have become an important phenomenon in our modern world. Social media have become important factors which affect public opinion. The impact of social media on the issues of freedom of expression and publishing, as well as democracy and human rights, has also been highlighted.

Since the January 25th Revolution, there has been a remarkable increase in the political involvement of young Egyptians who became more involved than ever before in the public sphere. This research attempts to address the following statement:

> New 'social' media, unlike traditional media, provided a platform on which citizens create their own version of news and updates on current events. Social media are believed by many to be single-issue oriented and lacking a consistent long-term impact and also their credibility is under question. Consequently, the extent to which social media helped represent and empower Egyptian youth for political participation as a vital step for establishing democracy needs to be further investigated.

Significance of the Study

During the 1990s, many commentators expected the Internet to have a profound impact on how democracy functions, transforming it into an ideal e-democracy with equal opportunities for all citizens. Despite the fact that the number of studies in the area of social media and political participation has been accelerating, further research still needs to be done in countries like Egypt.

According to Herrera (2012, p. 334), the Middle Eastern and North African (MENA) countries are of great significance to research in this area. The MENA countries represent communities of "wired youth" suffering from "political repression and economic exclusion" which act as a huge challenge that stands as an obstacle in the process of transitioning to democracy. With the increase in the numbers of Internet users, social injustice and lack of political representation increases as well under autocratic regimes. This acts as a strong justification to study and understand the notion of new media empowerment for youth in the MENA countries. There was a remarkable increase that occurred between 2008 and 2011, in which numbers increased from 822,560 Facebook users in 2008 to reach more than 5.6 million in 2011.

Recent statistics (Al Gazzar, 2013, p. 15) show that there is a massive growth in the number of Egyptian users of social media. The number of Facebook users is estimated at 13,010,580 users. This represents 16.2 percent of the population, putting Egypt in the 20th place in the ranking of the countries that use Facebook. Facebook users represent 60 percent of the online sites users. Most Facebook users are aged between 18 and 24 years followed by those in the age group of 25 to 34.

The study focuses on how social media started shaping and enhancing Egyptian youth's involvement in political life since the January 25th Revolution. It sheds light on the extent to which social media provide a platform through which citizens share their common concerns that result in collective real-life actions that can possibly define political participation. This reflects citizens' representation and empowerment which acts as a crucial step to democracy building.

Methodology

The study relies on a multi-approach (triangulation). It uses a combination of the survey as a quantitative method and the in-depth interview as a qualitative technique. Sample of the study, hypotheses and research question will be dealt with in the following lines.

The Sample

This study was carried out on a purposive sample, i.e. a non-probability sample. Subjects of the purposive sample are selected according to certain characteristics. Those who do not have these characteristics are excluded from the sample (Wimmer & Dominick, 2011).

The sample included 400 university students, aged 18 to 30 years, who are active users of the Internet and social media. Active users mainly refer to those who access their Facebook/Twitter accounts frequently, and interact with and react to the content they encounter. Respondents who did not meet the mentioned criteria were excluded from the study. Students (undergraduate and postgraduate) were selected from the American University in Cairo and Cairo University with an average of 200 students from each university. For the in-depth interviews, the purposive sample included those who are opinion leaders in the field studied (social media and political participation). The sample included three university professors, three journalists and three political activists. All three can be regarded as opinion leaders who may direct and lead others in their own domains and areas of specialty.

Hypotheses and Research Questions

Three hypotheses (H1a, H1b, and H2) and two research questions (RQ1 and RQ2) were set and tested through survey questions and in-depth interviews:

H1a: Egyptian youth utilize social media as primary sources of news.
H1b: Egyptian youth consider social media to be more credible news sources than traditional media.
H2: Social media empower Egyptian youth to turn online political participation to offline (real-life) political participation.
RQ1: Can social media potentially aid in the long term process of transitioning to democracy by enhancing Egyptian youth sense of political responsibility?
RQ2: Can social media have a role in Egyptian youth's assessment of the importance of being politically active citizens?

Discussion

The two most used social networking sites in Egypt are believed to be Facebook and Twitter. Consequently, the study focused on these two sites as representing social media in Egypt.

Over the past years, the Arab World has been witnessing turmoil as a result of the tyranny and repressiveness of the ruling regimes. Consequently, the peoples of different countries shared the same sufferings which resulted in several uprisings in some of the Arab countries. With the spread of the Internet and social media, Egyptian youth managed to identify their common problems and concerns. This came as a result of the characteristics of social media that enable user-generated content, continuous exchange and sharing of information and enhanced interactivity among its users. The content over social networking sites is mainly created by ordinary citizens, who act as citizen journalists by engaging in reporting on events. This occurs in different forms; pictures, videos, comments, reports, statuses or tweets. Consequently, according to scholars, this impacted the monopoly of traditional media on information providing. Traditional media outlets are no longer the sole gatekeepers or the only sources of information and news.

According to the interviewed opinion leaders, social media in many instances manage to set the priority of events in the minds of audiences as an impact of satisfying their needs.

When asked about their usage patterns, most respondents (82.3 percent) mentioned that they access Facebook and/or Twitter on a daily basis. This shows that accessing social networking sites became a daily habit to most students. The difference between Cairo University (CU) students and those from the American University in Cairo (AUC) was not significant when it comes to their usage patterns. However, in both universities, females (92.3 percent at CU, 85.9 percent at AUC) showed more regularity in using Facebook and/or Twitter than males (67 percent at CU, 83.3 percent at AUC). The majority of students mentioned that they spend more than four hours weekly online (51.8 percent) with a minority mentioning that they spend less than one hour a week (7 percent).

When asked about the type of information they obtain from social media, a large percentage (86.3 percent) of the study participants mentioned that they obtain political information; which comes in the second place after social and cultural information (93.5 percent). Respondents were also asked about the extent to which they trust or could count on Facebook and/or Twitter as a credible sources of news/information. More than one third (39 percent) of the respondents mentioned that they "strongly agree" that social networking sites can be considered a credible source of news and information. Also respondents mentioned that the type of political information they obtain from Facebook/Twitter the most is about demonstrations and protests (84.3 percent) followed by elections (56 percent) and then international issues (53.3 percent).

Based on these findings, H1a was supported. Social media consumption has become a basic activity which youth engage in on a daily basis. Accordingly, it can be inferred that their consumption of social networking sites exceeds that of traditional media. This leads to social networking sites in many cases becoming primary sources of news. This was highly supported by the interviewed opinion leaders who explained that social media have the advantage of rapid dissemination of news; information is published online before distribution through traditional media outlets. This characteristic of immediate/instant reporting on events gives social media the advantage of being a primary source to its users.

Furthermore, H1b was also supported. The researcher thought, based on other studies, that being created by peers, information over social media would be regarded as more credible than traditional media that in many instances, are known to follow owners/editors' agendas. However based on the findings this was found to be true only in some instances but not to be generalized. This has been emphasized by the interviewees as well. They highlighted the fact that professional journalists who work for specialized traditional media institutions have more credibility. This goes back to traditional journalists being familiar with professionalism; being objective leads to more audience. Furthermore, traditional journalists can be held accountable when violating any of the laws, regulations or set standards. On the other hand, it is difficult to hold citizen journalists who publish content on social media accountable. They may report news from their own personal perspective which can be affected by emotions and personal agendas.

When asked about the type of pages/accounts they like/follow, a majority (62.3 percent) mentioned that they are interested in political pages/accounts after social and cultural pages/accounts (85.1 percent). The majority of the study participants (95.3 percent) indicated they talk with friends/family members about the content they consume or obtain from Facebook and/or Twitter. This indicates that social media play a role in setting the public's agenda; though this role is somehow limited to a specific segment in the society.

According to the findings, social media do have an impact on motivating youth to participate in real life political events/activities. This was confirmed by those who indicated that discussions on Facebook/Twitter encouraged them to participate in January 25th revolution (89.3 percent), June 30th revolution (78.5 percent), Presidential Elections of 2012 (36.3 percent), January 2014 Constitutional referendum (26 percent). More than one third of the respondents (37 percent) "strongly agree" that they become politically active citizens when they participate on Facebook and/or Twitter.

Based on these findings, H2 is supported. Online political activities can be a significant motive to encourage youth for real life political participation however it is not enough. There are other requirements for youth to become actually active in political life. According to Sara El Khalili, one of the opinion leaders interviewed, political participation should be preceded by five essential steps. First, a citizen should be active in seeking information. Second, he/she should form an opinion and have the desire to share and discuss it. Third, there is an expression of public opinion, fourth, an actual action is taken and fifth, there is actual political participation. From these five steps, the role of social media would be prominent. Social media can have a role in the five steps, as it provides citizens with information which they share and express their opinion on, they can also be encouraged to take actual actions and so can enhance their political participation.

As mentioned, free expression of opinions is essential to achieve political participation. Almost half of the participants (49.5 percent) mentioned that they "frequently" express their opinions on Facebook/Twitter, while 27 percent "sometimes" do so. Also, more than two fifths of the respondents (41.2 percent) indicated that they "strongly agree" that Facebook/Twitter helps them realize the importance of voicing their opinions in political issues, besides the revolution. In addition, respondents were asked about the impact the disappearance of Facebook/Twitter would have on them. The majority mentioned that they will not be able to take part in political events (65.8 percent), they will not be active citizens (47.5 percent), they will not be able to express their opinions on political issues (45.5 percent).

Findings have shown that in answer to RQ1 social media can play a role in the long term process of transitioning to democracy by enhancing Egyptian youth's sense of political responsibility. Answers to RQ2 findings show that social media have a role in making Egyptian youth realize the importance of being politically active citizens. This can be inferred from the responses that have shown that the impact of social media can be long-term, cultivating values and beliefs, as well as short-term, single issue oriented. This has been agreed on by opinion leaders as well. They agreed that social networking sites have managed to implant ideas or beliefs that were not existent before, reflecting its long term impact. This illustrates social media's ability to aid in the democratic process.

Social media can help improve and sustain the existence of the two main pillars of any democracy; free flow of information and representing one segment in the society (social media users). A free flow of information is achieved in different ways. First, this occurs through citizen journalism enabled by the user-generated content. Citizens report and comment on current events. Second, traditional media outlets exist online in general and on social media specifically. This is obvious through the massive number of followers to institutions such as CNN, BBC and Al Jazeera. Through the continuous expression by youth on Facebook/Twitter, a crucial segment of the society will be represented and heard by those in power. Accordingly, based on the input of opinion leaders, the best way to pave the way for democratic transition in Egypt is for traditional and social media to work together. Social media complement the role of traditional media in the sense that it has the capacity of rapid/instant dissemination of news besides providing space for audiences/citizens to be represented and have their input valued.

References

Al Gazzar, N. (2013). The Role of Social Media in the Formation of Public Opinion Towards Islamists – A Content Analysis. *Arab Journal of Media and Communication Research*, 2, p. 15-22.

Feldman, T. (2009). *An Introduction to Digital Media*. South Africa: Blueprint.

Herrera, L. (2012). Youth and Citizenship in the Digital Age: A View from Egypt. *Harvard Educational Review*, 82(3), p. 333-352.

Klatch, R. (1999). *A Generation Divided*. CA: University of California Press.

Singer, J. B. (2006). Stepping Back From the Gate: Online Newspapers Editors and the Co-Production of Content in Campaign 2004. *Journalism and Mass Communication Quarterly*, 83(2), p. 265-280.

Wimmer, R. D. & Dominick, J. R. (2011). *Mass Media Research: An introduction*. California: Wadsworth Publishing Company.

Media Literacy and Political Campaigns in Nigeria

Adebisi O. Taiwo

Political campaigns done through all forms of media has been intensified since the beginning of the fourth republic in Nigeria. In fact, media has become a fundamental and indispensable tool for political parties to woo electorates during the build-up to elections. Hence the need for media and information literacy for everyone involved to know the type of message to disseminate and for the audience to know what type of message to expect. This is because in the process of political campaigns via the media, the content has been both constructive and calumnious in the attempt to persuade voters. This article examines the major issues in message dissemination in Nigerian media for political campaigns which brings out the important role of media and information literacy and suggests that media and information literacy projects in Nigeria should develop a comprehensive curriculum that would enable youth to understand healthy media content of political campaigns for both the audience and politicians.

Keywords: media literacy, political campaigns, media contents

Introduction

Media and information plays a vital role in politics and political campaigns all over the world. These are strong tools that have won some countries positive progress. This is not limited to developed countries. It is a known fact that the independence of Nigeria was achieved through the media, particularly the print media (Obafemi, 2012), who opined that "it was no accident that many of the political actors in the nationalist struggle for independence were themselves journalists or/and founders of print media corporations". Nationalists like Obafemi Awolowo and Nnamdi Azikuwe used the print media as tools to fight for the independence gained in October, 1960. This implies that media and information plays an important role for political activities.

It is essential that the political classes and their agents (source) understand the role and appropriate use of the media to deliver their message to their target audience and prospective voters (receiver). The receiver in turn should know what to expect from the candidates through the media and the extent to which information and political messages align with the code of conduct for political parties which sets the tone on the surrounding issues; the Rule of law, campaigns and elections which contains a set of rules of behavior for political parties and their supporters relating to their participation in an election process.

Therefore, the role of media and information literacy is vital for both the source and the receiver.

Nigeria runs a democratic system of government. At the time of writing this article this country was preparing for its fifth general election in March 28, 2015. Political campaigns with propaganda mixed in, were being carried out via various media platforms by the political classes, supposedly for the benefit of the electorate and other stakeholders. The effectiveness of the informational content and the embedded campaign propaganda may be dependent on the level of media and information literacy of the campaign management team on one hand and the public response to campaign messages. Also, the type of response given by audience to the campaign messages is determined by the level of media and information literacy of individuals and society on the other hand.

The National Association for Media Literacy Education defines media literacy as "The ability to access, analyze, evaluate, and communicate information in a variety of forms is interdisciplinary by nature. Media literacy represents a necessary, inevitable, and realistic response to the complex, ever-changing electronic environment and communication cornucopia that surround us." Also, The American Association of School Librarians (AASL), a precursor in the information literacy field, and the Association for Educational Communications and Technologies state that "information literacy – the ability to find and use information – is the keystone of lifelong learning" (Lau, 2006; Byerly & Brodie, 1999, p. 7). Hence, media and information literacy is the ability to find, access, absorb, analyze, evaluate and communicate information in any form which can be intrapersonal, interpersonal, group or mass.

Media creates a strong link between politics and the audience. It is necessary for the sources and the receivers to understand this link. Voltmer (2009, p. 139) points out that "Since the media are the main source of information and a vital link between the government and citizens they are an indispensable precondition for both government accountability and social accountability. The daily flow of news generates a "running tally" of government policies, political events and the actions of political officials on the basis of which citizens make their choices." To achieve sustainable development, the government needs the media to be accountable to the citizens. They need to be able to pass adequate and useful information to the citizen – this should get the citizens to contribute meaningfully to the society through the choices they make.

The type of information and messages disseminated to the public via media in the name of adverts, press release, press conferences, interviews, posts on social media and blogs has resulted in various (mostly negative) response and attitudes from the public.

This article analyzes the types of content from various forms of media and the role of the media in political campaign as well as the importance of media literacy for political campaigns in Nigeria.

The Political Landscape in Nigeria

Nigeria, also referred to as the heart of Africa, got its independence from British colonialism in 1960. The country possesses some interesting features that affect the political and economic landscape. Its approximately three-hundred and seventy-four ethnic groups make it a multi-ethnic state par excellence (Ojo, 2011). Amidst constant agitation for resource control and distribution, power rotation amongst the six geo political zones, she remains a nation divided among many lines. Salawu and Hassan (2010, p. 28) state that "In all political activities in Nigeria, the factor of ethnicity is reflected. It is particularly obvious in areas like voting, distribution of political offices, employment and government general patronage of the citizens."

Political alliances therefore require major considerations to meet common goals and while efforts are made to wed the interest of a diverse group democratically, this remains a daunting task. Because of the multi-cultural nature of Nigeria, there may be different approaches and thoughts to situations; in this case, political conditions of the society. In this context, the need for wider consultation and connection with the electorates is highlighted. It is important to note that the institutional weaknesses, infrastructural gaps and uneven economic growth and development may influence the political arrangement of the country.

This creates a huge need for access to adequate and beneficial information and the role of the media in educating and enlightening the citizens. Therefore, media and information literacy plays a huge role for sustainable development.

Political Campaigns in Nigeria

An average Nigerian citizen is an indigene of a Nigerian community or ethnic group, whose citizenship guarantees fundamental human rights, as well as other civil rights such as access to education and employment opportunities, political participation or the right to choose who he or she wants to be the head of a community, or a governor, or the president (Orji, 2014; Adesoji & Alao, 2009). However, over the years, the human rights of citizens of Nigeria have been violated. This was obvious during the period of military rule. During the General Abacha dictatorship for example, there was a complete ban on political activities: political associations, social groups or socio-political movements were outlawed. However, after the death of Abacha, General Abdulsalami Abubarka took over and shortly after handed over power to civilians in May 29, 1999.

In Nigeria today, citizens are able to make the decision during elections as a result of the democratic structure of the Nigerian government.

Political associations, social groups, youth groups and civil rights groups have begun to make their voices heard, with the mass media and the Internet becoming the major means of participating in political debates.

Nigeria's April 2003 elections were a watershed for its democracy, with an outcome that broadly reflected the electorate's wishes and was neither followed nor interrupted by a coup (Smith, 2005). But, the 2007 general elections were widely adjudged as generally flawed (Suberu, 2007; Ibrahim & Ibeanu, 2009; Onapajo, 2014). This forced the Independent National Electoral Commission (INEC), the government, civil society groups and Nigeria's development partners to initiate and implement electoral reforms. These reforms contributed largely to the success of the 2011 elections, yet the risk of flaws affecting Nigerian elections still remains (Akhaine, 2011; Lewis, 2011).

Human Rights Watch (2011) opined that besides the risk of irregularities, elections in Nigeria are imperiled by threats of violence. The 2011 general elections witnessed a scale of violence unprecedented in the country's history, with more than 800 people killed and 65,000 displaced. This same fear also applies to the 2015 general election as security measures appear to be shaky.

At the time of this study, the fifth general election which was scheduled on February 14, 2015 was moved to March 28, 2015 by INEC due to security reasons. The process was seen as controversial by individuals and groups all over the world.

Media Contents for Political Campaigns in Nigeria

Traditionally, the media comes in print format including newspapers and magazines and electronic which include radio and television. The mass media landscape in Nigeria shows tremendous improvement from the emergence of Reverend Henry Townsend's Iwelrohin in 1859, through the independence era till now. With the emergence of media outlets daily in Nigeria, the nation to say boasts of mass media of high reckoning, both government and privately owned. Such television stations as the Nigerian Television Authority (NTA), African Independent Television (AIT) and Channels Television among others, are beginning to have a truly global audience, having embarked on satellite broadcast operations. Radio stations such as Radio Nigeria, Ray Power FM, and the numerous state and privately owned outlets provide interesting news and current affairs programmes that impact on the society in one way or other. Numerous dailies such as *The Guardian, The Punch, Daily Sun, This Day, Vanguard, The Nation* and *Daily Independent*, among others, have become dominant communication channels in Nigeria, providing diverse hard and soft news that keep the society informed (Nwabueze & Ebeze, 2013, p. 863). Currently, new media which include online journalism, and social media have emerged. Internet penetration in Nigeria currently stands at about 30% with over 50 million Internet users. All the forms of media are accessible to a large extent in Nigeria[1].

The extent to which the political parties in Nigeria use the new media is minimal and therefore, political parties in Nigeria should give due attention to the use of the new media for the dissemination of political activities (Asemah & Edegoh, 2012). Also, Independent National Electoral Commission is making appropriate use of the new media during election and electioneering. This use includes registration of voters through the use of data capture technology, detailing election constituencies, contacting candidates, publishing the rules and regulations of elections and guidance for the voters and promoting news splash (Oyebode, 2014, p. 49).

The media plays a vital role in the process of politics regardless of the ruling system the country runs. Media is said to be the driving force for bringing changes in the society and world and therefore, it must, once again, realize its responsibility and adopt a proactive approach and launch a similar campaign collectively (Yadav, 2014).

The political classes use the mass media for campaigning through sponsored direct access spots, paid political advertising, televised debates, use of social media, and other mechanisms. They also hope the media will voluntarily cover them because of the newsworthiness of their campaign activities. The media in turn will disseminate political contents with consideration for the audience.

The primary concern of the media for any political campaign should be the recognition and consideration of the right of citizens to have full and accurate information, and their rights to participate with politicians on political matters. Inherent to this task is the entitlement of parties and candidates to reach out to the people through any medium of their choice. The media themselves have a right to report freely and provide healthy content. They should also abide by the code of conduct for political parties preamble put together by Independent National Electoral Commission (INEC, 2013) of Nigeria. However, one may wonder if these codes are followed. The seventh statement in the CODE OF CONDUCT FOR POLITICAL PARTIES' PREAMBLE state;

> *No political Party or candidate shall during campaign resort to the use of inflammatory language, provocative actions, images or manifestation that incite violence, hatred, contempt or intimidation against another party or candidate or any person or group of persons on grounds of ethnicity or gender or for any other reason. Accordingly, no Political Party or candidate shall issue any poster, pamphlet, leaflet or other publication that contains any such incitement.*

(http://www.inecnigeria.org/wp-content/uploads/2015/01/Code-of-Conduct-2013-.docx)

Source: www.nigeriaeye.com

The picture above is a presidential campaign advert put up by a member of a political party, Peoples Democratic Party (PDP). It shows pictures of late heads of states and includes the picture of the presidential candidate of APC, the opposition party it was accompanied by a suggestive statement:

> Nigerians be warned! Nigeria…I have set before thee Life and death. Therefore, choose life that both thee and thy seed may live," it said, suggesting that Mr. Buhari represents death while his rival, President Good luck Jonathan represents life."

(The Punch, 19 Jan, 2015: 1, copied from www.nigeriaeye.com)

This advert suggests provocative actions, and contempt against the opposing candidate which clearly goes against the seventh code of conduct.

Source:www.124news.tv

The picture above shows a poster of the presidential candidate of All Progressive Congress, the leading opposition, pasted over the poster of the current president and candidate of the ruling party, Peoples Democratic Party. This clearly does not comply with the fourteenth statement in the CODE OF CONDUCT FOR POLITICAL PARTIES PREAMBLE which states that;

> No Political Party or candidate shall prevent other parties or candidates from pasting their posters or distributing their leaflets, hand bills and other publicity materials in public place. Furthermore all parties and candidates shall give directives to their members and supporters not to remove, destroy the posters and other campaign materials of other parties or candidates.

(http://www.inecnigeria.org/wp-content/uploads/2015/01/Code-of-Conduct-2013-.docx)

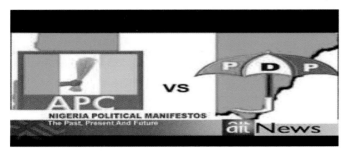

Source:www.google.com

The picture above is a screen shot of a news caption from a television programme which portrays the two major parties about to present their manifestos for the country in order to get people to vote for them at the 2015 general election. The picture shows objectivity as the two major parties are shown. The media should be objective and avoid bias. As Aghamelu (2013, p. 157) puts it "One of the main constitutional roles of the media in a democracy is to objectively monitor governance while remaining consistent, preserving an objective stance in holding those involved in the democratic process accountable to the people."

Media Literacy and Political Campaigns

The relevance of media and information literacy on political campaigns for youth is great. They should be aware of the political happening in their society. It is also important for current and future politicians and political agents to be media and information literate. With the media evolution, campaign groups have been seen to develop web pages for their candidates to showcase salient features of the candidate and political party. These range from interactive social media accounts for personal interaction with the public, to conducting independent online opinion polls as a technique for collecting information on public opinion.

Campaigns will oftentimes make wild claims about their opponents, hoping to get more votes. Some of these claims can be true, but some can also be false. Media and information literacy education can help us determine whether these claims should be taken seriously or not (Baker, 2012). Also, Richardson (2009) explains that "as the tide of political communication becomes a tsunami, citizens are in greater need than ever of the analytical and intellectual tools by which they can draw meaning from the maelstrom. There is, in short, a greater need than ever for media literacy in political communication". Information is important because it leads to knowledge, analysis, evaluation and enlightenment. Media literacy will help fulfill them.

In Nigeria, one third of the population is youth (National Population Commission, 2006). This implies that it is youth who are significant in terms of consideration for media and information literacy of political campaigns. Media and information literate youth and adults are better able to decipher the complex messages we receive from television, radio, newspapers, magazines, books, billboards, signs, packaging, marketing materials, video games, recorded music, the Internet and other forms of media[2].

Baker (2012) identified important points that young people should know about political campaign. He stated that candidates need the media to make sure the media captures their every move and keep them in the public eye; candidates work hard to control their images to create and keep a good impression; candidates depend on media consultants to help them appeal to various audiences; political adverts resemble traditional adverts; political adverts (produced by the candidates) are considered "free speech"; new media have already proven themselves to be important and necessary communication tools to reach voters.

Baker (2012) in his study identified important points that young people should know about political campaign. He stated that candidates need the media to make sure the media captures their every move and keep them in the public eye; candidates work hard to control their images to create and keep a good impression; candidates depend on media consultants to help them appeal to various audiences; political adverts resemble traditional adverts; political ads (produced by the candidates) are considered "free speech"; and new media have already proven themselves to be important and necessary communication tools to reach voters. With access to such information particularly in their educational curriculum, it will help them understand political activities better and make good choices.

Conclusion

One of the major functions of the media is to inform the audience. The audience needs to know how to get information, what kind of information to expect, how to verify the integrity of the information, how to analyze and evaluate information and determine how to constructively give feedback when necessary.

This assessment revealed that it is important for youth to know how important it is for them to have access to political information, the type of media content for political campaign they should expect, how to analyze the information they get on the media, how to evaluate the information, determine the type of feedback to give if necessary. These should be considered in the preparation of media and information literacy curriculum. Also, media and information literacy through responsible media engagement, supported by strong independent national regulatory institutions on the code and conduct of stakeholders can greatly improve electoral processes in Nigeria.

References

Adesoji, A.O. & Alao, A. (2009). Indigene ship and Citizenship in Nigeria; Myth and Reality *The Journal of Pan African Studies,* Vol. 2(9), pp 151-165.

Aghamelu, F. C. (2103). The Role of the Mass Media in the Nigerian Electoral Process. UJAH: Unizik *Journal of Arts and Humanities*, Vol. 14(2), pp 154-172.

Akhaine, S. (2011). Nigeria's 2011 Elections: The "Crippled Giant" Learns to Walk?, *African Affairs*, Vol 110(441), pp 649-655.

Asemah, E. S. & Edegoh, L.O. (2012). New Media and Political Advertising in Nigeria: Prospects and Challenges *African Research Review*. Vol. 6(4), ISSN: 1994-9057. Retrieved from http://www.ajol.info/index.php/afrrev/article/view/83610

Baker, F. M. (2012). Political Adverts and Media Literacy Skills. *W. Library Media Connection*. Vol. 30(5), pp 18-19.

Byerly, G. & Brodie, C.S. (1999). Information Literacy Skills Models: Defining the Choices. In Barbara K. Stripling, Englewood (Eds): *Learning and Libraries in an Information Age. Principles and Practice,* pp.54-82. Littleton: Libraries Unlimited.

Human Rights Watch. (2011). *Nigeria: Post-Election Violence Killed 800.* New York: Human Rights Watch.

Ibrahim, J. & Ibeanu O. (2009).Direct Capture: The 2007 Nigerian Elections and Subversion of Popular Sovereignty, Abuja: Centre for Democracy and Development.

Independent National Electoral Commission (INEC). (2013). *Code of Conduct for Political Parties Preamble*. Retrieved from http://www.inecnigeria.org/wp-content/uploads/2013/03/Code_of_Conduct_For_Political_Parties_Preamble.pdf

Lau, J. (2006). *IFLA Guidelines on Information Literacy for Lifelong Learning Final draft*. Retrieved from http://www.ifla.org/files/assets/information-literacy/publications/ifla-guidelines-en.pdf

Lewis, P. (2011). Nigeria Votes: More Openness, More Conflict. *Journal of Democracy*, Vol. 22(4), pp 60-74.

National Population Commission http://www.population.gov.ng/

Nwabueze, C. & Ebeze, E. (2013). Mass media relevance in combating insecurity in Nigeria, *International Journal of Development and Sustainability*, Vol. 2(2), pp 861- 870.

Obafemi, O. (17, November, 2012). Retooling the media culture for conflict/peace management in Northern Nigeria (Part I). *Weekly Trust*. Retrieved from http://www.dailytrust.com.ng/weekly/index.php/opinion/10735-retooling-the-media-culture-for-conflictpeace-management-in-northern-nigeria-part-i

Ojo, E. O. (2011). The politics of the formation of alliance governments in multi-ethnic states: a case study of the Nigerian first alliance government1954-57. *Canadian Journal of History*, ISSN 0008-4107, pp. 333-366.

Onapajo, H. (2014). Violence and Votes in Nigeria: The Dominance of Incumbents in the Use of Violence to Rig Elections, in: *Africa Spectrum*, Vol. 49(2), pp 27-51.

Orji, N. (2014). *Nigeria's 2015 Election in Perspective*. GIGA German Institute of Global and Area Studies, Institute of African Affairs in co-operation with the Dag Hammarskjöld Foundation Uppsala and Hamburg University Press. Vol. 49(3), pp121-133. Retrieved from http://www.academia.edu/9945854/ Nigeria_s_2015_Election_in_Perspective

Oyebode, M. O. (2014). *Use and Misuse of the New Media for Political Communication in Nigeria's 4th Developing Country Studies* ISSN 2224-607X (Paper) ISSN 2225-0565 (Online) Vol. 4(2), pp 44-53.

Richardson, G. W. (2009). Media Literacy and Political Communication. *The Journal of Media Literacy* 56(1-2).

Salawu & Hassan (2010). Ethnic politics and its implications for the survival of democracy in Nigeria. *Journal of Public Administration and Policy Research,* Vol. 3 (2), pp. 28-33.

Smith, A. M. (2005). Fractured Federalism: Nigeria's Lessons for Today's Nation Builders in Iraq. Harvard Law School, *The Round Table*, USA, Vol. 94(1), pp 129-144.

Suberu, R. (2007). Nigeria's Muddled Elections. *Journal of Democracy*, Vol. 18(4), pp. 95-110.

Voltmer, K. (2009). The media, government accountability and citizen engagement. In Pippa, N. (Ed.), *Public Sentinel: New Media and the Governance Agenda,* pp 137-159. The World Bank. Retrieved from http://www.hks.harvard.edu/fs/pnorris/Acrobat/ WorldBankReport/Chapter%206%20Voltmer.pdf

Yadav, A. R. (2014). Media Lacking Aggression to Report Environment-Related Issues. *International Journal of Multidisciplinary Approach and Studies,* Vol. 1(4), ISSN 2348 – 537X, pp 147.

Notes

1   The Social Media Landscape in Nigeria (2014). http://www.africapractice.com/wp-content/uploads/2014/04/Africa-Practice-Social-Media-Landscape-Vol-1.pdf Accessed May 25, 2015.

2   Introduction to Media Literacy-Media Literacy Project https://medialiteracyproject. org/sites/default/files/resources/Intro_to_Media_Literacy.pdf

WeOwnTV: Survivors Speak Out in Sierra Leone

Kathleen Tyner

WeOwnTV is a long-term collaborative media project with local residents of Sierra Leone, North American filmmakers, and regional humanitarian organizations. Located in Freetown, the center launched its first media education workshop in Sierra Leone in 2009. Workshop participants were chosen from young men and women who were survivors of more than a decade of war. Building on youth media traditions of access, voice, and collaborative production skills, WeOwnTV provides participants with a creative outlet for sharing stories of culture, trauma and survival. The workshop curriculum balances intensive film production and computer skills training with classes in narrative and creative self-expression. In the process, WeOwnTV supports the media analysis and production skills that facilitate workforce development and civic participation for citizens in Sierra Leone. With the mandate that no one is more qualified to help Sierra Leoneans than the people who live there, these activities have taken on new resonance as WeOwnTV works in the context of the Ebola crisis. In collaboration with the Sierra Leone Film Council, the National Health Ministry, and the World Health Organization, WeOwnTV contributed to the production of an educational media series that raises awareness about urgent care and prevention protocols for those infected with the Ebola virus. The health messages are broadcast by radio and television to rural and urban populations in Sierra Leone and surrounding countries. This article is a case study of international collaboration and its impact on activities related to the dissemination of local media and information resources. Based on ethnographic interviews with key stakeholders, the study intends to contribute to research related to the design and sustainability of community media programs and activities around the world.

Keywords: Africa, community media, documentary filmmaking, voice, health communication, media literacy

Introduction to WeOwnTV

WeOwnTV is a dynamic community media center based in the capital city of Freetown, Sierra Leone. It serves the community through media and information literacy workshops, public service messaging, distribution, and activities that build the supportive infrastructure for a developing regional filmmaking industry in Sierra Leone.

WeOwnTV was launched in 2009 after a seven-year collaboration between an international coalition of artists and humanitarian organizations. The coalition evolved from the worldwide success of an award-winning documentary film *Sierra Leone's Refugee All Stars* (2004) directed by U.S. filmmakers Zach Niles and Banker White in collaboration with artists and musicians in Sierra Leone.

The documentary was based on the story of resilience for the members of a popular band in Sierra Leone in the context of a civil war that began in 1991 and lasted for over a decade. The award-winning documentary has been broadcast for millions of viewers around the world. The production and reception of *Sierra Leone's Refugee All Stars* proved to be a life-changing event for the filmmakers who were inspired by the region's spirit of self-reliance and the power of filmmaking for positive social change. They envisioned a community Media Center that could capture survivors' stories in Sierra Leone and support more pro-social filmmaking in the country.

Filmmaker Banker White partnered with Alhaji "Black Nature" Kamara, a rapper and member of the Sierra Leone Refugee All Stars band to form a media center in the capital city of Freetown to continue and support inspirational media production in Sierra Leone. WeOwnTV was born. They were joined by a local team that includes filmmaker and youth organizer Arthur Pratt, who manages all education programs and creative initiatives for WeOwnTV, and Lansana Mansaray, a filmmaker and rapper, also known as "Barmmy Boy," who manages production.

Based on the core premise that no one is more qualified to help Sierra Leone than Sierra Leoneans themselves, WeOwnTV builds on the "transformative processes they [media] bring about within participants and their communities" (Rodriguez, 2002, p. 79). As scholar John L. Hochheimer notes, community media begins by supporting "an existing desire to communicate to establish a sense of personal and community power" (Hochheimer, 1999, p. 451).

WeOwnTV media education activities began by facilitating a month-long filmmaking workshop for 18 young men and women survivors just outside the capital city Freetown. Workshop participants represent a wide-range of participants – from young media professionals and students, to Ebola survivors, people with physical disabilities, ex-combatants, street kids and former prostitutes who come from all areas of Sierra Leone to tell their stories of resiliency in the face of disaster (Odugbemi, 2014, p. 520).

Drawing from cultural traditions of oral storytelling as a way to share and process social experiences, it is important to note that workshop participants are not chosen for their technical skills. Most have never operated a computer or a camera. Due to the disruption of civil war, many of them have never completed school. Instead, these aspiring filmmakers are selected based on their passion for film, eloquence, and resolve in the face of crisis.

The mission of WeOwnTV is to give people a "voice" that can express their authentic experiences in the public sphere. It is equally important that their voices are heard and broadcast to a wider audience. With distribution and exhibition support through its website and licensing agreements, as well as through connections with news, broadcast and screening venues in Sierra Leone and abroad, WeOwnTV provides the continued technical support for its producers to share their stories on a regional and international scale.

Participation in WeOwnTV workshops also offers a potential workforce development component. Some workshop participants have worked as film editors, actors and audio producers after participating in WeOwnTV activities. Their films have been broadcast in the capital and large areas of the country through the government's Sierra Leone Broadcast Corporation (SLBC). WeOwnTV-produced media also screens at festivals and in museums worldwide.

Through these media education programs and field-building activities, WeOwnTV has become a vital cultural resource that offers a public sphere for Sierra Leoneans to practice the media and information literacy skills that allow them to create their own stories in their own words.

Scaling up the Infrastructure for Media Production in Sierra Leone

Like community media centers around the world, WeOwnTV is challenged to meet the growing demand for its services. To inform their strategic plan for capacity building and sustainability, the team researched successful models of film production in other countries such as Nigeria, Ghana, Kenya and the United Kingdom.

From the beginning, the founders concluded that it was critical for all participants and members to feel a sense of ownership in this new entity. The name itself, WeOwnTV, reflects this very concept as it is derived from the Sierra Leonean Krio phrase *weyone tv*, which means "Our Own TV." Accordingly, to build an infrastructure with growth potential, the initial strategy was to create not just a sense of ownership from the beginning but to also formalize a partnership between a US-based non-profit organization and a Sierra Leonean owned and managed media center. Defining this formal relationship became important as the Sierra Leonean team began to think of their involvement with the group not just as participating in a one-time workshop, but instead as part of a long-term process of gaining new skills, building agency and taking charge of their own futures.

Access to WeOwnTV messages is customized for the region. A large-scale United Nations peacekeeping mission provided broadband Internet access in 2001 and, through the support of the World Bank, a fiber optic cable was installed in the country in 2009. Although Internet access exists, the cost of service is so high that most of the population cannot afford it. It is more common in Sierra Leone to use pre-paid plans on mobile phones, and the use of social networking platforms such as WhatsApp, Twitter and Facebook are popular communication tools on mobile devices. However, streaming video and large downloads and file transfers are cost prohibitive on mobile devices and so media content is seldom streamed or downloaded.

Instead, the vast majority of citizens in Sierra Leone access film, video and radio content through the use of broadcast media, DVDs and the cheaper VCDs, a video CD with a lower resolution than the DVD format. On the one hand, distribution through lower cost media such as DVDs and VCDs offers an affordable distribution strategy for filmmakers to reach a wide audience. On the other hand, the circulation of DVDs and VCDs in Sierra Leone is also a liability due to a high incidence of media piracy that undercuts the intellectual property rights and profit margins for producers.

Surprisingly, audience development for documentary film was also an important step in building an infrastructure for the reception of independently produced films in Sierra Leone. At the onset of the WeOwnTV media center, documentaries were seldom screened in the country and so the audience for documentary films in Sierra Leone was relatively small. Since then, the growing popularity of film festivals in the country is increasing. The Freetown Film Festival has been running since 2007 with festival director Ian Noah. In 2010, WeOwnTV successfully ran a film festival in Freetown. Since then, the organization has partnered with other groups including the Sierra Leone International Film Festival, established in 2011, and Opin Yu Yi, two newer festivals that screen both locally produced content and award winning international titles. The Opin Yu Yi festival (Krio for Open Your Eyes) is the country's first human rights focused festival, founded in 2012 by filmmaker Idriss Kpange and human rights lawyer Sabrina Mahtani. WeOwnTV filmmakers have won many awards at these festivals and have played a major leadership role helping to grow the popularity and demand for documentaries in Sierra Leone.

Strategic partnerships are key to the success of WeOwnTV. The organization works to connect and build affinity networks that support and sustain independent production and distribution in the region. Through its community outreach efforts, WeOwnTV was instrumental in connecting a cadre of competitive media organizations who came together to build consensus around issues that affect economic development for the emerging film industry in Sierra Leone.

With help from the government's Ministry of Information and Communications, competing factions in the film industry came together in 2014 to form the

Sierra Leone Film Council (SLFC), a union of film industry advocates and organizations who have been officially recognized by the government. WeOwnTV manager, Arthur Pratt, was a founding member and serves as acting president in 2015. The SLFC, sometimes known as "The Union," works to support filmmakers through activities that help to standardize and mediate issues related to distribution costs, payment schedules and contracts. In addition, the SLFC works with the government on legislation and policy work that helps to block the piracy of intellectual property. The SLFC also builds international partnerships with non-governmental organizations, news outlets and other stakeholders to improve citizen access to both digital and analog media content. The inauguration of the Sierra Leone Film Council in 2014 proved fateful as a key player in the fight against Ebola that ensued that year.

Public Information in the Ebola Crisis

In early 2014, the Ebola virus spread to the population of Sierra Leone with tragic public consequences. By the end of 2014, the virus was rampant, creating mass public anxiety and confusion about the correct protocols that the public should use to contain and treat the virus. Sierra Leone's Ministry of Health and Sanitation (MHS) and the World Health Organization (WHO) partnered with the Sierra Leone Film Council (SLNC) and WeOwnTV to create a series of public service announcements (PSAs) that provide accurate health information related to the Ebola crisis for broad distribution to urban and rural residents across Sierra Leone.

WeOwnTV's small bureaucratic structure allowed for the flexibility and quick response time needed to produce their partners' urgent health messages in a rapidly changing environment of crisis management. Building on its base of community trust and grounded in its mission to rely on the voices of Sierra Leoneans, WeOwnTV constructed stories that could engaged the public with vital information that countered widespread confusion, misinformation and distrust of the government and medical establishments (Haglage, 2014).

In the process, WeOwnTV identified important best practices that contributed to the dissemination of their health communication messages. Using the organization's prior research about the everyday uses of media by Sierra Leoneans, WeOwnTV quickly identified diverse distribution strategies that allowed these messages to efficiently reach a broader public. WeOwnTV was invited to participate in a think-tank that linked local media-makers and journalists with the Health Ministry, WHO, CDC and networks of other international NGO's. The group was tasked with creating and disseminating culturally sensitive educational material. Sensitization materials were distributed via texts and social networks to raise awareness about resources and facts about the virus. WeOwnTV was particularly instrumental in formulating materials that helped combat the massive mistrust of government and international NGOs, as it proved more difficult for people to believe the messages being distributed than it was to reach the populations. WeOwnTV produced educational content using local actors and directly addressed many of the arguments that were happening in the neighborhoods it needed to reach.

The team also knew that streamed video on mobile devices was not a viable option for the WeOwnTV public service announcements, especially in rural areas. As a result, WeOwnTV worked closely with the recently privatized Sierra Leone Broadcasting Corporation (SLBC) to create and disseminate public service announcements that were widely broadcast via television and radio. The team produced over 30 educational assets for television that were translated into 11 local languages for broadcast on radio.

WeOwnTV also learned that word of mouth was one of the primary ways that people received health information about the Ebola outbreak. As a result, the organization undertook an innovative, grassroots strategy to leverage the success of word of mouth communication. In the style of community organizing, WeOwnTV engaged with community leaders in schools, churches and other key community centers to disseminate their public service messages about Ebola treatment and care in face-to-face situations. The grassroots distribution of health communication messages on DVDs was a vital enhancement to the word of mouth strategy. It proved to be a promising practice that can be used in future public media campaigns.

In addition to educational material, the team continues to produce documentary content for both local and international audiences. Short documentary portraits that present the stories of everyday heroes from the sub-region focus on community members, nurses, doctors, burial team workers and survivors. These films present a much-needed human face to the pandemic that encourages compassion and understanding as they counter the representation of Sierra Leoneans as victims of another catastrophe rather than as resilient individuals capable of solving their own problems. SLBC has agreed to include this material alongside the team's educational content for broadcast in 2015. Internationally, WeOwnTV work has been broadcast on BBC, NHK, and covered by *The Guardian*, *McCleans* and other news agencies. There is strong distribution interest from the *New York Times*, *OpDocs*, *PBS Interactive*, *Al Jazeera* (AJ+) and *BBC World Stories*. In 2015, the team began production on a documentary feature called "Survivors," which will add an authentically African voice to the representation of this critical piece of their history. This documentary has recently received support by the Sundance Documentary Fund and the Catapult Film Fund and is expected to receive wide international distribution.

Conclusion

Working from the belief that no one is more qualified to represent events in Sierra Leone than Sierra Leoneans themselves, WeOwnTV focuses on media and information literacy practices that build on the public's passion to find a voice and to share their authentic stories of survival, resiliency and hope with the world.

WeOwnTV provides a case study of international collaboration for media and information literacy activities that support the dissemination of local, pro-social media and information resources in communities with high demand and low capacity. Based on ethnographic interviews with key stakeholders, the study intends to contribute to research related to the design, best practices and sustainability of community media programs and activities across cultural and geographic boundaries.

References

Haglage, A. (2014, August 20). Courageous filmmakers are fighting Ebola on screen. *The Daily Beast*. Retrieved from http://www.thedailybeast.com/articles/2014/08/20/courageous-filmmakers-are-fighting-ebola-on-screen.html

Hochheimer, J. L. (1999). Organising community radio: Issues in planning. *European Journal of Communications Research*, 24(4), 443-455.

Odugbemi, F. (2014). *African Documentary Film Fund (ADFF) West Africa (Anglophone): The Gambia, Ghana, Liberia, Nigeria, Sierra Leone, (pp. 516-573)*. The Bertha Foundation. Retrieved from http://adff.org/wpadff/wp-content/uploads/2014/04/Anglophone_West_Africa_ADFF.pdf

Rodriguez, C. (2001). *Fissures in the mediascape: an international study of citizens' media*. Creskill, NJ: Hampton Press.

Media and Information Literacy in Bangladesh: A Case Study of East West University

Dilara Begum

This present study has been undertaken to ascertain people's awareness of media and information literacy (MIL), and the difficulties being faced by them in accessing information. It is a survey research. It uses both quantitative and qualitative methods. In quantitative method, data have been collected through a questionnaire and in qualitative method data have been extracted from the stakeholders through interviews. The present study focuses on MIL initiatives of East West University (EWU) library, Dhaka, Bangladesh only. This article also discusses the initiatives taken, and challenges faced by Bangladeshi library professionals in promoting media and information literacy in Bangladesh. It also puts forward a few suggestions for organizing more MIL events for University students.

Keywords: media information literacy, information literacy, information gap, East West University, Bangladesh

Introduction

Media literacy focuses on the need for a better understanding of the roles and functions of media in democratic societies (UNESCO, 2011). Today libraries are shifting their roles from the custodian of traditional information resources to the provider of service-oriented digital information resources. Library and information science (LIS) professionals are working with media and information literacy. Particularly, LIS professionals and journalists are actively pursuing the spread of information and media literacy in our society. Bangladesh is a country with a vast population. However, it is quite difficult to sensitize people about the importance of media and information literacy. Fortunately, Government of Bangladesh has taken various steps for promotion of media and information literacy for the society. East West University in Bangladesh is also playing a significant role in increasing awareness about media and information literacy (MIL).

East West University – an Overview

East West University (EWU) was established in 1996. It is one of the top ranked private universities in research achievements. EWU maintains a large team of very highly qualified faculty members. The primary mission of EWU is to provide education at a reasonable cost. It provides tertiary education in a range of subjects that are particularly relevant to current and anticipated societal needs. EWU provides students with opportunities, resources and expertise to achieve academic, personal and career goals within a stimulating and supportive environment.

IL and MIL Initiatives

In Bangladesh many information providers are trying to develop MIL amongst their patrons. Various types of workshops, seminars, and training programs on information literacy (IL), health information literacy (HIL), media and information literacy (MIL) have been organized since the last few years. Major events are as given below:

- International Workshop on Information Literacy, organized by Independent University, Bangladesh (IUB), from 22-26 June 2009, sponsored by International Federation of Library Associations and Institutions (IFLA).

- Workshop on Information Literacy, organized by East West University, Bangladesh from 5-6 January 2010, sponsored by International network for the availability of scientific publications (INASP).

- A two-day training course on Information Literacy and UN Literacy jointly organized by the Centre for Information Studies, Bangladesh (CIS, B) and United Nations Information Centre (UNIC), Dhaka, for the students of Haji Md Ekhlas Uddin Bhuiyan School at Ekhlasnagar in Rupganj, Narayanganj (south of Dhaka) in 2010.

- Centre for Information Studies Bangladesh (CIS, B) conducted another training program on Information Literacy from 23-24 January 2010 at Ratanpur Abdullah High School, Nabinagar, Brahmanbaria.

- International Workshop on Health Information Literacy (1st Phase), organized by East West University from 27-30 July 2011, sponsored by IFLA.

- International Workshop on Health Information Literacy (2nd Phase), organized by East West University from 12-13 February 2012, sponsored by IFLA.

- International Workshop on Health Information Literacy (3rd Phase), organized by East West University on 20 July 2012, sponsored by IFLA.

- A Seminar on media and information literacy was jointly organized by East West University and University of Rajshahi, Bangladesh on 13 December 2010 at Rajshahi.

Purpose of the Present Study

The present research has been carried out to assess the present state of media and information literacy among Bangladesh library professionals as well as to put forward recommendations for improvement. In a mass mediated and media saturated society media messages and their structures must be taken seriously, and Bangladesh is no exception. The literacy rate of the country is 57.7 % (Human Development Index 2014) and there has been a growing recognition for the need and importance of media and information literacy among cross sections of people. Assessing youngsters' perception of media and also their understanding of information flow via media is crucial to help them move forward in this increasingly media-centric information society.

Objectives of the Study

The main objectives of this study were to:

- Assess the level of media and information literacy of East West University community in Bangladesh.
- Examine the initiatives of media and information literacy organized by Library and Information Science (LIS) professionals in Bangladesh.
- Identify the obstacles for implementing media and information literacy in EWU, and other information providers.
- Suggest recommendations for enriching and strengthening the media and information literacy campaign among LIS professionals.

Research Sample and Data Collection

Most of the earlier studies of media and information literacy have used survey method utilizing questionnaire and interview as data collection techniques. A review of earlier studies has shown that the questionnaire has been used successfully. It was, therefore, decided to use a self-administered questionnaire in this study. The available literature was examined to prepare a questionnaire which was peer-reviewed.

Questionnaire method was used for East West University community in which respondents were 50. The respondents of questionnaire method consist of 25 undergraduate students, 15 graduate students and 10 faculty members. Besides, the interview method was used for five LIS professionals who live in

Dhaka city at different locations. Hence the total respondents of two methods were 55. With the help of a structured questionnaire and interview schedule, the respondents were asked to give their views. Respondents provided their answers directly on answer sheets. All answer sheets were reviewed to make sure that they marked correctly. The answer sheets were processed directly using Excel program by the researcher.

Limitations of the Study

The survey was conducted in East West University and most of the respondents are well educated. But there is little awareness regarding MIL especially with regard to empowering the citizens. In the mean time, survey has shown that Bangladesh LIS professionals face great difficulties in implementing this topic for their working institutions. The study included only one university to assess the level of MIL and five LIS professionals of Dhaka city to examine their initiative for organizing MIL programs and to identify obstacles and suggestions. So this study does not depict the total scenario of Bangladesh.

Data Analysis and Discussion

Questionnaire Method

The majority of the respondents belong to the age group ranging from 25-41 years. In the context of Bangladesh, this number is believed to be highly productive segment of population. In terms of educational qualifications, 25 were undergraduate students, 15 possessed bachelor degree, five possessed Masters degree in different faculties and five possessed Ph. D degrees.

When asked to mention the awareness among the respondents about information literacy, and media and information Literacy, the following responses were found and tabulated below:

Table 1.

Respondent Category	Number of Respondents	Awareness about Information Literacy				Awareness about Media and Information Literacy			
		Yes	%	No	%	Yes	%	No	%
Undergraduate students	25	15	60	10	40	10	40	15	60
Graduate students	15	10	67	5	33	6	40	9	60
Faculty members	10	10	100	0	0	8	80	2	20

The respondents of all three categories were more aware about information literacy than media and information literacy. On the other side the graduate students and faculty members were more aware about information literacy than undergraduate students.

From the responses of another several questions, it is found that 45% of respondents admitted that they were totally unaware of the importance of media and information literacy in the context of socio-economic development of Bangladesh. 55% respondents informed that they were aware of media and information literacy, but lacked a clear understanding of the implications and ramifications of the concepts. Faculty members were more aware about MIL (80%). When asked the question whether they believe that media and information literacy can positively contribute in sustainable development, 60% answered positively.

It is also found that the majority of respondents agreed that media can play a vital role in improvement of access to information, transparency and accountability of the Government. The interesting fact is that respondents (45%) are not getting most of the information from the Internet. 86% of the respondents believe that receiving information is a fundamental human right.

50% of the respondents informed that they learned about media and information literacy by self learning whereas 35% learned through training on information literacy program conducted by the EWU library or other organization and 15% through academic study. It shows the necessity to include MIL in regular academic curricula.

The questionnaire included another question about the awareness and their following status of plagiarism, the answers are tabulated below:

Table 2.

Respondent Category	Number of Respondents	Awareness of plagiarism				Avoid plagiarism			
		Yes	%	No	%	Yes	%	No	%
Undergraduate students	25	15	60	10	40	5	20	20	80
Graduate students	15	10	67	5	33	5	33	10	67
Faculty members	10	8	80	2	20	8	80	2	20

The table above shows that graduate students and faculty members are more aware about plagiarism than the undergraduate students. This proves that the regular academic syllabus and information literacy program conducted by EWU library helps to increase the awareness about the plagiarism. The table above also shows that 36% of respondents avoid plagiarism in their practical work. So it may be said that if MIL can be taught to people in general, especially for undergraduate students, the outcome will be more sustainable in a long run.

Only 25% of the respondents know well about mass media policy where only 40% know that government is going to formulate mass media policy which will cover the radio, TV and Internet news agencies. This proves that most of the respondents who claimed to have awareness about MIL have very basic knowledge on the subject.

68% of the respondents opined that government interferes on the activities of the media in Bangladesh. 25% indicate that weak telecommunication infrastructure of the country is to be blamed for this predicament. Other notable responses are: widespread illiteracy, corruption, political turmoil, lack of proper support from the government, lack of proper legal support, weakness of mass media, etc. 65% of respondents believe that launching a massive awareness campaign in educational institutions is the key to overcoming these problems and to make people more media and information literate. A majority of them think that the government must link media and information literacy to their ongoing campaign for creating a Digital Bangladesh by the year 2021. They also advocated for carrying out similar interventions like the developed world to strengthen the state of media and information literacy in Bangladesh.

Interview Method

An interview was conducted among five LIS professionals to know their initiatives in increasing awareness among the students and faculty members, strategies in conducting different types of training, workshop, seminar, symposium and obstacles to achieve their goals. All five respondents possessed Master degree in library and information science. It is found from the interview that most of them lack detailed knowledge to conduct such workshop, they do not get support from authority for financial and infrastructural limitation, and they also face problems of inadequate skilled library staff. It is found from the study that in most of the university the students and faculty members attain knowledge about media and information Literacy by self learning. Hence it becomes difficult for them to utilize their knowledge at right time when they need. It can be said that in present perspective in Bangladesh inclusion of MIL in regular academic curricula is difficult. It is easier for the libraries to adopt effective strategy to make the university stakeholders more aware about MIL.

Recommendations

In light of the findings of the study, following recommendations are put forward for promoting media and information Literacy in Bangladesh. Here is the list of the most pressing ones:

- Government must allocate adequate funds for carrying out media and information literacy training programs, seminars, workshops at national as well as international level. Government should take initiatives for designing infrastructure of MIL for the universities.

- Government must take an active role in promoting media and information literacy. It should take initiatives for setting up well equipped libraries and other information institutions. Hence, an optimistic role from the government is the main solution to promote media and information literacy in Bangladesh.

- In most of the private universities, the problems are acute. Some of these universities function as high-end coaching centers with no regard to the aim of knowledge dissemination, research and development. The proper knowledge dissemination methods should be strengthened and more new and evolving technologies should be applied in the sector.

- All academic institutions including schools, colleges and universities should include MIL in their regular curriculum library and information science, and journalism and mass communication departments should conduct these courses so that students can attain in-depth knowledge on media and information literacy.

- Syllabi and teaching materials should be more contemporary and supervision must be involved. Library and information professionals can play a crucial role in this case.

- Sufficient funds need to be provided for training of LIS professionals and journalists for implementing MIL in their working institutions. Professional organizations should actively be involved in this sector.

- Standard curricula of MIL considering different levels of citizens should be developed that can be followed nationally in academic institutions and libraries.

Conclusions

Media and other non-media information providers, such as libraries, museums, archives, Internet information providers, and other information organizations play a central role in information and communication processes. They are one way of communicating information, although their role is much broader. At present, there is a vide variety of resources and services available on the Internet varying greatly in accuracy, reliability, and value. In addition, this information is in a variety of forms (e.g. as text, image or statistic, electronically or in print), that can be made available through online repositories and portals, virtual and physical libraries and documentary collections, databases, archives, museums, etc. MIL should be promoted to make effective use of these resources.

References

Bawden, D. (2001). Information and digital literacies: A review of concepts. *Journal of Documentation*, 57(2), 218 – 259. Doi: 10.1108/EUM0000000007083

Begum, D. (2013). Promoting media and information literacy: A case study of Bangladesh public sector. *Media and Information Literacy for Knowledge Societies* (pp. 292-299). Moscow: UNESCO.

East West University Library. (2012). Health information literacy. Retrieved from http://lib. ewubd.edu/hil1 (2015, March 24).

Hooks, J. (2005). Information literacy for off-campus graduate cohorts. *Library Review*, 54(4), 245-256. Doi: 10.1108/00242530510593434

Horton, Jr., F. W. (2007). *Understanding Information Literacy: a Primer*. Retrieved from http://unesdoc.unesco.org/images/0015/001570/157020e.pdf

Johnson, A., Sproles, C. & Detmering, R. (2013). Library instruction and information lite-racy. *Reference Services Review*, 41(4), 675-784. Doi: 10.1108/RSR-07-2013-0040

Joint, N. (2005). eLiteracy or information literacy: Which concept should we prefer? *Library Review*, 54(9), 505 – 507. Doi: 10.1108/00242530510629506

Maitaouthong, T., Tuamsuk, K. & Techamanee, Y. (2010). Development of the instruc-tional model by integrating information literacy in the class learning and teaching processes. *Education for Information*, 28(2-4), 137-150. Doi: 10.3233/EFI-2010-0897

National Association for Media Literacy Education (2008). Media and information literacy. Retrieved from http://www.unesco.org/new/en/communication-and-information/ media-development/media-literacy/mil-as-composite-concept/

Nijboer, J. & Hammelburg, E. (2010). Extending media literacy: a new direction for libraries. *New Library World*, 111(1/2), 36-45. Doi: 10.1108/03074801011015676

Singh, D. & Joshi, M K. (2013). Information literacy competency of post graduate students at Haryana Agricultural University and impact of instruction initiatives. *Reference Services Review*, 41(3), 453 – 473. Doi: 10.1108/RSR-11-2012-0074

Thorne-Wallington, E. (2013). Social contexts of new media literacy: mapping libraries. *Journal of Information Technology & Libraries*, 32(4), 53-65.

UNDP. (2014). Human Development Report. Retrieved from http://hdr.undp.org/sites/ default/files/hdr14-report-en-1.pdf

UNESCO. (2011). Media and information literacy. Retrieved from http://www.unesco.org/ new/en/communication-and-information/media-development/media-literacy/mil-as -composite-concept/

University Grants Commission of Bangladesh. (2015, January 15). List of private universi-ties. Retrieved from http://www.ugc.gov.bd/university/?action=private

Wallis, J. (2005). Cyberspace, information literacy and the information society. *Library Review*, 54(4), 218 – 222. Doi: 10.1108/00242530510593407

Wilson, C., Grizzle, A., Tuazon, R. et al. (2011). *Media and Information Literacy Curriculum for Teachers*. Retrieved from http://unesdoc.unesco.org/images/ 0019/001929/192971e.pdf

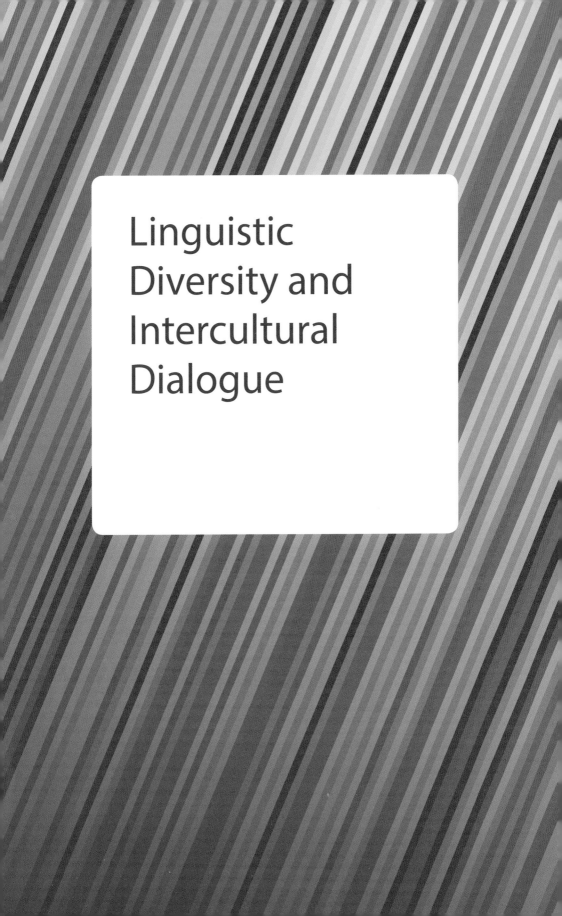

Linguistic Diversity and Intercultural Dialogue

Measuring Linguistic Diversity in Indian Online Scenario

K S Arul Selvan

Regional language-based content is dominating every sphere of mass media in India. The most highly circulated dailies are in regional languages, the highest number of television channels are regional language-based ones, regional language-based radio stations form vast networks, and the film producing industry in India (Hindi, Telugu, Tamil are leading players along with other regional language films) is the highest globally. Native speakers of Indian languages are in millions. Yet, no Indian regional languages are visible in global rankings of online language measurement. In order to find out details about the representation of Indian languages in the online world, this study uses three online indicators to measure the popularity of Indian languages. The results are showing significant representations.

Keywords: multilingualism, linguistic diversity online, languages in India, measuring linguistic diversity, language popularity

Regional language newspapers dominate the readership market of India. Out of the top 10 highly circulated editions, nine slots are for regional language dailies and only one for English daily (Hindi is leading with five dailies, two Malayalam, one each of Tamil, Marathi and English). The case is the same with the magazine section (India Readership Survey, 2014). In the television industry, regional language channels are ruling the roost. There are about 400 news channels in regional languages alone, English news channels are fewer in numbers. Each English channel has a regional language channel in its networks to maximise its reach and business. The regional language-based film industry in India is vibrant and it produces highest number of films in the world with 1,602 produced films in 2012 (745 in China, 476 in US) (McCarthy, 2014).

In every mass media in India, regional language-based outlets are predominantly popular.

The Internet Users in India

There are many factors associated with the profile of the Internet in India. Primarily, the Internet was an urban phenomenon until recently; the expansion of the Internet has touched semi-urban and rural areas too.

Figure 1. Internet connections in India (in millions)

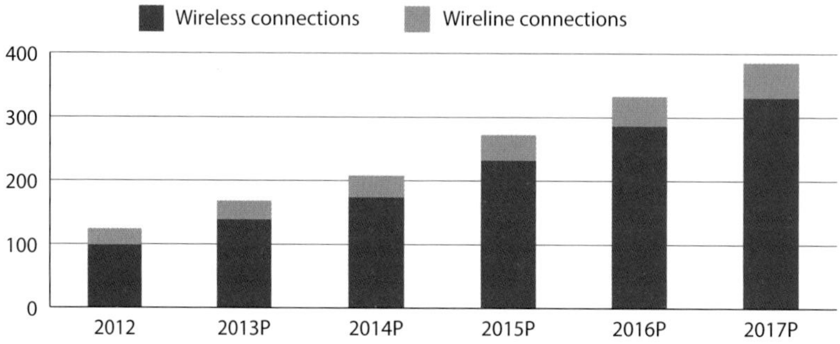

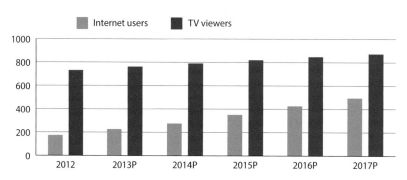

Source: FICCI-KPMG Report, 2013

Figure 2. Internet vs TV penetration in India (in millions)

Source: FICCI-KPMG Report, 2013

In India, 22% of the population has Internet connections. Out of this user base, nearly 12% of the population has mobile net access. At the national level, 79% of India's total population own or use a mobile device. Closer to 900 million mobile phone subscribers are in India, but there is a vast difference between urban and rural sectors – the urban teledensity is 163% and rural teledensity is just 38% (FICCI-KPMG, 2013, COAI).

According to the *LiveMint* newspaper report (quoting IAMAI and IMRB data[1], 2012), "Internet users in India could increase by 24% if local language content is provided" (D'Monte, 2014). This statement implies a lack of adequate representation of Indian language based online content. There are few factors, associated with the Indian online scenario, which might have favoured the dominant presence of English language and comparatively low visibility of Indian regional language contents. These factors are: a large section of Indian population (78% as on 2014) has no online access due to various issues of access factors, low adapting level of regional language based computing among active Internet users, and content-generating institutions like media companies are reluctant and investing less in this segment due to small size of regional language market and its lesser revenue scope.

India is known for its diversity of languages. The online medium, a convergence platform, has the capacity to embrace such linguistic diversity, and a multilingual content scenario can be expected. However, that is far from the reality. This article makes an attempt to map this scenario.

About Indian Languages

The Eighth Schedule of the Indian Constitution lists 22 languages, which are considered to be official languages. According to the Census of India, 2001 there are 122 languages spoken in India and 234 mother tongues exist. However, the People's Linguistic Survey of India states that there are about 780 languages in India.

The following information shows (Census of India, 2001) the number people who speak the 22 official Indian languages:

Table 1. List of Indian official languages and size of speakers

S No.	Language Name	Number of Speakers in Millions
1	Assamese	13
2	Bengali	83
3	Bodo	1.2
4	Dogri	2.2
5	Gurajati	46
6	Hindi	422
7	Kannada	37
8	Kashmiri	5.5
9	Konkani	2.4
10	Maithili	12
11	Malayalam	33
12	Manipuri	14

S No.	Language Name	Number of Speakers in Millions
13	Marathi	71
14	Nepali	2.8
15	Oriya	33
16	Punjabi	29
17	Sanskrit	0.014
18	Santali	6.4
19	Sindhi	2.5
20	Tamil	60
21	Telugu	74
22	Urdu	51

Source: Census of India, 2001 data

Measuring Linguistic Diversity

In the UNESCO funded Language Observatory Project, Mikami et al. (2005) identified three methods to assess the usage level of each language in cyberspace: 1. User profile; 2. User activity; and 3. Web presence. Analysing all these three methods, Gerrand (2007) identifies "web presence as the most practical indicator for estimating actual language use in cyberspace". By following established ways to measure linguistic diversity and identify the position of chosen languages in the online platform, this study adapted the web presence method to measure Indian languages in the online world.

For this article, three indicators have been identified to measure the language position online:

1. Wikipedia articles in Indian languages

2. Using Google search techniques

3. Using third party online language measuring algorithm

Wikipedia Details

Wikipedia is one of the top ten popular websites of the world (6th position in Alexa ranking). The entire content of this free online encyclopaedia is created by the user community. The details about the number of Wikipedia language editions, and the articles in each language edition are available at the wiki statistics. All data about the Indian language based Wikipedia editions were fetched, based on this data a ranking list has been created (Figure 3).

Figure 3. Ranking of Indian languages based on Wikipedia Articles

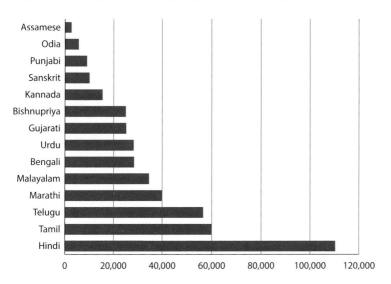

Source: Data collected from Wikipedia website[2]

As per data retrieved from wiki statistics, Hindi is leading with highest number of articles (more than 100,000 articles), followed by Tamil (60,000) and Telugu (57,000). The number of articles in Marathi, Malayalam, Bengali, Urdu, Gujarati and Bishnupriya range from 20,000 to 40,000. Kannada, Sanskrit, Punjabi and Assamese have less than 20,000 articles.

Hindi language dominates with other languages in this list, mainly due to large section of Hindi speakers in India cutting across individual states. Remaining language speakers are mainly concentrated in their respective states – for example, Gujarati in Gurajat, Kannada in Karnataka, Bengali in west Bengali etc. The size of speakers in these languages is more or less having similar number except Sanskrit and Bishnupriya, however there is a variation in their contribution to wiki articles. Literacy rate is uneven in the country (national average is 74.04%), literacy rate among Telugu speakers (language of then undivided Andra Pradesh) is well below national average, 67.66%, whereas the Assamese is closer to national average, 73.18%. Kannada is another surprise, India's equivalent of Silicon Valley is in Karanata where Kannada language is an official langauge, however their contribution is significantly less in comparison with the Telugu and Tamil (languages in neighbouring states). Due to liberal government policy on telecommunication sector, infrastructure for Internet network is much better than India was in decades ago, 76% of teledensity of mobile penetration is evidence to it.

Hence size of language speakers, literacy rate and infrastructure may not be the limiting factors to influence the position of respective language representation in online. However, online access and skills required for it might be the potential issues that restrict the proliferation of respective language content in the online world.

In the global context, there are 4.5 million English articles. Dutch, German, Swedish and French languages have articles around 1.5 million. Italian, Russian, Spanish, Polish and Waray-Waray have close to one million articles.

Google Search Details

The top 10 popular search keywords from the news category of 2013 were collected from Google Trends (2014 data is not yet released for the news category). All these keywords were translated into available Indian languages through Google Translate. While translating, three keywords were removed due to the non-availability of translated words in one or more languages. The translated keywords in each language were searched through Google individually, and the respective total figures were collected for ranking purposes. For each keyword, the data was sorted by language. The highest search result for a language was given 8 marks and lowest 1. The popularity was measured based on the total marking of each language (Table 2 and Figure 4).

Table 2. Google search results of popular news category of 2013

	Indian Economy	Election	Airlines	Bad-minton	Cricket	Mobile	Prime Minister
Bengali	2,310,000	2,330,000	49,000	104,000	855,000	2,830,000	1,480,000
Gujarati	272,000	151,000	21,300	18,300	1,630,000	1,390,000	171,000
Hindi	1,490,000	1,690,000	23,100	602,000	2,240,000	3,080,000	570,000
Kannada	388,000	2,260,000	302,000	250,000	211,000	69,900	414,000
Punjabi	65,600	234,000	446,000	57,800	815,000	315,000	3,740,000
Tamil	4,850,000	1,620,000	2,400,000	97,700	1,060,000	1,020,000	889,000
Telugu	308,000	325,000	42,900	76,100	2,320,000	1,560,000	413,000
Urdu	485,000	349,000	149,000	47,200	335,000	21,200,000	17,900,000

Source: Data retrieved from Google search[3]

Figure 4. Ranking of Indian languages based on Google search results

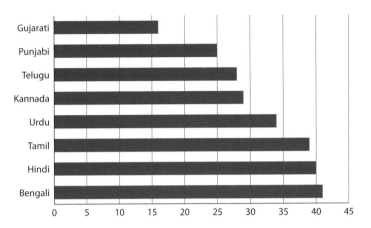

Source: Data retrieved from Google search

Bengali language dominates with the highest score (42), Hindi (40), and followed by Tamil (38). Other languages: Urdu (34), Kannada (28), Telugu (27), Punjabi (25) and Gujarati (16).

There are two possibilities for why Bengali is comparatively having a higher score:

1. Bengali script is being shared by other neighbouring state languages, such as Assamese and Bishnupriya. It may be the same for the next indicator too where Bengali takes lead web presence among other languages. Both Google search as well as website algorithm give results based on automatic computer intervention, there is a possibility of tagging similar scripts under one language.

2. As mentioned elsewhere, Bengali is a national language of neighbouring country Bangladesh.

Hindi is predominantly used and a connecting language in India along with English, Hindi takes five slots in among top 10 dailies, and is an early adaptor of online world compare to other languages. Tamil is another vibrant language, official language of Sri Lanka and Singapore, yet another early adaptor of the online world.

Website Details

A website[4] uses a computer algorithm which monitors recognisable languages in the sampled websites (top 10 million sites). Individual web pages and sub-domains were not considered in their monitoring. This site fetches web data directly from the websites like any search engine, through a crawler as well as using publicly available data from Alexa and Google. Based on the data from this website, a ranking was made for top 10 languages of India (Figure 5).

Figure 5. Ranking of Indian Languages based on web algorithm data

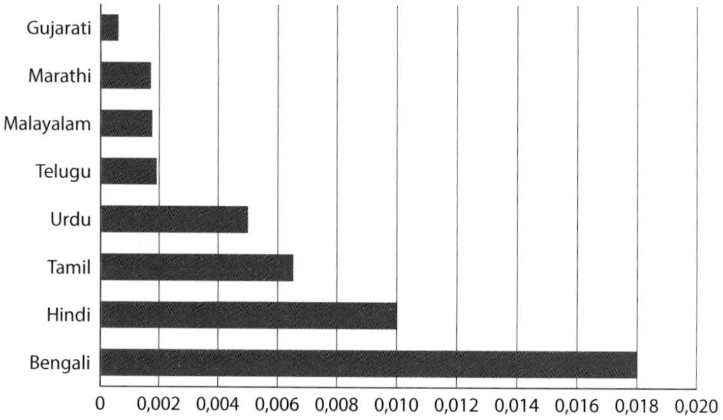

Source: Data retrieved from www.w3techs.com[5]

Based on the data from the website, Bengali has higher online content (0.024%), Hindi comes second highest share (0.018%), followed by Tamil (0.013%). Urdu, Telugu, Malayalam, Marathi and Gujarati are the remaining available languages with meagre shares (0.001%) of online content. English has dominant presence (55%) of online content. Russian, German, Japanese, and Spanish are other popular languages with online content share of less than 5%. In the global context, the Indian languages share is insignificant.

Comparison of Three Data Sets

Data from three sources are arranged based on the popularity of Indian languages. Languages which are commonly available in all three data sets are taken for final comparison; languages which are not listed in any of the data sets are removed from the comparison list. Interestingly, the Google and website-based rank list matches exactly and in the Wikipedia rank list, Bengali and Urdu were rearranged (Table 3).

Table 3. Consolidated ranking of Indian Languages based on three data sets

Google Search	W3tech	Wikipedia
Bengali	Bengali	Hindi
Hindi	Hindi	Tamil
Tamil	Tamil	Telugu
Urdu	Urdu	Bengali
Telugu	Telugu	Urdu
Gujarati	Gujarati	Gujarati

Source: Combined data from Wikipedia, Google search and w3techs.com

Analysis and Discussion

Some of the Indian languages are national languages of other countries too, e.g. Bengali in Bangladesh, Urdu in Pakistan and Tamil in Sri Lanka and Singapore. There would be significant contribution from these countries in their respective languages. An important factor is the sizable population of Indian diaspora, who may have better resources in terms of content and technological facilities.

Out of the 22 official languages and 234 mother tongues of India, only six languages feature in the final comparison chart. This shows the hard realities of Internet accessibility in the Indian context. As per the FICCI report, in 2017 at least 35% of the Indian population is going to be Internet users (FICCI-KPMG, 2013). Internet access through mobile is increasing rapidly due to the steps taken by a few multinational online firms in collaboration with the national telecommunication networks to provide free/affordable data access to some of their online services.

Other regional language-based mass media entities have huge popularity in India. The case of less web presence of Indian languages indicates the significant role of the digital divide in determining the market for regional language content. Not having a big audience size for regional language content forces online institutions to invest less. At the same time, not having adequate regional language content is restricting the expansion of potential user base in India. In New Delhi, the author personally witnessed the national media entities having strong online teams for the English version of their web operations, whereas their regional language edition is managed by thin editorial teams. This shows that the media firms put less human resources due to lack of profit from regional language content.

Cue to Enhance Web Presence

There is a potential for the massive expansion of user base of those who prefer regional language content. The lack of a significant web presence of regional language content is the ideal case for media and information literacy interventions to enhance regional language content in the Indian context. Policy level measures to meet the aforesaid target include:

1. Technological interface for language inputs was the biggest issue for non-Roman letters in the initial period of Internet use. Thanks to advances in computing, the Unicode made that issue simpler for many languages including many Indian languages. However, the lack of skills of the Unicode-based keyboard operation is one of the biggest hurdles among many Indian net users.

2. The Internet population in India is young. The national as well as state level school curriculum boards should incorporate media and information literacy (MIL) in the secondary level onwards. In the MIL curriculum, a good mix of skills development about language computing would increase the user base for language content. A sizable section of the tech-savvy users interfaces with the online world by transliterating their language into English, this is evident in many Indian regional languages. One of the main reasons for transliteration is due to lack of required skills to use regional language keyboard. If the school ICT curriculum incorporates this skill component, the users would take full advantages of the digital medium.

3. National and state governments should initiate efforts to create online resources on a wide range of subjects. If the governments publish its information for the public in the officially listed languages, it will boost public engagement with the online content in regional languages. There are visible efforts undertaken by volunteers and communities for creating online resources for many Indian languages, however the national and state governments need to push this factor vigorously.

4. Higher learning institutions should make efforts to create regional language content through its faculties and learners in a sustained manner over a period of time. Universities and colleges are the main hub of knowledge developments, and if those outputs are made available in the chosen languages, they will boost the web presence of respective languages.

5. As per the Government of India's policy, 2% of any business entities budget needs to be allocated to corporate social responsibility (CSR). Civil societies should make the case to tap financial support from the huge budget available through CSR for online language content creation.

References

COAI – Cellular Operators Association of India. (ND). National telecom statistics. Retrived from http://www.coai.com/statistics/telecom-statistics/national (May, 2015).

Census of India. (2001). Abstract of speakers' strength of languages and mother tongues. Retrieved from http://www.censusindia.gov.in/Census_Data_2001/Census_Data_Online/Language/Statement1.aspx (May, 2015)

D'Monte, L. (2014, March 10). 'Need more local language content for Internet to bloom in India.' *Mint* newspaper, LiveMint.com. Retrieved from http://www.livemint.com/Opinion/zCFoFUXebEbxBOVq8a2UUJ/Need-more-local-language-content-for-Internet-to-bloom-in-In.html (May, 2015).

FICCI-KPMG. (2013). *The power of a Billion. Realizing the Indian dream.* Indian media and entertainment industry report. Retrieved from http://www.ficci.com/spdocument/20217/FICCI-KPMG-Report-13-FRAMES.pdf (May, 2015).

Gerrand, P. (2007). Estimating linguistic diversity on the Internet: A taxonomy to avoid pitfalls and paradoxes. *Journal of Computer-Mediated Communication,* 12:1298–1321. doi: 10.1111/j.1083-6101.2007.00374.x

Indian Readership Survey. (2014). Retrieved from http://mruc.net/sites/default/files/IRS%202014%20Topline%20Findings_0.pdf (May, 2015).

McCarthy, N. (2014, September 3). Bollywood: India's film industry by the numbers. Forbes.com. Retrieved from http://www.forbes.com/sites/niallmccarthy/2014/09/03/bollywood-indias-film-industry-by-the-numbers-infographic/ (May, 2015).

Mikami et al. (2005). Language diversity on the Internet: An Asian view. In Paolillo, J. et al., (Eds). *Measuring Linguistic Diversity on the Internet,* pp. 91-103. Retrieved from http://eprints.utm.my/3407/2/Measuring_Linguistic_Diversity.pdf (May, 2015).

Notes

1 IAMAI (Internet and Mobile Association of India) and IMRB (Indian Market Research Bureau) data and reports are available in this URL – http://www.iamai.in/reports1.aspx

2 Figure 3 data (as on March 2014) collected from Wikipedia website – http://en.wikipedia.org/wiki/List_of_Wikipedias

3 Table 2 data (as on March 2014) retrieved through Google search based on 2013 popular keywords – https://www.google.co.in/trends/topcharts#date=2013

4 Third party website is www.w3techs.com.

5 Figure 5 data (as on March 2014) collected from this URL – http://w3techs.com/technologies/overview/content_language/all

Muses on Information Literacy, Media Literacy and Intercultural Dialogue: A Coffee and Tea Shop Application

From an 85 year old stalwart in the field (Editors' Title)

Forest Woody Horton, Jr.

This brief article tries to squarely address the inter-relationships between three very important concepts that are absolutely critical to the ability of people to fully exploit the benefits of what is often called the "Global Information Society". The author frankly admits that his writing style is highly informal – written in a first person, storybook telling manner, which is certainly not characteristic of scientific articles! Rather, this article is written based on the writer's own extensive personal travels, visits, work and living experiences, in the course of perhaps fifty years, worldwide, in 144 different countries, on all continents. He believes that the ability to communicate and explain these three crucial concepts and skills to a very wide audience, not just to practicing professionals, will be more fruitful and effective by using this highly personalized anecdotal approach than the more conventionally prescribed retrospective scientific literature research approach usually used for articles of this kind.

Keywords: information literacy, media literacy, intercultural dialogue

Introduction

Given the very turbulent world in which we live today, where understanding, tolerance and forbearance are in extremely short supply, information literacy, media literacy and intercultural dialogue are unquestionably three strategic and closely interrelated concepts which must be learned, and practiced effectively, if people are to ever be able to live, work, and prosper together, harmoniously, and become empowered to enjoy the benefits of the Global Information Society, especially given the very turbulent world in which we live today, where understanding, tolerance and forbearance are in extremely short supply.

The Thesis

I believe very strongly that the three main topics in this article's title are interdependent and no single one of the three elements can or should control or dominate the other two. To truly maximize their ultimate effectiveness – their advance planning, their use, and their periodic evaluation – they must be very closely synchronized. On the contrary, if they are viewed, antithetically, as largely independent and autonomous elements, which are defined, learned, practiced and assessed largely separately, then the potential benefits of all three will be correspondingly minimized. The challenge is that they traditionally and historically have been researched, developed, tested, applied, and evaluated largely in a disconnected manner, by both theorists and practitioners. Moreover, they each traditionally fall under a different academic discipline (or under different professional "turfs" to use a common everyday phrase), and they are seldom closely coordinated in the context of a collegiate level course of study.

The foregoing is the author's thesis, which he tries to defend in this brief article. Moreover, he hopes to relate, and make this discussion relevant to UNESCO's "Media and Information Literacy and Intercultural Dialogue" (MILID) initiatives. The article concludes with a few conclusions and a single recommendation.

Why are these Three Concepts Critically Important?

Perhaps a ready answer to this can be found in the "Proclamation on Information Literacy" which was issued in 2009 by the current American President, Barack Obama:

> Everyday, we are inundated with vast amounts of information. A 24-hour news cycle and thousands of global television and radio networks, coupled with an immense array of online resources, have challenged our long-held perceptions of information management. Rather than merely possessing data, we must also learn the skill necessary to acquire, collate, and evaluate information for any situation. This new type of literacy also requires competency with communication technologies, including computers and mobile devices that can help in our day-to-day decision making. National Information Literacy Awareness Month highlights the need for all Americans to be adept in the skills necessary to effectively navigate the Information Age[1].

What is an "Intangible Cultural Expression"?

Let me try to introduce my discussion in the context of a real life personal anecdote. A few years ago some friends of mine and I were discussing the challenge of why it's so important for every country to preserve what UNESCO formally calls "intangible cultural expressions", in contrast to (or more accurately, in addition to) a country's historically significant tangible possessions – it's buildings, it's documents, it's monuments, it's man-made artifacts, it's natural resources, etc., which are considered "tangible cultural expressions".

My friends and I began by talking very generally about this, but soon we found ourselves talking specifically about "coffee and tea houses" (perhaps, no doubt, in part because we were at the time sitting in one) as well known kinds of places where friends meet regularly to share their views about almost everything and anything, talking animatedly, sometimes for hours, all the while enjoying each other's friendship and camaraderie. And they do this frequently, very often daily, or every few days, and often while being entertained in some way such as listening to music, playing a game, watching a video, watching passers-by, hearing a lecture or story being told, perhaps even dancing or singing, and so on.

What are Coffee and Tea Houses?

My friends and I defined "coffee and tea houses," and similar friendly "meeting and greeting" places, very broadly. Clearly beer, or consuming some other beverages, alcoholic or non-alcoholic, instead of coffee or tea, served with or without food, would supplement and serve the same basic socialization purpose in many countries. In short, widely different kinds of inside or outside areas, from park benches to the cocktail lounges of elaborate and expensive restaurants, would qualify, depending on whether the purpose of people gathering together was exclusively, or mainly, functional (i.e. to eat breakfast, lunch or dinner) rather than mainly to socialize.

For example, the British, Irish, Welsh and Scottish often serve beer and therefore the Pub must be included in addition to their Coffee Houses. The *Biergarten* in Germany and Austria are the Anglo Pub equivalency, but the *Konditorei* are also very popular in those countries if you want sweet tortes with your coffee (or *Torten* as they're called there). Tea houses, rather than coffee houses, are more common in the Orient and much of Asia. In China, for example, they are called tea and dining houses. In Japan, they are called *Kissaten*.

Starbucks claims the leadership coffee house role in the USA. Americans tend to often add a lot of other things to their coffee in order to make their *lattes*. And doughnuts and muffins are the preferred accompaniment. But beer and bars are also very popular in America, especially sports bars, before and after big games.

Coffee houses are called a *Café* in Latin America and in Latin-oriented countries in Europe such as Spain, France, Belgium and Italy; a *Botequim* in Portuguese speaking countries; a *Kaffehus* in Sweden and a *Koffiehuis* in the Netherlands but spelled differently, but quite similarly, in other Nordic and European countries; in Arabic countries they are called *Kahwa; Kofeinya* in Russian speaking countries; *Kaufee Ghar* for coffee house and *Chai Ghar* for tea house in Hindi speaking lands; and so on across the globe!

Wikipedia defines what we are talking about in this way: "A tea house or tea room is an establishment which primarily serves tea and other refreshments. Although its function varies widely depending on the culture, tea houses often serve as centers of social interaction. Some cultures have a variety of distinct tea-centered houses or parlors that all qualify under the English language term "tea house" or "tea room"[2].

Why We are Using Coffee Houses as the Vehicle for Advocating the Interdependence of Information, Media and Intercultural Dialogue?

Coffee and tea houses, in my view, are a very special kind of opportunity not only for preserving "intangible cultural expressions" but also because they are virtually universal, occurring in every country, and in every kind of local community within a country, down to quite small villages. And the more remote and isolated the villages are, the more important and unique they are as a central social center for sharing news and socializing.

Moreover, and more directly relevant to our thesis, coffee houses are an excellent example of a venue where information literacy, media literacy and intercultural dialogue all come together. Coffee houses all over the world have in common bringing people together very regularly and quite often to communicate with each other, often people with different demographic profiles, to talk, to laugh, to frown, to argue, to debate, sometimes even to cry, and to interact with each other in other ways such as playing games or dancing, listening to music, listening to a story, etc. And we can safely presume that most readers will have been in coffee or tea houses and know what they are, what to expect, how to behave, what kinds of people they are likely to meet there, and so on. While they virtually all serve locally appropriate snack type food and drinks (except perhaps the remote park bench or grassy slopes near a distant river or lake), and very often there are radios and television sets, games, and other diversions and distractions available.

Many such places also often feature actors and performers specializing in "intangible cultural expressions" that are indigenous to, and representative of, one or more ethnic, sectarian, tribal, religious, racial, national or other kinds of social groupings. These groups or customers frequent those houses because they live nearby and the facilities are usually easily and conveniently accessible.

Finally, the author frequented coffee and tea houses in virtually all of the 144 countries he travelled to, worked in, or lived in. He learned very early that they were a wonderful and virtually unique place to meet the local people, ask questions, hear opinions (solicited or not), find out about local cross-cultural "no no's" (we don't do this, we don't say that, don't go there, we never act that way, don't eat the pomegranates, and so on). These exhortations and admonitions, received first hand largely from strangers – people whom one has just met – are rooted deeply in the local cultural fabric, which is why they are so valuable to visitors from a practical, real life standpoint.

In sum, the author's many personal forays into local community coffee houses is why this article is based primarily on his personal experiences, not on a formal literature search and review.

National Culture Defined and Illustrated

Before I go further with my coffee house story, let me first try to do two things. Firstly, to define "national culture". Second, to define and illustrate with some examples of "intangible cultural expressions".

In the authors view, national culture – at least a working definition for purposes of this article – is:

A subtle and very diverse blend of both implicit than explicit, intangible than tangible, morphous and amorphous, visible and invisible, and both covert and overt characteristics, attributes and qualities.

No two national cultures are exactly alike, even if two adjacent countries speak the same languages, are in the same geographic region, are populated by peoples of the same race, religion, ethnic group, celebrate the same or similar holy days and feasts or festivals, and so on. Examples of these adjacent countries are India vs. Nepal, China vs. Vietnam, Peru vs. Chile, Australia vs. New Zealand, etc.

This is why it may be more appropriate to speak of "co-cultures" in countries which are multicultural.

Intangible Cultural Expressions

The exact nature of intangible cultural expressions often found in coffee houses, and how they are performed, acted out, or otherwise "implemented", will ultimately depend, partly, on some very practical matters such as budgetary considerations, space availability, the availability and interest of performers, and other factors. Amateur and/or professional teachers, tutors, mentors, "wise men" and performers, who are trained in one, or perhaps several forms of the above list of expressions, or other expressions, are typically hired and then they are positioned in these houses in either adjacent, or often separated areas of a single large room.

In local communities which are densely inhabited by majorities – a single race, religion, ethnic group, sect or caste, and a single language or dialect is spoken – there is understandably a concentration of intangible cultural expressions which are indigenous to and representative of that particular native majority group.

In other communities where there is a rich and fairly harmonious co-existing mixture of minority races, religions, nationalities, ethnic groups, sects, tribes, castes, etc., and many different languages and/or dialects are spoken, such a facility, and its menu of specific offerings, both food and drink, as well as its intangible cultural expression performances, are usually multicultural rather than unicultural, and more inclusive rather than exclusive. This is especially true where there are large sized minorities present, even if they don't technically constitute a majority (in other words, percentages are less important in my context than absolute numbers).

This is because of many reasons in my view.

First, the owners don't wish to openly offend minority cultures. Second, often customers arrive who reflect multicultural backgrounds. Third, the local customs traditionally favor inclusivity rather than exclusivity. Fourth, even in the absence of a strong multicultural local customs, there may be laws that punish, in some way, exclusivity behavior and practices. Finally, in small, isolated and remote villages, the coffee house may be the only venue where people can meet together informally and socially.

How Information, Media and Culture Interact with Each Other

Returning to our coffee house with its performers, Wikipedia's performing arts definition makes some relevant observations. "The means of expressing appreciation can vary by culture. Chinese performers will clap with the audience at the end of a performance; the return applause signals "thank you" to the audience. In Japan, folk performing arts performances commonly attract individuals who take photographs, sometimes getting up to the stage and within inches of performer's faces."

"Sometimes the dividing line between performer and the audience may become blurred, as in the example of "participatory theatre" where audience members get involved in the production."

We also have this wonderful example provided by Jane Wright about a square in Morocco, called Jemaa el-Fna Square, which UNESCO inscribe several years ago on their list of World Intangible Heritage. It eloquently reveals how multi-faceted and important these cultural spaces are to a society's functioning in general.

> The Jemaa el-Fna Square is one of the main cultural spaces in Marrakesh and has become one of the symbols of the city since its foundation in the eleventh century. It represents a unique concentration of popular Moroccan cultural traditions performed through musical, religious and artistic expressions.
>
> Located at the entrance of the Medina, this triangular square, which is surrounded by restaurants, stands and public buildings, provides everyday commercial activities and various forms of entertainment. It is a meeting point for both the local population and people from elsewhere. All through the day, and well into the night, a variety of services are offered, such as dental care, traditional medicine, fortune-telling, preaching, and henna tattooing; water-carrying, fruit and traditional food may be bought.
>
> In addition, one can enjoy many performances by storytellers, poets, snake-charmers, Berber musicians (mazighen), Gnaoua dancers and senthir (hajouj) players. The oral expressions would be continually renewed by bards (imayazen), who used to travel through Berber territories. They continue to combine speech and gesture to teach, entertain and charm the audience. Adapting their art to contemporary contexts, they now improvise on an outline of an ancient text, making their recital accessible to a wider audience.
>
> The Jemaa el-Fna Square is a major place of cultural exchange and has enjoyed protection as part of Morocco's artistic heritage since 1922. However, urbanization, in particular real estate speculation and the development of the road infrastructure are seen as serious threats to the cultural space itself. While Jemaa el-Fna Square enjoys great popularity, the cultural practices may suffer acculturation, also caused by widespread tourism.
>
> http://www.unesco.org/culture/ich/RL/00014

We are very happy to be able to report that this square still exists and is operating to serve the public today!

Conclusions

First, coffee and tea houses are a truly unique institution at the local community level. There are no other institutions at this grassroots level, political, economic or social, that are designed and serve primarily to bring people together in a multicultural setting, often with different backgrounds, to interact daily, with no other "agenda" other than to encourage them to communicate freely and openly with each other, and enjoy their time together in an unsupervised, unobserved and uninhibited manner. Virtually all other meeting places at this level have an "agenda" of some kind – hospitals, senior centers, day care centers for children, libraries, museums, galleries, commercial stores and shops of all kinds, post offices, restaurants, etc.

Second, coffee and tea houses very often bring a few or many minority and underserved populations together, not just members of the same majority groups. This applies to races, religions, ethnic groups, linguistic groups, and so on.

Third, the atmosphere or ambiance of coffee and tea houses is friendly, warm, informal and conducive to a free, open and amicable exchange of views and ideas in all spheres of life – political, economic and social.

Fourth, new ideas, views or issues (e.g. the electability of emerging leaders, community projects being considered and other kinds of community problems and issues) are implicitly "tested" in coffee house cross-cultural dialogues and conversations. However they are not, in any "official" way intentionally or deliberately "captured, distilled, summarized" and then presented to any kind of governing local level, provincial level or national level institutions.

Fifth, bearing in mind the immediately preceding item, there are obvious and serious privacy and security concerns that are raised if the informal, unsupervised, unobserved and uninhibited atmosphere of coffee house dialogues were ever to be compromised. At the same time, it must be conceded that very often this local institutional domain is the first, and oftentimes the only place, where critical and sensitive issues of importance to not only the local community level, but to higher levels as well, are discussed and debated.

Recommendation

That UNESCO use the context and vehicle of its MILID project as a constructive and timely opportunity to explore how the coffee and tea house institution can be researched and studied with the goal of learning how it's operation and its societal benefits could help countries to improve their information literacy, media literacy and intercultural dialogue competencies, but without risking raising privacy or security concerns as mentioned above.

There are many practicing library and information science, media and culture studies professionals who are, and many academic centers which are, very well qualified for this purpose and which may have well already studied this specific area, or, if not, would welcome such an initiative. Preparing one or more videos to help explain such projects could be very helpful. And small but focused international conferences on intangible cultural heritage could be very useful. A series of well designed projects, using participating MILID higher education institutions, is recommended. The author believes a group of such research projects clearly falls within the purview of "Post 2015 Sustainable Development Goals" as that admonition is specified in instructions to authors for preparing these articles. For example, a study to address the problem of gender discrimination against women being barred from entering coffee houses in many parts of the world could be an excellent central focus.

Notes

1   Barack Obama, The White House, Washington D.C., USA, 2009, Proclamation, Information Literacy Day.
2   Tea House. http://en.wikipedia.org/wiki/Tea_house

Media Wise: Empowering Responsible Religious Leadership in the Digital Age

Ogova Ondego

The African Media Development Initiative states that fostering stronger mass media "is an indispensable part of tackling poverty, improving development and enabling Africa to attain its development goals" (BBC World Service Trust, 2005). Several organizations are stepping in with Media and Information Literacy and Intercultural Dialogue (MILID) as the tool for arbitration that will lead to common purpose and unity for the good of the whole region. It was for this reason that a four-day media education training for senior religious leaders was held in Nairobi, Kenya, November 15-18, 2014.

The training, dubbed Media Wise: Empowering Responsible Religious Leadership in the Digital Age, was meant to expose religious leaders – Christians, Muslims, Sikhs, Coptics – to the practice of media operations so as to minimize misunderstanding and to equip them with the skills for participating in the media operation. The training also aimed to help minimize, if not eliminate, any misrepresentation or bias the media harbored against their communities. The curriculum used for training was a pilot adaptation of UNESCO's Media and Information Literacy: Curriculum for Teachers, and UNESCO: Media and Information Policy and Strategy Guidelines.

Specifically developed to meet the needs of religious leaders, the training explored how news is produced, delved into the risks and opportunities associated with the Internet, examined how representations shape perceptions, and looked at how religious leaders can best respond to misinformation in the media about religious groups.

Keywords: religion, religious leadership, media education training, news

Religion is a major shaper of opinion in modern Eastern Africa. It is not only considered progressive to belong to a faith community, but a person who subscribes to a particular religion and attends worship regularly is usually taken as an honest and virtuous individual. Perhaps it was for this reason that John S Mbiti, the Switzerland-based, Kenyan theologian and philosopher concluded in his book, *African Religions and Philosophy*, that "Africans are notoriously religious" (Mbiti, 1969).

The people of Kenya, one of the most progressive countries in East Africa, are ranked among the "Top 10 Most Religious Populations in the World", according to a 2012 report by Red C Opinion Poll, part of WIN-Gallup International, a world-wide network of leading opinion pollsters, that showed that 88% of Kenyans considered themselves "a religious person" (WIN-Gallup International, 2012).

The poll not only appeared to corroborate Mbiti's assertion about the religiosity of Africans, but also confirmed the results of the Population and Housing Census 2009 that were released in 2011 and that showed that 47.7% of Kenya's total population of 38.6 million in 2009 and 41 million in 2011 said they were Protestant Christians, 23.5% Roman Catholic Christians, 11.9% Other Christians, 11.2% Muslims and 1.7% belonged to African Traditional Religions (Kenya National Bureau of Statistics, 2009).

The census showed that adherents to the Bahá'í Faith, Buddhism and "Other Religions" accounted for 1%, 0.3% and 2%, respectively. But 2.4% of those counted indicated they subscribed to "No Religion" (Kenya National Bureau of Statistics, 2009).

At the time of writing this article, there is a stand-off between civil servants on one hand and the Government of Kenya on the other. The former have since the beginning of 2015 refused to report to work in the volatile and largely Muslim north-eastern part of the country fearing for their safety and security; they want the government to provide them with ample security (IRIN, 2014; Standard Media, 2015).

Another problem is over the Islamic community's claim that it is marginalised in Kenya, a secular state that guarantees freedom of worship to every citizen (Constitution of Kenya, 2010). Muslims claim they are overlooked when it comes to the allocation of national resources on the account of their faith. The large Muslim population in the coastal region of the country has been threatening to secede from Kenya on the account of marginalisation (Richard Lough and Joseph Akwiri, 2012). This makes an already bad situation worse even without bringing in the fact that several outspoken Muslim clerics have been killed under suspicious circumstances. In fact, the Muslim faith community has pointed a finger at state security agents but the government has denied ever killing its own citizens (IRIN, 2014).

From the foregoing, it appears that a section of the citizenry of Kenya is under siege from its own political leadership. As this happens, the government, too, points a finger at Muslim leaders, accusing them of fomenting civil disobedience and radicalising the youth against the government (Akwiri, 2014).

Critical observers, both within and outside government, question how an influential group, such as religious leaders, a group that shapes perceptions in their communities as teachers, guides, advisers, counselors and role models, cannot prevail against those who are getting radicalised. It is stressed that religious leaders need to be equipped with the skills to critically analyse media content, and understand the risks and opportunities of media, especially with regard to the Internet, so they may become responsible and informed consumers and transmitters of information and opinion.

In addition to religion, the mass media have been the other cog in the wheel of unity and development in this part of Africa. Yet never in the history of eastern Africa has religion and mass media been as divisive; and at loggerheads with each other.

Faith communities, especially the Muslims, accuse the media of fueling differences or even inventing and perpetuating non-existent disagreements between religious communities on one side and government and the general citizenry on the other. The media, that should play the role of independent and objective 'ears-and-eyes' of society', are instead being accused of harbouring biases and prejudices against religious communities (Dialogue Days, 2014).

As the main socialising agents of the 21st century, the media both shape the understanding of reality and provide identity to individuals and societies (Ondego, 2011). Consequently, every human being needs access to the media and must feel welcome to be actively participating in the way the media function.

The African Media Development Initiative states that fostering stronger mass media, "is an indispensable part of tackling poverty, improving development and enabling Africa to attain its development goals" (BBC World Service Trust, 2005).

Organizations like the United Nations Educational, Scientific and Cultural Organization (UNESCO) and King Abdullah bin Abdulaziz International Centre for Interreligious and Intercultural Dialogue (KAICIID) of Vienna, Austria are stepping in with Media and Information Literacy and Intercultural Dialogue (MILID) as the tool for arbitration that will lead to common purpose and unity for the good of the whole region.

It was for this reason that a four-day media education training for senior religious leaders was held in Nairobi, Kenya, November 15-18, 2014.

The training, dubbed Media Wise: Empowering Responsible Religious Leadership in the Digital Age, was meant to expose religious leaders – Christians, Muslims, Sikhs, Coptics – to the practice of media operations so as to minimise misunderstanding and to equip them with the skills for participating in the media operation. The training also aimed to help minimize, if not eliminate, any misrepresentation or bias the media harbored against their communities.

Two practising journalists who also manage media organisations, were chosen to facilitate the training; Victor Bwire of Media Council of Kenya and myself, as manager of the Lola Kenya Screen audiovisual media festival, skills-development programme and marketing platform for children and youth in eastern Africa. Lola Kenya Screen has also been conducting MIL training programmes for children and youth since 2005.

The curriculum used for training was a pilot adaptation of UNESCO's Media and Information Literacy: Curriculum for Teachers, and UNESCO: Media and Information Policy and Strategy Guidelines.

Specifically developed to meet the needs of religious leaders, the training explored how news is produced, delved into the risks and opportunities associated with the Internet, examined how representations shape perceptions, and looked at how religious leaders can best respond to misinformation in the media about religious groups.

Mike Waltner, Head of KAICIID, which developed the curriculum and organised the training in Nairobi in collaboration with UNESCO, said the training sought "to equip religious leaders with the skills with which "to navigate the media landscape in the digital age" (Waltner, 2014).

That religious leaders exert enormous influence on their communities as teachers, bridge-builders and conflict mediators in the conflict-prone 21st century is not in doubt. It therefore makes sense that they be equipped with the skills to guide those around them to consume and produce media in what KAICIID calls "an informed and responsible manner" (KAICIID, 2014).

KAICIID, which says its "programmes strive to improve media engagement and strengthen reporting while upholding freedom of expression and the press", further says it developed its curriculum that was used for the first time in Nairobi and New Delhi, India in November 2014, "at the request of renowned religious authorities of several faiths...[who] were concerned that media representations of their faiths and communities are often inaccurate, distorted or incomplete" and that "Social media, while providing opportunities for engagement and dialogue, has also become a forum for hate speech" (KAICIID, 2014).

Naomi Hunt, Project Officer for the KAICIID Media Programme, said of the Nairobi workshop: "Religious leaders are a vital conduit of information and opinions to their communities, and we hope that this course will help them understand how media operate, give them an opportunity to reflect on the way that perceptions are shaped, and think about how they can best approach, within their communities, the challenges and opportunities afforded by the digital age."

Project Highlights

- First Media and Information Literacy (MIL) training for Religious Leaders in eastern Africa
- Successful adaptation of UNESCO MIL Curriculum
- Successful implementation of pilot curriculum
- High level of appreciation of the training by participants

Project Overview

The four-day media education training for senior religious leaders that was conducted in November 2014 was a ground-breaking event in the region where conflict resulting from religious differences is getting more pronounced.

Though the 2009 census statistics showed that almost 85% of Kenya's population is Christian with those subscribing to Islam accounting for about 12%, the training conducted in Nairobi had more Muslim composition than Christian. African Traditional Religions, Baháʼí Faith and Buddhism were not represented in the training, but the Sikh faith, which is part of 'Others', was represented. Perhaps this could be rectified in future training so that each faith may feel that it is recognised and appreciated.

The training started by discussing the rationale for Media Education. The trainer explained why the 21st century is referred to as the Information Era that is driven by information and knowledge, gave examples of mass media, stressed that mass media are the main socialising agent of the century, explained why every human being must not only have access to the media but must also participate in the way the media function, and then concluded by stating that "Fostering stronger mass media in Africa is an indispensable part of tackling poverty, improving development and enabling Africa to attain its development goals" (African Media Development Initiative, 2005).

Having observed that mass media are social systems that are affected by the social, economic, political and cultural environments in which they operate, the trainer asked the class: "In whose interest do the media work?" – a question that led to some animated debate.

In a later module, the trainer discussed how media symbols are shared through:

• Sound

• Camera angles

• Lighting

• Types of camera shots

• Icons

• Dress

• Action, and

• Figurative language

It was in this module that concepts such as stereotypes and prejudices against the 'Other' were tackled:

• We understand and accept people according to our experience of them

• We form an opinion of people on the role they play in society

• Stereotypes can be both positive and negative

Stereotypes are formed from:

• Inquiries about people

• Hearsay about people

• Appearance of people

• Behaviour of people

• Dress of people

• Living standards of people

"Can prejudice be eliminated? " was the question that participants were left with as the trainer moved on to Module 7 that deals with young people and the Internet and its Web 2.0 function.

Though the web abounds in opportunities, it is also replete with risks; how does one use it responsibly?

A highly interactive session, it ended with a brief moderated debate on how to use the Internet responsibly, stressing the terms and conditions of use and the privacy of users.

The module addressing media ownership and media content generated as much debate as prior modules.

It was here that participants got into robust discussion on issues such as 'media-ownership interests' versus 'editorial independence', 'mission-driven' versus 'profit-driven' objectives, media ownership types, emergence of alternative media in 1990s Kenya, and the place and role of religious media.

All the modules presented during the training generated equal interest from all the participants. But perhaps the modules that generated the greatest interest were those that touched on the values of news, what constitutes news and how news is prepared and presented.

The participants wanted to be taught how to select, process and present information that is news in the form of media releases. Due to time constraints, there wasn't time for that!

Since there was so much ground to cover within a limited time, the co-trainers, in consultation with KAICIID, had to devise the best methods to ensure that as much knowledge as possible was imparted to the participants in the most economical manner.

The methods employed in the training were role plays, demonstrations, group work, moderated debate, plenary presentations, video and newspaper-cutting analyses, straight-lecture delivery, question-and-answer, Microsoft PowerPoint, and activity as framed in the pilot curriculum.

Overall Impact

- Participants developed a better definition for information and how it is accessed through different media platforms

- The concept of Freedom of Expression as a right and the importance of self-regulation versus regulatory bodies for the press became clearer to them

- The 5Ws & 1H (who, what, when, where, why and how), which participants referred to playfully as '5 Wives and 1 Husband') plus the right-side up and inverted pyramid for news reports and features was highly appreciated

- Participants developed an understanding of the difference between the spaces and operations of traditional media and new media and the value of the latter in today's world

- Participants gained a better understanding regarding freedom and rights in the cyber world

Recommendations

While KAICIID's pilot curriculum is well summarised, some sections appeared to be repetitive and thus called for the trainers to combine some Modules, such as Modules 3 (Representation of media and information) and 4 (Language in media and information).

The trainers also observed that the pilot curriculum is 'heavy' as if it were designed for a rigorous academic study using a straight lecture approach rather than being presented in a light, non-formal, highly interactive seminar-like arrangement.

As presented in the pilot curriculum, a class of 25 participants wouldn't cover even half of the content in the course modules in three or four days if the trainers employed the highly interactive, participatory and engaging approach suitable for media education.

For contextualisation in Africa, the data – statistics, spending habits, electronic media clips, and newspaper/magazine cuttings – for illustrating lessons to use has to come from outside the prepared course work.

It would be best if future trainings did not have to skip any modules. Additionally, it would be helpful to upgrade the curriculum to be used at diploma and degree levels that could be covered over a semester of 16 weeks instead of over four days.

The trainers noted some varying levels of grasping concepts among the participants of varying academic qualifications ranging from PhD to bachelor's and even diploma level. It is recommended that a minimum academic level be set for participants undertaking this MIL training in future.

Successful MIL sessions in Kenya – where they exist, as in the case of Lola Kenya Screen – are usually conducted as interactive seminars led by a moderator and not as a classroom in which the teacher dispenses knowledge to the learners. Use of Microsoft PowerPoint presentation methods do not generate great results. It was gratifying when KAICIID allowed the trainers to use any visual aid for presentation rather than be confined to the rather slow and cumbersome PowerPoint. This flexibility is something that KAICIID should be commended for, especially when it comes to cross-cultural and intercultural interaction.

As required by KAICIID, participants not only learned about MIL, but also had a chance to reflect on the way they use media and information.

Drawing lessons and examples from the local setting and always with a view to ensuring balance and sensitivity toward the diversity of religious opinions in the room during the training is a practice worth maintaining in all future interaction.

The KAICIID MIL curriculum adopts a non-prescriptive approach that can be used for various groups, not just religious ones. It identifies the main aims of each module, identifies the skills and knowledge that participants should demonstrate after completing each module and is adaptable to any situation.

Besides being used in workshops, this curriculum has the potential of being used in formal training at certificate, diploma or even degree level.

As if to demonstrate that the MILID training had worked, KAICIID ended the training with a public forum dubbed Dialogue Days 2014 in Nairobi that was held in cooperation with Arigatou International – Nairobi. The gathering brought together religious leaders, dialogue practitioners, policy-makers and media experts for training and discussion on these groups' roles in shaping perceptions of the religious 'Other' in the Horn and Great Lakes region of Africa.

Here in eastern Africa, MILID is not offered as a course in school. The closest the region comes to MIL is the seasonal civic education conducted by Non-Governmental Organisations (NGOs) in the run up to general elections. Yet well-formulated and implemented MIL programmes would not only empower voters but also equip citizens with holistic life skills.

References

Akwiri, J. (2014, November 4). Pro-government Kenyan Muslim cleric shot dead in Mombasa. Retrieved March 27, 2015, from reuters.com

BBC World Service Trust (2005). African Media Development Initiative. London, United Kingdom: BBC World Service Trust.

DPPS. (2015, February 8). North Eastern teachers given last chance to resume work, says DP William Ruto Read more at: Http://www.standardmedia.co.ke/article/2000151018/dp-north-eastern-teachers-given-last-chance-to-resume-work Retrieved March 27, 2015, from standardmedia.co.ke

IRIN News. (2014, July 28). Gunned down in Mombasa – the clerics that have died. Retrieved March 27, 2015, from irinnews.org

IRIN News. (2014, November 28). Terrorism hits education, health in Kenya's marginalized Mandera. Retrieved March 27, 2015, from irinnews.org

KAICIID Dialogue Centre (2014). Media Wise: Empowering Responsible Religious Leadership in the Digital Age. Vienna, Austria: King Abdullah Bin Abdulaziz International Centre for Interreligious and Intercultural Dialogue.

Kenya National Bureau of Statistics. (2011, January 1). Population and Housing Census 2009. Retrieved March 27, 2015, from knbs.or.ke

Lough, R. & Akwiri, J. (Reporters). (2012, September 2). Kenya Muslim riots expose political, economic rifts. Retrieved from http://www.reuters.com/article/2012/09/02/us-kenya-riots-idUSBRE88101L20120902

Mbiti, J. S. (1969). *African Religions and Philosophy*. Nairobi, Kenya: Heinemann Kenya Limited.

Ondego, O. (Reporter). (2014, November 16). Eastern African Religious Leaders Train in Media and Information Literacy. Retrieved from http://artmatters.info/books/2014/11/eastern-african-religious-leaders-train-in-media-and-information-literacy

Ondego, O. (2011). *How to Write On 1001 Subjects!* Nairobi, Kenya: ComMattersKenya.

Red C Research. (2012, July 12). Press Release: Religion and Atheism. Retrieved March 27, 2015, from redcresearch.ie

The Constitution of Kenya (2010). Nairobi, Kenya: National Council for Law Reporting with the Authority of the Attorney General

Wilson, C., Grizzle, A., Tuazon, R., Akyempong, K. & Cheung, C. K. (2011). *Media and Information Literacy: Curriculum for Teachers* (2011). Paris, France: UNESCO.

Intercultural Dialogue and the Practice of Making Video Letters between Japanese and Chinese Schools

Jun Sakamoto

This article advocates that raising critical thinking skills and the ability to analyze images mass media produces for children and young people is essential for future education. But raising critical viewing and thinking skills does not directly affect mutual understanding between countries. For understanding to improve, we need to connect inter-cultural understanding education and international exchange education with media and information literacy skills. I accomplish this via exchanging video letters and digital storytelling practices between Japanese and Chinese schools. Prior to the practice, Japanese students had negative preconceptions of China. But just one exchange of video letters has changed their attitude.

Exchange learning of video letters and digital storytelling works as the beginning stage of an intercultural collaboration approach in the context of developing children. MIL (media and information literacy) is an expanded definition of literacy and a powerful tool to enable intercultural dialogue, tolerance and cultural understanding. From this standpoint, the important thing is not establishing a formal subject or curriculum, but embedding the ideals and practices of MIL into all kinds of subjects. In order to do this, establishing an international network of collaborative research and practice is necessary.

Keywords: video letter, digital storytelling, intercultural dialogue, intercultural collaboration approach, media and information literacy

Introduction

One of the issues facing the world today is obviously the struggle among cultures. For instance, terrorist activities of ISIS (the Islamic State of Iraq and Syria) are galvanizing people all over the world against the horrors. Meanwhile, the frequency of terrorist acts and the violent conflict between Islamic and Western cultures produces prejudice and discrimination.

There are the same problems in East Asia. For instance, politically difficult problems such as territorial or historical disputes cause conflicts among East Asian countries. An especially big problem in Japan is the hate speech directed at Korean residents in Japan. Some rightwing groups, which include young people, hold demonstrations with hate speech everywhere in Japan and they voice opinions filled with prejudice toward Koreans and Chinese. The spread of the Internet not only connects people who have different cultures but also spreads prejudice and insecurity.

A survey of public opinion in Japan and China conducted by the Genron NPO showed that the respondents have an unfavorable impression of each country (The Genron NPO, 2014 September). 93.0% of Japanese respondents have an "unfavorable" (including "relatively unfavorable") impression of China. And 86.8% of Chinese respondents have an "unfavorable" impression of Japan. Responses to another question on the degree of interaction between Chinese and Japanese people revealed that only 3.5% of Japanese get information about China from direct communication with Chinese people. 96.5% of Japanese get information about China from Japanese media (TV programs, newspapers or the Internet). Likewise, 1.0% of Chinese get information about Japan by direct communication, and 91.4% of Chinese get this information from Chinese news media. One can see that the news media shape the image of the other country or at least has a strong effect on it.

Consequently, one has to advocate that raising critical thinking skills over and above those prejudiced preconceptions produced by the mass media to children and young people is essential for future education. But difficult points must be considered.

Firstly, many governments in the world have backwards thinking on media literacy education, which raises essential critical viewing and thinking skills among their own people. Regrettably, this is also applicable to East Asia. Secondly, raising critical viewing and thinking skills does not directly affect mutual understanding between countries. It is necessary for these skills to connect to programs that focus on inter-cultural understanding education and to international exchange programs. Thirdly, it is necessary to build international relationships and a multilateral framework because it is difficult for one country to solve these problems alone.

It is the Media and Information Literacy (MIL) program and movement by UNESCO and the United Nations Alliance of Civilizations (UNAOC) that offers this framework to the world. UNESCO states that it has "introduced the new concept of MIL into its strategy, thereby bringing together several interrelated concepts – such as information literacy, media literacy, ICT and digital literacy and other related aspects – under one umbrella concept" (UNESCO Global MIL Assessment Framework, 2013).

MIL not only includes critical viewing and thinking skills but "Expanded Literacy". MIL is regarded as an important tool of intercultural dialogue. "MIL can be a powerful tool to enable intercultural dialogue, tolerance and cultural understanding" (UNESCO MIL Policy and Strategy Guidelines, 2013). It is no wonder that UNESCO promotes such educational policies and movements because they are one of the organizations of the UN. Taking into consideration that discussions in Japan about media literacy or ICT education tend to be lacking a global viewpoint that includes developing countries, it stands to reason that Japan needs to adopt the MIL theory to promote new educational practices. In my program, I promote MIL by exchanging video letters and digital storytelling programs between Japanese and Chinese schools.

I started the practice in 2009. The Japan Forum (TJF) was introduced to the Dalian No.16 Middle School in China because it has a Japanese language course; a relationship with TJF, and one of my colleagues has a relationship with the Dalian University of Foreign Language (DLUFL). I coordinated the academic exchange agreement between DLUFL and Hosei University in 2012. This enabled me to hold the workshop at DLUFL.

In Chinese secondary schools, classes use computers, but there is no media literacy education, or analysis of the media and production. Since it is hard to do workshops in regular classrooms or computer classrooms, I was allowed to use a meeting room with a large display to conduct my workshops.

Meanwhile, the Hosei Daini Junior High School in Japan at which I hold workshops didn't have a media literacy course or curriculum either. I have run the program with these schools in a circumscribed way for about five years.

Digital Storytelling Workshop at Chinese University

In 2013, I held my workshops using an iPad mini at University and Secondary levels. I also taught digital storytelling production in the Japanese language course at DLUFL for the first time. Digital storytelling is the best way for students to create films of their own lives. It started out as a way to tell a story about their own roots. I currently teach a digital storytelling workshop in the "Introduction of Lifelong learning and Career studies" class that has about 300 freshman students every year. I provided a similar workshop at DLUFL.

Currently 33 students learning Japanese at DLUFL attend my workshop. I hold a workshop in cooperation with Ms. Yan Sun, who is a lecturer in the Japanese language department. Students expressed an interest in works Japanese students had made and this challenged them to produce their own works. As digital storytelling is composed of images and narration, narration has a key role. In the case of recording in a foreign language, it requires not only language skill but also the ability to express ideas clearly. In contrast, as a video letter is composed of moving images, narration and subtitles, students don't need foreign language skills. The main point is the movement. For this reason, video letters made for foreign schools are more suitable for secondary and elementary schools.

Video Letter Workshop at a Junior High School in Japan

In July 2014, I held a workshop making video letters at the Hosei Daini Junior High School with my students for 3 days. 70 third grade students participated in the workshop and were divided into 14 groups of 5 members. I taught it in tandem with Mr. Kan-ichi Ohba, a teacher of the school. University students from my seminar supported each group.

On the first day, I showed the objective of the workshop to the students, which got them talking about images of China. It was found that they had negative images of it, such as air pollution or fake products based on the comments they wrote. Certain students had preconceptions that Chinese people disliked Japanese people. Relying on the students existing information resources and knowledge of China, 25 of them answered that they got their information from TV, 6 of them from the newspaper, 2 of them from the Internet, but nobody answered that their information came from a Chinese acquaintance. Therefore, their negative images of China come mostly from TV.

After that, I taught them how to make a video letter, and got them to think of topics on which their video letter should focus. Most of the themes they picked were the introduction of the city or school. Some of them picked play or anime in Japan. After picking the theme, I explained how to create a storyboard, how to use an iPad mini, and how to shoot images. University students supported the groups as they picked their themes and created their storyboards.

On the second day, after creating a storyboard, each group began shooting, recording narration and editing their footage. The last day, we had a presentation meeting. Each group presented the results of their creation. I found that they had made concerted efforts to improve their new skills in making video letters to convey their messages.

Video Letter Workshop at the Dalian No.16 Middle School

I visited the Dalian No.16 Middle School to do a workshop on making video letters on October 31 and November 3. First, I sent a DVD of the video letters the Japanese students had made. Because the class periods in China only lasted 50 min, I sent it in advance. 14 high school students (2 of them boys) in their second year participated in the workshop. I divided them into seven groups with seven iPad minis for making the video letters.

Almost all of the students pointed out that the Japanese school was clean, school life seemed interesting, and Japanese students seemed to be courteous. Since they were taking a Japanese class, the class might have already given them a very positive preconception of Japan. But there was a big difference between the perceptions of the Japanese students of China versus the Chinese students perception of Japan.

I conducted the class in cooperation with Ms. Wang Hu a teacher of Japanese language. Two students of DLUFL also supported us in the same way as before. They had experience in making digital storytelling works and had supported students at this school in 2013. As a result, the workshop ran as smoothly as expected. Students could get advice directly from students of DLUFL when they had questions even over the weekend, as these students were well respected as learners of Japanese and video makers. For the middle school students, the University students were role models because the middle school students wanted to learn Japanese just like the older students. For the University students, they gained great teaching experience from the middle school students.

On November 3, we had an edit and presentation meeting. I found that though they struggled on production, the students enjoyed the workshop just as much as the Hosei Daini Junior High School students had. They understood each other as classmates, and they focused on conveying their messages as plainly as they could. The university students looked back on their experience as enlightening as they were able to produce their own digital storytelling by supporting the junior students.

I sent the works of the Chinese students to the teacher of the Hosei Daini Junior High School students. The teacher showed the students the videos. What did they get and feel from them? The most popular comment was that the Japanese spoken by Chinese students in the video letter was good. Some of them wrote "It's nice Japanese with such enthusiasm", "I felt bad that I only speak Japanese even though that they spoke Japanese", "We can understand Dalian No.16 Middle School because they spoke Japanese well for us".

Other students pointed out that the quality was very high. Some of the comments were: "Their works are more intricate than ours", "They are very good and ingenious", "They are easily understood", and "The students are good at editing". In this instance, high quality meant that the Chinese students' messages got through distinctly to the Japanese students.

Others wrote about Chinese towns or daily life of the students as follows: "I understand the daily life of Chinese students", "The works transmitted the appealing Chinese culture", "They seem to be having fun at the night food stalls or karaoke", or drew a comparison between each culture as follows: "I see both similar and different items, but most of them look similar because China is a cultural neighbor", "There are foods that are not in Japan, they look yummy", "I am glad there is Japanese culture even in China".

There are no negative comments on China or Chinese culture. The following comments represent the voice of the Japanese students, "I want to visit China", "The image that I had before has changed". Just one exchange of video letters changed the Japanese students' attitudes.

Conclusion

I advocate an intercultural dialogue process in three phases, namely *Correspondence*, *Communication*, and *Collaboration*. I call it "the Intercultural Collaboration Approach". In this instance, correspondence means exchange of letters. At this phase, students need to have skills creating messages and analyzing them as a part of MIL. The exchange of video letters and digital storytelling works are also a phase of correspondence. But from the point of the intercultural dialogue developing process, it is just a beginning stage. We have to reach to the phase of Intercultural Collaboration as the goal.

For those of whom study abroad opportunities are scarce, communication with students who live in other countries is difficult. But tablet devices provide a chance to overcome this difficulty, by making a simple way to create and analyze movies.

It is best to exchange video letters and digital storytelling works at the beginning stage of the intercultural collaboration approach in the context of developing children. This cultivates the power of expression, imagination, cooperation with others, and cultivates reading skills by requiring that students analyze video letters that others produce. After the phases of correspond and communication are completed, children who have different cultural backgrounds can work together toward one goal like a joint project or co-production of a work. This brings in the phase of collaboration. The goal of intercultural collaboration is creation of new value by intercultural dialogue.

The collaboration phase needs teachers and students with specific abilities and bringing what they learned from their experiences from the correspondence and communication phases. I think that the goal of MIL education is to spread the learning of the Intercultural Collaboration method to the world and establish the Borderless Learning Community.

It is challenging for Chinese researchers to introduce an MIL curriculum into the formal schooling system. Qinyi Tan and her co-researchers included a quotation from Chen Changfeng's stating, "The awareness of media literacy education is important, but it is quite difficult to introduce it to the formal schooling system. Because the establishment of an independent discipline, the training of teachers, curriculum system settings, the establishment of the examination and evaluation system, and the cultivation of social cognition, require a long development process" (Tan. Q et al., 2012). The MIL situation in Japan is almost the same as in China.

As mentioned at the beginning of this article, MIL is an expanded definition of literacy and a powerful tool to enable intercultural dialogue, tolerance and cultural understanding. From this standpoint, it is possible to practice MIL education even though it is not in a formal curriculum. This situation was made possible mainly due to sharing an educational ideal between teachers and students of both countries. In other words, the important thing is not establishing a formal subject or curriculum, but embedding the ideals and practices of MIL in to all kinds of subjects, and in order to do this, establishing an international network of collaborative research and practice is necessary.

References

The Genron NPO. (2014 September). The 10th Japan-China Public Opinion Poll Analysis Report on the Comparative Data. Retrieved March 2015 from http://www.genron-npo.net/en/pp/archives/5153.html

UNESCO Communication & Information Sector. (2013). *Global MIL Assessment Framework: Country Readiness and Competencies*. Paris, France:UNESCO. p.30. Retrieved March 2015 from http://www.unesco.org/new/en/communication-and-information/ resources/publications-and-communication-materials/publications/fulllist/global-media-and-information-literacy-assessment-framework/

UNESCO Communication & Information Sector. (2013). *MIL Policy and Strategy Guidelines*. (Eds. A. Grizzle & M. C. Torras.) Paris, France: UNESCO. p.18 Retrieved March 2015 from http://www.unesco.org/new/en/communication-and-information/ resources/publications-and-communication-materials/publications/full-list/media-and-information-literacy-policy-and-strategy-guidelines/

Sakamoto, J. & Murakami, K. (2013). The 'Culture Quest' Project Media and Information Literacy & Cross Cultural Understanding, In Carlsson, U. & Culver, S. H. (Eds): *Media and Information Literacy and Intercultural Dialogue. MILID Yearbook 2013*. Gothenburg, Sweden: Nordicom. p.387-397.

Tan, Q., Xiang, Q., Zhang, J., Teng, L. & Yao, J. (2012). Media Literacy Education in Mainland China: A Historical Overview. *International Journal of Information and Education Technology*, 2(4).

Towards a Global Strategy for Media and Information Literacy

José Manuel Pérez Tornero, Santiago Tejedor
& Marta Portalés Oliva

This article describes the recent activity of the Gabinete de Comunicación y Educación (Communication and Education Research Group) in cooperation with the UNESCO-UNAOC International University Network on Media and Information Literacy and Intercultural Dialogue (MILID University Network). Some of these activities were implemented while the Autonomous University of Barcelona (UAB) served as Chair of the MILID University Network. In this context, the article describes the recent research efforts completed in 2014 by describing the outcomes of two major European projects EMEDUS – European Media Literacy Education Study and FilmEd – Film Education in Europe: Showing Films and other audiovisual content in European Schools – Obstacles and Best Practices. It also gives a snapshot of UAB's strategy for the period 2013/3014 which aimed to: a) Support efforts to unify globally the actions being pursued among researchers, universities, organizations and other stakeholders through the creation of different events and the outlines of common work paths and b) Contribute to the transmission of MIL among students for their professional development and the fostering of intercultural dialogue among them.

Keywords: media and information literacy, EMEDUS, FilmED, MIL observatory, MIL global strategy

Introduction

The Communication and Education Research Group (*Gabinete de Comunicación y Educación*)[1] was constituted in 1994 and belongs to the department of Journalism and Communication Sciences at the Autonomous University of Barcelona (UAB). The members are specialized in research, development and scientific transfer related to media and information literacy (MIL). Major projects have been granted to the group by the Spanish Ministry of Culture, Sport and Education, and the European Commission and their work has been recognized by the Government of Catalonia (*Generalitat de Catalunya*). Their aim is to encourage research on communication and education by studying the integration of new communication technologies and development of MIL pedagogical methodologies into society.

European Research Projects – the Five Things You Should Know about EMEDUS and FilmEd

EMEDUS – European Media Literacy Education Study[2]

1. Policy recommendations: EMEDUS proposes national educational policies after analyzing the areas formal education, informal education and disadvantaged groups of 27 member states.

2. Overview reports: Individual country reports have been published, which explore the actual inclusion of MIL in each of the states in relation with their educational policies.

3. Databases on media literacy: Research has also advanced in the exploration and gathering of data composed of organizations and institutions, literature related to media literacy, international and national experts, and audio-visual records of the EMEDUS research.

4. Final conference: First European Media and Information Literacy Forum in Paris.

5. MIL observatory launch: European Media and Information Literacy Observatory (EMILO).

These activities were funded with the support of the European Commission. The project was coordinated by the Autonomous University of Barcelona with the following partners: European Association for Viewers' Interest (EAVI) in Belgium, Minho University in Portugal, Institute for Educational Research and Development (OFI) in Hungary, the Institute for Political, Social and Economic studies (EURISPES) in Italy, and the School of Communication and Media and Pedagogical University of Krakow in Poland.

FilmEd – Showing Films and Other Audio-Visual Content in European Schools – Obstacles and Best Practices[3]

1. Policy recommendations: FilmEd supports the European Commission within the context of film literacy policies by identifying the existing situation concerning the use of audio-visual content in primary and secondary schools.

2. Overwiev of the report: The report reflects on film literacy pedagogical practices: the acquisition of audio-visual media production and creativity

skills, the creation of young European audiences and the educational value of European heritage film. The study maps current copyright policies in each of the countries, ensuring reliable data on the situation of the educational use of films from the perspective of both consumers and creators of content.

3. Methodology: FilmEd provides statistical evidence from a survey of 6,000 teachers and in-depth consultation with experts and stakeholders. National analysis was carried in each member country of the European Union about the pedagogical use of audiovisual-content in schools. The following factors were considered: technology and infrastructures, content, intellectual property right use, and pedagogical activity.

4. Databases: FilmEd reports on good practices and initiatives that have been implemented in different European countries within the field, considering three angles: the educational, the legal, and the relationship with the film industry.

5. Conference: FilmEd Learning Experiences Seminar in Barcelona. Different stakeholders were gathered to put in common film literacy initiatives.

The study was carried out among the 28 Member States of the European Union. In addition, the European Economic Area Member States and Switzerland component of the study was undertaken by a Consortium composed by the Autonomous University of Barcelona, the European Think Tank on Film and Film Policy (Denmark), CUMEDIAE – Culture and Media Agency and Europe (Belgium) – and AEDE, the European Association of Teachers (Belgium).

A Global Strategy for MIL – the Path to the Launch of a MIL Observatory

During 2014 the Communication and Education Research Group of the Autonomous University of Barcelona has organized and supported different events in order to unify globally the efforts being pursued among researchers, universities, organizations and other stakeholders.

European Media and Information Literacy Forum[4] (Paris – May 2014)

The Forum was held on May 27 and 28, 2014 at the UNESCO Headquarters in Paris. This conference was funded by the European Commission and UNESCO within the Media Literacy Action. It registered approximately 350 participants from around 50 different countries, who attended the following 14 sessions: "New world, new literacies", "Formal education: new curriculum", "MIL and intercultural dialogue", "Research and assessment on MIL", "New action lines:

249

European project's recommendations", "Regulatory authorities and MIL", "Family, media and MIL", "MIL and policy implications", "The European context: Building the new media and information literacy paradigm", "Global Alliance for Partnership on Media and Information Literacy – GAPMIL", "Promoting film literacy", "Informal education, social inclusion and MIL", "Media industry and MIL", "Conclusions, adoption of Paris Declaration on MIL, and Launch of the European chapter of GAPMIL and Closing sessions".

The event ended with the adoption of the Paris Declaration[5] and served to encourage the creation of diverse collaborative platforms such as the European Chapter of the Global Alliance for Partnerships on Media and Information Literacy (GAPMIL) and the European Media Information Literacy Observatory (EMILO).

Global Alliance for Partnership on Media and Information Literacy (GAPMIL)[6]

This initiative of UNESCO Communication and Information Sector was born during the Global Forum for Partnerships on MIL, Incorporating the International Conference on MIL and Intercultural Dialogue which was held from 26th to 28th June 2013 in Abuja (Nigeria). GAPMIL aims to promote cooperation among organizations, enterprises and associations in order to ensure access to media and information competences to all citizens.

FilmEd Learning Experiences[7] (Barcelona – June 2014)

This conference organized on 12th to 13th June 2014 gathered film education experts, industry professionals and international students at the Filmoteca de Catalunya in order to discuss and propose film literacy initiatives in Europe and pedagogical implementation of films in schools.

In the following sessions different themes related to the legal framework of copyright and the obstacles faced by schools to develop film literacy were debated: "Learning and teaching audiovisual language", "The place of cinema in European education", "Case studies: Presentation of experiences in Spain", "Case studies: Presentation of experiences in Europe", "School and cinema – literature, art, music, history", "Promoting film literacy in Europe", "FilmEd project presentation", "Discussion on copyright and licenses obstacles relating to film education" and "Film literacy and film industry".

Latin American and Caribbean Media and Information Literacy Forum[8] (Mexico Distrito Federal – December 2014)

This conference was held from December 10 to 11 in Mexico City. It was hosted by the National Autonomous University of Mexico (through TV UNAM) and the National Public Broadcasting System of Mexico, with the Autonomous University of Barcelona and UNESCO as co-organizer. More than 300 international stakeholders, mainly from Latin American and Caribbean countries gathered at the Centro Cultural Universitario Tlatelolco. They debated the assumption of new technologies among educational contexts in their countries. During the event the Mexico Declaration on MIL[9] was adopted and the Observatorio Latinoamericano y del Caribe de Alfabetización Mediática e Informacional (OLCAMI)[10] was lauched.

European Media and Information Literacy Observatory (EMILO)[11]

EMILO aims to explore and systematize the European activity being achieved by organizations, experts and policy makers in the field of MIL. The research platform disseminates the exploration of the actual MIL policies in 27 European Countries (EMEDUS) and monitors different databases of recent publications, organizations and experts. Different Universities will build together a core of research to foster exchange and cooperation among different MIL actors in order to be a reference for policy-making.

Educational Transmission of MIL

The Communication and Education Group has been offering professional development in the field of MIL during 21 years. Since 1994 international students from all around the world come to study MIL theory and practical methodologies in order to implement them at their home countries.

Media and Information Literacy and Intercultural Dialogue (MILID) Summer School[12]

The MILID Summer School is organized since 2013 during the first week of June and has as its main topic MIL and intercultural dialogue. Participation is open to all international students and counts on the yearly participation of the Arab Academy represented by Professor Samy Tayie from Cairo University.

Within the framework of the MILID Summer School students collaborate at the Young Journalists Platform[13] divided into groups of radio, online press and television production. It was created as a part of a UNESCO supported project that was connected to the second MILID Week celebration in Egypt in 2013. It aims to set up an intercultural network of young journalists and information specialists with alternative views and research approaches embedded in intercultural dialogue.

Master's Degree in Communication and Education[14] (on-campus and online editions)

The classes highly rely on theory and practice through seminars, lectures and workshops, that encourage debate, critical and analytical thinking. The syllabus is based on three areas: educational media and technology, knowledge society and media and digital society, and project management.

Tahina-Can[15]

For 10 years the journalistic expedition Tahina-Can awakens cultural diversity awareness by implementing workshops about radio, television and photography among the participating students, which are selected for their outstanding performance in university subjects. The academic programme of the expedition involves cooperation and development activities, which allow them to discover and analyze media perspectives and cultural representations of the country they visit. Uzbekistan, Thailand, Morroco, Chile, Ecuador, Peru, Dominican Republic and Mexico, are among the visited countries.

Olympics on Cyberjournalism

A project developed in the Dominican Republic and Mexico, it aims to bring the concept of MIL to students from different universities. The initiatives simulates the structure of the Olympic Games, the different editions of this competition have provided theoretical and practical training to the students. The main objective is to enhance the participants' sensitivity towards a critical and qualitative use of: communication media, their messages, and the different collaborative platforms in the web. Under the project's framework, students had to create their own media and promote democratic values, train their critical thinking and ethical use of ICT.

Recent Publications

The Communication and Education Research Group stands out for its dissemination of numerous reports and monographs, based on their research and projects. The following recent titles are related to MIL:

Media Literacy and Intercultural Dialogue[16] (Ediciones Sehen)

This book presents a selection of texts discussed at conferences, seminars and reflexive sessions during the MILID Week 2012 and 2013. Each of these texts starts with the idea of MIL in relation with issues regarding strategy, debates and good practices.

Media Literacy and New Humanism[17] (*Alfabetización Mediática y Nuevo Humanismo* – Universitat Oberta de Catalunya Editorial)

This book is the result of a seven-year collaboration between José Manuel Pérez Tornero (UAB, Spain) and Tapio Varis (University of Tampere, Finland), both are European Commission experts in digital literacy policies. The work is an approach to media literacy in a holistic, critical and sociocultural approach. The authors formulate basic principles and point out an agenda to enhance the contribution of media literacy to intercultural dialogue.

Media Literacy and the General Law on Audiovisual Communication in Spain[18] (*La Alfabetización mediática y la ley general de comunicación audiovisual en España* – Universitat Oberta de Catalunya Editorial)

The book written by Juan Carlos Gavara and José Manuel Pérez Tornero presents a systematic study framed in the European legislation about the right to MIL in Spain exposed in the General Law on Audiovisual Communication (LGCA), promotes the right to education, active citizenship and participatory democracy. The reach of the law's development in the actual information society is decisive among economic, creative, culture, education and participatory issues.

Technology Guide on Communication and Education for Teachers: Questions and Answers[19] (*Guía de Tecnología, Comunicación y Educación para profesores: Preguntas y Respuestas* – Universitat Oberta de Catalunya Editorial)

The guide is a tool for teachers and researchers wishing to approach MIL from a theoretical and practical perspective. The book includes recommendations, explanations and reflections on the pedagogical use of Internet in and out of the classroom. It is presented as an everyday working tool for any teacher or researcher interested in the use of ICT at educational environments. The book was written by the students of the Communication and Education Master students under the guidance of José Manuel Pérez Tornero and Santiago Tejedor.

Notes

1. Communication and Education Research Group (*Gabinete de Comunicación y Educación*): http://www.gabinetecomunicacionyeducacion.com/ Retrieved May 6, 2015.
2. EMEDUS available at: http://www.eumedus.com/ Retrieved May 6, 2015.
3. FilmEd available at: http://filmedeurope.wordpress.com/ Retrieved May 6, 2015.
4. European Media and Information Literacy Forum: www.europeanmedialiteracyforum.org/ Retrieved May 6, 2015.
5. Paris Declaration Document available at: http://www.unesco.org/new/en/communication-and-information/resources/news-and-in-focus-articles/in-focus-articles/2014/paris-declaration-on-media-and-information-literacy-adopted/ Retrieved May 6, 2015.
6. GAPMIL: www.unesco.org/new/en/communication-and-information/media-development/media-literacy/global-alliance-for-partnerships-on-media-and-information-literacy/ Retrieved May 6, 2015.
7. FilmEd Learning Experiences: www.filmedlearningexperiences.blogspot.com Retrieved May 6, 2015

8   Latin American and Caribbean Media and Information Literacy Forum: http://www.foroamilac.org/ (Spanish) http://www.lacmilforum.org/ (English) Retrieved May 6, 2015.

9   Mexico Declarationon on MIL (Spanish): http://www.gabinetecomunicacionyeducacion.com/files/adjuntos/Declaracion_Mexico.pdf Retrieved May 6, 2015.

10   OLCAMI: http://latinamericanmedialiteracy.com/index.php?lang=es Retrieved May 6, 2015.

11   EMILO: http://www.europeanmilobservatory.org/ Retrieved May 6, 2015.

12   MILID Summer School: https://milidsummerschool.wordpress.com/ Retrieved May 6, 2015.

13   Young Journalists Platform: http://youngjournalists.org/index.php/en/ (English) http://youngjournalists.org/index.php/es/ (Spanish) Retrieved May 6, 2015.

14   Master's Degree in Communication and Education: www.mastercomunicacionyeducacion.wordpress.com/ Retrieved May 6, 2015.

15   Tahina-Can available at http://www.tahina-can.org Retrieved May 6, 2015.

16   Media Literacy and Intercultural Dialogue available at: http://www.gabinetecomunicacionyeducacion.com/files/adjuntos/Libro.pdf Retrieved May 6, 2015.

17   Media Literacy and New Humanism available at: http://www.editorialuoc.cat/alfabetizacinmediticaynuevohumanismo-p-984.html?cPath=1 Retrieved May 6, 2015.

18   Media Literacy and the General Law on Audiovisual Communication in Spain available at: http://www.editorialuoc.cat/laalfabetizacinmediticaylaleygeneraldecomunicacinaudiovisualenespaa-p-1044.html?cPath=1 Retrieved May 6, 2015.

19   Technology Guide on Communication and Education for Teacher- Questions and Answers available at: http://www.editorialuoc.cat/guadetecnologacomunicacinyeducacinparaprofesores-p-1334.html?cPath= Retrieved May 6, 2015.

Gender Equality
and Persons
with Disabilities

Communication Strategies for Effective Participation of Women in Healthcare Programmes in Rural Nigeria

*Adebola Adewunmi Aderibigbe
& Anjuwon Josiah Akinwande*

*The well-being of the rural population is important for the continued sustenance of the ur-
ban dwellers. This is because the survival of the latter is dependent on the former. Important but often neglected populations are the rural women. Several studies show that rural
women in Nigeria are poor and deprived of requisite social resources for development. Their
participation in development efforts has been low over the years. However, certain factors
determine how effectively they participate in development programmes. Primary amongst
them are the choice of communication methods employed to reach them. This study evaluated the communication and information strategies employed at the rural level to encourage participation of women in selected development programmes. Women in selected
states in the south west geopolitical zone were target population. The states that presented
substantial rural indices were given priority. Qualitative methods were used to obtain data.
The study found that radio is most effective for encouraging participation of women in development programmes. The market as a venue-oriented communication medium showed
significant prospect as an important interpersonal avenue for dialogue on development.
Finally, the study found that communication messages are more localized on radio than
they were in the print medium.*

Keywords: women empowerment, participation, healthcare programmes, localism

Introduction

The Millennium Development Goal Initiative is perhaps an outstanding principle of the United Nations that has had a significant effect on developing nations
since its launch. A critical look at the eight goals shows that six of these goals
are focused on women. How? The first goal statement is to eradicate poverty

and hunger. Women are adjudged the poorest socio-economically and by access to productive opportunities. The second statement is to achieve universal primary education. The ratio of the girl/boy child education has always been a contending issue. The third statement is to promote gender equality and empowerment of women. A lot of work has been done here, but there is a lot more to be achieved. The reduction of child mortality and the improvement of maternal health are the fourth and fifth respective statements, while the fight against HIV/AIDS, malaria and other diseases makes the sixth goal. We can heave a sigh of relief on the HIV/AIDs pandemic; it appears that the war is near a state of peaceful resolution with great management going on across Africa. But, some scholars have only adduced this to mere reduction in the volume, while the music lingers. We have yet to win the war on malaria however.

An unpopular assumption in Africa is that the empowerment of women is a prerequisite for an improved development of the family, particularly the children and the extended family at large. Before effective empowerment can be achieved, the well-being (physical as a matter of priority) of the women is sacrosanct. And this is perhaps a fundamental challenge in Nigeria. The question of quality of and access to good health infrastructure and security has over the years become a nagging issue in our national polity. The most affected of course are the rural women in the country, where there is a disparaging setup of health facilities for the rural populace. Yet, amidst this condition, women still eke out a living and in some cases serve as bread winners.

These authors are of the opinion that democratic participation is perhaps the only avenue by which sustainable development can be attained in Africa. However, several forms of participation are noticeable from the development programmes that are directed at the rural populace. The discussion on participation has moved beyond integrating the people in development. The discussion now is how locally involving are the communication content/strategies employed to reach the rural populace? Who decides the contents, the recipient or the development planners? Discussion on localism is advanced in this article as a way to alert the United Nations for future goal implementation, especially in Africa.

Research Questions

With a view to proffering solutions to the problem of the study, the following questions were raised:

1. What form of communication methods (print, broadcast, traditional media or interpersonal) was/were employed to reach the women in the last ten years?

2. To what extent were these communication methods useful in moving the women into adopting the health development programmes?

Review of Literature

Akinwunmi (2013) advanced that a nation whose rural areas remain undeveloped is definitely backward. The rural area is perhaps the most important section of any forward-looking country. This is because the continued survival of the urban area is largely dependent on the wellbeing of the rural population. Also, the major economic survival of the urban is a function of how truly healthy the rural area is. For instance, the raw materials for food, clothing and shelter are an import from the rural area.

Against this backdrop, Okunna (2002) notes that development is a change for the better that must benefit a majority of the people and should entail a process that is participatory in nature, involving the people as closely as possible. Development has to be ruralized, people-centred and human-focused. Development should be planted and nourished in the rural areas with the support of locally generated and natural resources. To corroborate this, Salawu (2008) states that the purpose of development communication is to understand the needs and social realities of the people and to mobilize them towards the development goals.

According to Lasiele (1999), women can be described as an indispensable group in the development of any nation. Also, according to National Population Commission in National Bureau of Statistics (2010), the 2006 population statistics put the number of Nigerian women at about 69 million, which is almost fifty percent of the total population of 140 million. Apart from that numerical strength, women have great potential that is necessary to evolve into a new economic order, to accelerate social and political development and consequently transform the society into a better place to live. Olawoye (1985) described Nigerian women as a crucial factor for development. They assume this status because they are largely responsible for the bulk production of crops, agro-based food processing, preservation of crops and distribution of yields from farm centres to urban areas.

The adoption of the Primary Health Care (PHC) model by Nigeria since 1987 ensures that every rural community has a primary health centre post, bringing healthcare almost to the doorstep of the rural dwellers. This model has an in-built mechanism for community ownership and participation in the healthcare delivery at the centre specifying who should be involved in the community meetings. According to the PHC model, the Chief, a police officer, a headmaster of a school and the primary care coordinator (usually a nurse; in charge of the primary health care centre) constitute the Community Health Committee (CHC) of the health centre.

The complex nature of the relationship between the rural community and the supposed expert representative made scholars conclude that the model was incongruous. This brought about the incongruous paradigm. Scholars however proposed the community participation model, which is an integrative system that engages community members in the collection of meaningful and reliable qualitative and quantitative data through community forums, observations, interviews, town hall meetings, focus groups, and video/photo voice methodologies for community groups, community health workers as well as the Community Health Committees (CHC) of all health centres (Ndep, 2014).

The democratic participant theory was given the needed popularity by Denis McQuail. This was to meet the unique peculiarities of the developing nations, as they were not adequately addressed by the four theories of the press advanced by Siebert, Peterson, and Schram in the 1950s. The principles of the theory as given by Denis McQuail in Anaeto (2008, p. 68) are as follows:

- Individual citizen and minority groups have rights of access to the media (right to communicate and right to be served by the media according to their own determination of need).

- The organization and content of the media should not be subject to centralized political or state bureaucratic control.

- The media exist primarily for the audience and not for media organizations, professionals, or clients of the media.

- Groups, organizations, and local communities should own their own media.

- Small-scale, interactive, and participative media forms are better than large scale, one-way, and professional media.

The democratic participant theory calls for devolution of media authority. It seeks pluralism of the media rather than the needs, interests, and aspirations of the receiver. It calls for democracy in the media, i.e., the media should be interactive and participative – the people should be involved. It also calls for the establishment of small media by local communities and groups, so they can meet their own needs; and that potential users of the media can have access to them.

In line with the idea of localism in communication for development, one of the principles of the democratic participant theory states that local communities should have their own media. This is referred to in this article as localism in media channel, i.e. using community media (rural community radio, rural community newspaper, community viewing centre) and the traditional media (theatre, dance, story-telling, etc.) in communication for development. Another principle which favours the idea of localism states that the media should serve the people according to their own needs. This is referred to as localism in media content, packaging and presenting information according to the development needs of the people to help bring about development.

Method of the Study

Data for the study were obtained through the qualitative method of focus group discussion. To achieve this, some of the respondents were recruited as moderators. A total of 912 women were selected from 40 wards within 20 local government areas across three states of the south-west geopolitical zone. The states are Osun, Ogun and Oyo. The choice of these states was informed by the presence of substantial rural indices of density of rural population and availability of the development programmes. The multi-stage cluster sampling approach was employed. The interview was conducted in the local dialect with competent research assistants employed in the selected wards. The rationale for the adoption of this method is simply because the researchers consider it to be the most appropriate. Appropriateness here simply refers to the linguistic competence of interviewers in their local dialect.

Summary of Findings

The study found that a variety of communication methods were used for development programmes. They included indigenous, group and conventional media of radio, television and community newspaper where they are available. The study found that methods that involved literacy skills did not drive participation. Radio stood out as an important medium for involving women in development programmes and opportunities. Also, the market showed amazing prospects for encouraging participation in development programmes. The women valued an interpersonal encounter more than a mediated one.

These findings support a number of research studies carried out before this one. Moemeka (2012) advocated the use of an integrated strategy, which he calls a combination of interpersonal and mass media strategies, blending into one with the aim of eliminating their limitations and problems and maximizing their potentials and strengths. It is on record as captured by Akinwande (2009) that both government and international development agencies have used the mass media in combination with interpersonal and media channels to stimulate dialogue among the otherwise passive viewers to speak and discuss burning issues in rural development and social change.

The finding also shows that radio still has a great reach to the women, but with an outstanding gap to reach the others. This is in agreement with FAO (Food and Agriculture Organization) Documentary Repository (2012) that states that radio remains the most powerful, and yet the cheapest mass medium for reaching large numbers of people in isolated areas because it can be used for training and the transfer of technologies. It can promote dialogue and debate on the major issues of need for rural women including their opinions and aspirations.

Much as the above is true and in agreement with the findings of the work, the second part of the FAO documentary is not applicable. The second part states that "radio enables women to voice their concern and speak about their aspirations with the external partners, such as national policy makers and development planners". The FAO is speaking from the position of the democratic participant theory that articulates democracy in media. The theory states that media should be interactive and participative and should exist primarily for their audiences and not for media organizations, professionals or clients of the media. There is, however, a question as to the level of participation the media gives to women in Nigeria. There is no doubt that radio is effective in reaching women, but there is however a concern as to the level of participation and contribution the women have through radio as they are expected to be involved in the content production process.

Conclusion and Recommendations

Knowledge and information are essential for people to respond to the opportunities and challenges of social and economic changes. But, this will not make significant meaning except if they are communicated. It is when they are communicated that they become useful. Communication is basically about sharing meanings and trying to affect or influence behavior. MacBride et al. (1981) in Laninhun (2003, p. 72) opine that communication should pursue three aims:

1. Increase understanding of development problems

2. Build up a spirit of solidarity in a common effort; and

3. Enlarge the capacity of men and women to take charge of their
   own development

In light of the findings outlined above, it is safe to conclude that the rural population in south-west Nigeria receive health information messages and to an extent participate in same. But there is a need to encourage further participation through localism of the communication directed to them. The following is a succinct guide into the understanding of localism through outlined recommendations.

1. **Localism in message content:** The message of our communication for development should be focused on things particular to the community and their development needs. The development needs of one community are undoubtedly different from another. The prognostic conception that African communities are bereft of commonsense should be discarded. The community, regardless of their level of literacy, should form an important variable in the decision-making process and the communication content.

2. **Localism in media channel:** The communication for development should be localized in terms of channels. Nigeria is ripe for a holistic community media (radio in the interim). Through such form of medium, the people can then participate further in solving their own problem.

Appendix

Table 1. List of examined health development programmes

S/N	Health Development Programmes
1.	Baby Friendly Initiative
2.	Prevention of Mother-to-Child Transmission of HIV/AIDS
3.	Female Genital Cutting
4.	HIV/AIDS Prevention
5.	Roll Back Malaria Initiative
6.	Breast Cancer Awareness

Table 2. List of examined communication/information methods for encouraging participation

S/N	Communication Methods	Features
1.	Electronic	Radio, Television
2.	Print	Newspapers, Pamphlets, Flyers
3.	Traditional Media	Dance, Drama, Folktales, Festivals
4.	Interpersonal	Market

References

Akinwande, A. J. (2009). Media Techniques in Adult Education and Community Development. In Bamisaye, O. A, Nwazuoke I. A. & Okediran A. (Eds), *Education this Millenium-Innovations on Theory & Practice*. Ibadan: Ibadan University Press.

Akinwunmi, O. A. (2013). An Appraisal of Communication Strategies Used for Women's Participation in Development. *Journal of Communication and Media Research*. 5(2), p. 66-69.

Anaeto, S. G. (2008). Localism in Communication for Development in a Globalized World. In Mojaye, E. C. et al. (2008). *Globalization and Development Communication in Africa*. Ibadan: Ibadan University Press.

FAO Corporate Document Repository in http://www.fao.org/docrep/x2550e/x2550e04.htm Retrieved on April 14, 2015.

Laninhun, A. (2003). Communicating for Development Purposes: A Gender Perspective. In Soola, E. O. (Ed.): *Communicating for Development Purposes*. Ibadan: Kraft Books Limited. pp.72-79

Lasiele, Y. A. (1999). Women Empowerment in Nigeria: Problems, Prospects and Implications for Counselling. *The Counsellor*. Downloaded on May 04, 2015 from http://www.google.com.ng/url?q=https://www.unilorin.edu.ng/publications/lasiele/Women%2520Empowerment%2520in%2520Nigeria.pdf&sa=U&ei=RhpHVZCII4HwUqiUgZgE&ved=0CBEQFjAA&usg=AFQjCNEg0JNf1H4oa-_AAWmf7HFU0439DQ

Moemeka, A. A. (2012). Development Communication: Strategies and Methods. In Moemeka, A. A. (Ed): *Development Communication in Action: Building Understanding and Creating Participation*. Maryland: University Press of America. p.113

National Bureau of Statistics (2010). Annual Abstract of Statistics. Retrieved on May 1, 2015 from http://www.google.com.ng/url?sa=t&rct=j&q=&esrc=s&source=web&cd=2&cad=rja&uact=8&ved=0CCEQFjAB&url=http%3A%2F%2Fwww.nigerianstat.gov.ng%2Fpages%2Fdownload%2F170&ei=lgNRVdblEIXD7gaZgoGgDQ&usg=AFQjCNF6_fjMGfa8fVpOROyLBWZT90i5uA&sig2=3QJh2eEY2lGtUKoBB0CuTQ

Ndep, A. O. (2014). Informed Community Participation is Essential to reducing Maternal Mortality in Nigeria. *International Journal of Health and Psychology Research*. 2, p. 29

Okunna, C. S. (2002). A Quick Look at Development Communication Systems. In Okunna, C. S. (Ed.): *Teaching Mass Communication: A Multi-Dimensional Approach*. Enugu: New Generation Books. pp. 292-294.

Olawoye, J. E. (1985). Rural Women's Roles in Agricultural Production: An Occupational Survey of Women from Six Selected Rural Communities in Oyo State. *Nigerian Journal of Rural Sociology*. 2(1). p. 18.

Salawu, A. (2008). Development Communication: The Preliminaries. In Mojaye, E. M., Oyewo, O. O., M'bayo, R. & Sobowale, I. A. (Eds.): *Globalization and Development Communication in Africa*. Ibadan: Ibadan University Press. pp. 14-15.

Women's Life-Skills Education through Local Cultural Arts: Enhanced by Media and Information Literacy

Mia Rachmiati & Syarif Maulana

The purpose of women's life-skills education through local cultural arts is to empower women in their environment. The model presented in this article is needed because there have been inequalities between men and women in education and working sectors in Indonesia. Furthermore, Indonesia is working hard to reach targets set in connection with the Millennium Development Goals. Local cultural arts are very essential means of women's life-skills education. They are valuable assets for any country and should be preserved. The media, technology, libraries and archives are indispensable tools to preserve, sustain and share local cultural arts. The result expected from the model is the improvement of women's life-skills through local cultural arts and media and information literacy. Learners will be able to earn money from their expertise in local cultural arts. They will be able to maintain their literacy skills by implementing the learning materials into daily life and by using the media such as the Internet, radio, television, and DVDs to improve their performance. The local cultural arts as part of identity and wealth of the country will be maintained through application of the indicators of empowerment in women's life-skills education which consists of open access, increased participation, control formation, and benefits for women learners.

Keywords: women's life-skills education, local art and culture, media and information literacy, literacy skill, Indonesia

Introduction

Education is a basic essence of human life, especially in the competitive era like nowadays. Education plays a strategic human empowerment role in political, social, economic, and cultural contexts. The purpose of education is to handle human reality and methodologically focus on the principles of action and total reflection as action principles to change the oppress reality, and to grow the awareness on reality and desire on change the oppress reality. The awareness process is inherent in the whole education process itself.

In Indonesia, media and technology are often implemented in learning programmes, especially in non-formal education. The Internet is quite accessible in Indonesia. The users of Internet in Indonesia were 71 million in 2014, where 41 million of them have accessed through smart phones and 70 million of them have accessed social media, such as YouTube, Facebook, Twitter, Path, Instagram, LinkedIn and Google+[1]. So the implementation of media and technology aids in learning programmes, including life-skills programmes is possible through the social media. Besides, the usage of media and technology in learning programmes can create interactive learning, where learners can learn new perspectives through the media and technology.

Media and information literacy (MIL) is about life-long learning and mirrors the empowerment process in education described above. It enables us to recognize how information, media and technology influences what people know about themselves, their culture, the world around them and that different versions of "human's life reality" that exists. Media, information and technology are part of today's environment and together forms the public sphere that fuels open discussion about one "environment's problem" and opportunities provided one has access to "step in". This awareness through MIL spurs women and men of all ages to become active and ethical citizens who seek "positive" change.

In Indonesia, as listed in paragraph 31 of The Constitution 1945, each citizen has a right to education. The importance of education is reinforced in The Regulation Number 20, Year 2003 on National Education System, especially stated in paragraph 5, article (1) that each citizen has a right to obtaining qualified education. Besides, paragraph 5 article (5) states that each citizen has a right to opportunities in improving lifelong education. So that development can be carried out by all residents with better education quality without discriminating men and women.

In fact, there have been imbalances between women and men in education and occupation. According to Profile of Indonesian Women 2012[2], the percentage of women and men population aged 10 years and over which have not been at school is 8.05%, and 3.38%, respectively.

On the other hand, according to The Employment and Social Trend in Indonesia 2013 released by ILO Office for Indonesia (2013), there has been the gender disparity in labor force participation. The participation level of workforce for men and women has been 84-85% and 52-53% during 2012 and 2013. In all occupations, about 62% men worked in 2013, and 38% women worked.

In 2000, 189 member countries of United Nation have agreed The Millennium Declaration to reach Millennium Development Goals (MDG's) by 2015. There have been eight key commitments in MDGs, one of them being to promote gender equality and empower women, MDG "[3].

The purpose of women's empowerment is to improve women's productivity in increasing family and community income to improve the ability and quality of individual, family and community life. The improvement of women's productivity can be reviewed in the attitude change indicators which will be more positive. Besides, they can improve their life-skills and attainment competencies for their personal and community requirements. To empower women also means empower and transmit positive spirit to next generations who learn more from their mothers.

To realize the women's empowerment as stated in MDG Goals, The Ministry of Education and Culture through Directorate General of Early Child, Non-formal and Informal Education has provided women life-skills education programme. In 2014, the program has served 7,000 people in 33 provinces[4].The main target of women's life-skills education is women in productive age with lower education background, coming from economically and socially marginalized communities, and the unemployed. The rationale is that equipping them with skills will improve their well-being. As we will show later, media and information literacy with its combined and related competencies could enhance this life-skills education programme.

One important life-skill that can be useful to earn money is service skills. Skills which can be explored in local cultural arts are varied: fine arts, dance arts, music arts and theatre arts. Indonesia has many ethnic teams which develop local cultural arts in each area. Local cultural arts are valuable asset. These have to be preserved. Unfortunately, some parties have "stolen" the intellectual property rights on the original artworks of Indonesia. For example, *reogponorogo* dance and *angklung* instrument which are rich of local wisdom and local tradition of Indonesia have been taken as the intellectual property of other countries. It means the local cultural arts of Indonesia have the potential for livelihood given that other countries have interest in these arts.

The role of many parties – including women – is needed to preserve local cultural arts and economic opportunities therein. Women's life-skills education through local cultural arts can be an intervention in reaching MDG[3]. Of course, a learning programme should be designed well, based on a multi-disciplinary and integrated approach where multiple media and technology are used to explore their talents and skills as well as to maintain their literacy skills.

Below is a bird's-eye-view of a framework that could be applied.

Targets Groups

1. Learners' categories
   a. Women in productive age 18-45 years old, but prioritized 18-35 years old
   b. Unemployed
   c. With basic formal education background or drop-out of basic formal education
   d. Economic level of impoverishment
   e. Residing around the learning location

2. Learning team
   a. A learning team consists of ten learners
   b. A learning team is guided by one or two instructor(s)
   c. A learning team is organized by an organizer to facilitate learning needs

Learning Materials

The learning materials of women's life-skills education through local cultural arts are divided into three teams; personal skills, social skills and vocational skills. Here media and information literacy skills are embedded.

No	Core Competencies	Basic Competencies	Learning Hours (lh)
Personal Skills			
1.	Knowing self potencies	• Building confidence	2 lh
		• Recognizing self potencies in local cultural arts	2 lh
		• Recognizing ones power to shape information about ones culture and to shape cultural expression in and through media and technology	2 lh
2.	Analyzing the potencies of local cultural arts	• Exploring the potencies of local cultural arts	2 lh
		• Exploring the local cultural arts skills to solve problems in daily life	
		• Explore local information life cycle and the involvement of women	
		• Understand the power of media and technology to preserve and transmit and to package local culture for entrepreneurship	3 lh

No	Core Competencies	Basic Competencies	Learning Hours (lh)
Social Skills			
1.	Communicating with Indonesian and local languages	• Listening and delivering oral information and ideas in Indonesian and local languages • Delivering written information and ideas in Indonesian and local languages	5 lh
2.	Collaborating in developing the potencies of local cultural arts	• Collaborating in making decision for developing local cultural arts • Mutual understanding in collaborating • Use of radio, television, newspaper, multimedia tools, mobile devices and the Internet for collaboration to produce and disseminate cultural products	2 lh 4 lh
Vocational Skills			
1.	Mastering local cultural arts	• Being a professional performer of local cultural arts	42 lh (the mastery is adapted with the local cultural arts learned)
2.	Recognizing market opportunities of local cultural arts	• Use media and information skills for effective research critical analysis when: • Identifying market opportunities of local cultural arts • Determining markets of local cultural arts • Determining promotion strategies • A key market could be the media that has access to huge audiences, via content disseminators on the Internet or even for local communities to set up their own cultural arts dissemination platforms where people can view for a small fee or sponsored through advertisement	8 lh
3.	Managing finances in teams and households	• Basic financial literacy made simple through information and media competencies • Drafting the budget revenue and expenditure of local cultural arts team • Making cash income and expenditure of local cultural arts team • Planning family financial	6 lh
Total			**78 lh**

Learning Implementation

Learning implementation in women's life-skills education through local cultural arts combines the humanistic learning methods (confluent learning and co-operation learning) and information, media, and technological aids (radio, tele-vision, video, the Internet etc.). The combination can be described as follows:

1. **Confluent learning with media aids**

   Confluent learning combines affective experiences and cognitive learning in the classroom. This is a good way to initiate learners personally into the learning materials. An example of the implementation for 'self confidence' material:

   a. The instructor distributes the instructions and worksheet to all learners

   b. The instructor asks learners to read the instructions, and fill the questions in the worksheet

   c. The instructor asks learners to discuss the answer on the worksheet

   d. The instructor comments on the learners' answer

   e. The instructor divides learners into two teams and asks them to search some tips on the Internet about how to build self-confidence

   f. The teams monitors local media and search the Internet for local cultural expressions whether commercialized or not

   g. Each team presents their discussion result

   h. The instructor concludes the material

2. **Cooperative learning with media aids**

   Cooperative learning is a good foundation to improve the achievement of learners. Some techniques of cooperative learning implemented in the learning process are:

   a. Team-Games-Tournament

   Learners are divided into two teams. The instructor plays a DVD about the demonstration of a dance/performance in local cultural arts learned. Then each team practice with their friends based on the DVD. They learn from each other and after that the instructor asks each team to present their performance in front of the class. In the end of the learning process, the instructor tells the best team and the best performer. This could be done through the use of video online such as in YouTube and other social networks if Internet is available. This could enable many groups in various remote communities to practice at the same time.

   b. Learner Teams-Achievement Divisions

   The technique divides learners into two teams then each team discusses a topic given by the instructor through guides and worksheets. After that, the instructor asks each team to present their discussion result and take question-answer time.

c. Jigsaw

Learners are divided into two teams. Each team comprises five learners. The instructor distributes dictates and worksheet to each team. There will be two learners in the different teams which have the same task in the worksheet, so they are asked to form small teams based on the same task in the worksheet. The small teams discuss the question by using the dictate as the guidance. After that they come back to their previous team and teach each other about their task with their own team.

d. **Team investigation**

Team investigation is a technique where learners work in the small team to handle some class projects. Each team divides topics into sub topics. Then they take investigation by searching in the Internet, reading some dictates and interviewing some persons to reach the team's goal. After that each team presents the result of investigation in front of the class.

Mentoring

Mentoring is taken after the learning implementation. The duration of mentoring is 16 hours or approximately two months. Mentoring involves instructors, resource persons of local cultural arts, women organizations, and local government. Mentoring could be carried remotely via offline video or the Internet. This could save huge travel costs for hard-to-access or remote communities where more women are marginalized.

The activities of mentoring:

1. To facilitate learning group of women's life-skills education through local cultural arts to be a group or an organization of local cultural arts

2. To facilitate the study tour activities to museums and art galleries

3. To facilitate learners to perform in arts activities

4. To accompany learners in every performance

Outcomes

The goal of the programme is the improving women's life-skills through local cultural arts and enhanced by media and information literacy with the indicators:

1. Learners are able to earn money through their expertise in local cultural arts.

2. Learners can maintain their literacy skills by implementing the learning materials into daily life and using some media, such as the Internet and DVDs to improve their performance.

3. The women's team in local cultural arts is developed

4. The local cultural arts as a part of identity and wealth of the country is maintained

5. The indicator of empowerment in women's life-skills education through local cultural arts which consists of open access, increased participation, control formation, and benefits for women learners will be materialized.

Conclusion

The enhancement of media and technology information in women's life-skills education through local cultural arts is very essential in improving learners' competencies because they can learn new information and ideas which cannot be explained by the instructors. Learners can develop their abilities in making use of new technology in their daily life. The programme proves that the media, technology, libraries and archives are indispensable tools to preserve, sustain and share local cultural arts. After the programme, learners will be able to use media and technology information not only in solving problems, but also to improve their competencies in local cultural arts.

References

Asmani, J. M. (2009). *Buku Panduan Internalisasi Pendidikan Karakter di Sekolah.* Yogyakarta: Diva Press.

Dwijowijoto, R. N. (2008). *Kebijakan Publik.* Jakarta: Elex Media Komputindo.

Notoatmodjo, S. (2003). *Pengembangan Sumber Daya Manusia.* Bandung: Rineka Cipta.

Salahudin, Drs, M. Pd. (2011). *Filsafat Pendidikan.* Bandung: CV. Pustaka Setia.

Sadulloh, U. D. (2008). *Pengantar Filsafat Pendidikan.* Bandung: Alfabeta.

Slamet, P. H. (2002). *Kepemimpinan Kepala Sekolah,* Makalahdan Lokakarya Nasional.

Soemanto, W. (1998). *Psikologi Pendidikan (Landasan Kerja Pemimpin Pendidikan).* Jakarta: Rineka Cipta.

Sulistiyani, A. T. (2004). *Memahami Good Governance dalam Perspektif Sumber Daya Manusia.* Yogyakarta: Gava Media.

Suparno, A. S. (2001). *Membangun Kompetensi Belajar.* Jakarta: Direktorat Pendidikan Tinggi.

The article is based on the model developed by The Center for Development of Early Child, Non-formal and Informal Education Region I Bandung, Indonesia in 2014. The team consisted of: Mia Rachmiati, Waluyo Saputro, Haryono, Liesna Dyah, Erni Sukmawati Dewi and Edy Hardiyanto with Syarif Maulana as the resource person. The programme has been implemented at Kandaga Community Learning Center in Subang, West Java, Indonesia and Nur Alam Foundation in Cimahi, West Java, Indonesia. Enlisting media and information literacy to enrich the use of what the original authors call "media aids" model was added for the article.

Notes

1 www.tekno.kompas.com/pengguna Internet di Indonesia nomorenamdunia, accessed May 10, 2015.

2 Collaboration of The Ministry of Women Empowerment and Child Protection and Central Bureau of Statistics, 2012.

3 The Ministry of Women Empowerment and Child Protection, 2012, accessed June 7, 2014.

4 The Action Plan of Sub-Directorate of Learning Programs and Learning, Directorate of Community Education Development, Directorate of Early Child, Non-formal and Informal Education, 2014.

Information Literacy among People with Disabilities

Manukonda Rabindranath & Sujay Kapil

Disability in the India is varying from 2-3% as per the Census of 2001. However, the estimates of disability by Census and NSS differ significantly. According to Census 2011, male population has been found more prone to various kinds of disabilities as compared to females and population in rural areas had almost two fold disabilities than their counterparts in urban areas. Maximum disability has been found to be in movement followed by hearing and seeing. Age of the persons has been found to be directly proportional to the disability. A large number of legislations have been passed by the Government of India for minimizing the disability and their upliftment, but the results have been not very promising. People with disabilities either do not know or don't have access to information which would improve their day to day life. The information sought through Right To Information from the highest educational institutions in the state of Himachal Pradesh, India revealed that there are no learning resources suited to the needs of the students with disability. The libraries neither have the learning resources nor the physical infrastructure that aids the students with disabilities. Thus this section of the population finds itself at the bottom in terms of information literacy. There is an urgent need to give a fresh look into the basic requirements of persons with disabilities and to make serious efforts with accountability to fulfill their needs.

Keywords: information literacy, disability, library, educational resources

> *The problem is not how to wipe out the differences but how to unite with the differences intact.*
>
> Rabindranath Tagore (quoted in Alur)

Introduction

Disability is a multi-dimensional and intricate concept and there is no universally accepted definition of disability. The definitions vary across the world but these also differ and change within a country with evolving legal, political and social dialogue. It is an enormous task to get reliable data about the occurrence of disability in India. The various models used to define disability cover the medical, charity and social aspects of disability.

According to the social model; institutional, environmental and attitudinal prejudice is the real cause of disability. So, it is not the medical (physical or psychological) condition that impairs a person, it is the society which hinders the person with disabilities through bias, denial of rights, exploitation and creation of economic dependency. The rights based model of disability will not become effective until and unless the people who fall under this category rise against the discrimination perpetuated by the society. This is possible only with the liberation of thought and action. This liberation can be achieved through information literacy. The people who are disabled must have access to education and information, thus empowering them. Media and information literacy can be ensured through education.

Disability Estimates in India

The 2001 Census (Registrar General of India, 2001) and the 2002 National Sample Survey 58th Round (NSSO, 2003) are two early sources of data on the disabled population of India in the 21st century. The 2001 Census, recorded a rate of 2.13% i.e. 21.91 million people with the five types of disabilities out of a total population of 1,028 million.

According to the National Sample Survey Organization (NSSO) 58th round (July-December 2002) 1.8% of the Indian population i.e. 18.5 million suffered from disability. This appears to be a gross underestimation. The World Bank (2007) notes that "the real prevalence of disability in India could easily be around 40 million people, and perhaps as high as 80-90 million if more inclusive definitions of both mental illness and mental retardation in particular were used". Similar findings have also been reported by Kuruvilla and Joseph (1999) and Erb et al. (2002).

Table 1. Disability rates from Census and NSSO Survey

PWD	Census	NSS 58th
All individuals	**2.13**	**1.8**
All urban individuals	NA	1.50
All urban households	NA	6.1
All rural individuals	NA	1.85
All rural households	NA	8.4
All males	2.37	2.12
All females	1.87	1.67

Sources: Census 2001 and NSS 2002

The methodology of the 2011 Census (Registrar General of India, 2011) was different in comparison to that carried out in 2001 as the definitions and criterion of disabilities were changed in the Census 2011. The differences are mentioned in the table given below:

Table 2. Disabled population by sex and residence India, 2011

Residence	Persons	Males	Females
Total	**26,810,557**	**14,986,202**	**11,824,355**
Rural	18,631,921	10,408,168	8,223,753
Urban	8,178,636	4,578,034	3,600,602

Source: C-Series, Table C-20 Census of India 2011

Table 2 further clearly shows the disabled population by type of disability in India as per Census (2011). There were more male disabled persons than disabled females. The population with disabilities of sight, hearing and movement was above 500,000. The proportion of disabled males was higher than that of females in all the categories of disabilities. The number of people suffering from mental illness was found to be lowest among the various types of disabilities across both males and females.

In Movement

Specific mention of the following was made in the definition for Census 2011:

1. Paralytic persons
2. Those who crawl
3. Those who are able to walk with the help of aid
4. Have acute and permanent problems of joints/muscles
5. Have stiffness or tightness in movement or have loose, involuntary movements or tremours of the body or have fragile bones
6. Have difficulty balancing and coordinating body movement
7. Have loss of sensation in body due to paralysis, leprosy etc
8. Have deformity of body like hunch back or are dwarf

The proportion of the disabled population in various social groups as per Census 2011 is shown in Figure 1. The proportion of disabled among the scheduled castes is the highest overall as well as in both the sexes.

Figure 1. Proportion of disability by social groups in India, 2011

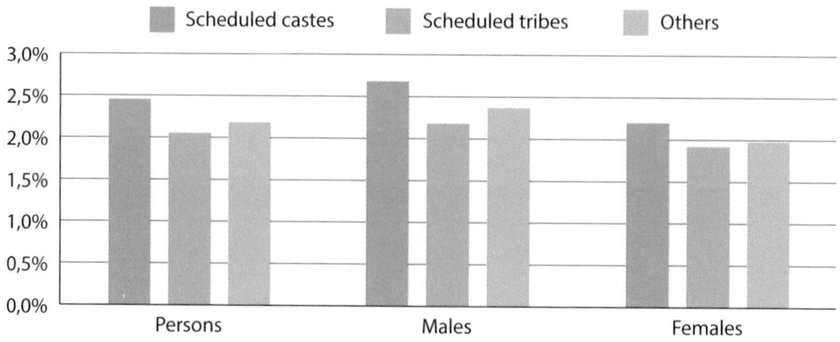

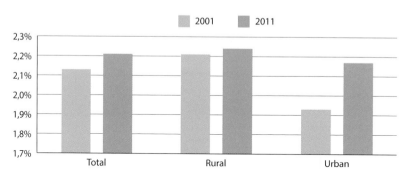

Source: C-Series, Tables C-20, C-20SC and C-20ST, Census of India 2011

The percentage of disabled persons in India has increased both in rural and urban areas during the last decade (Figure 2). The proportion of disabled population is higher in rural areas. However, the decadal increase in proportion is significant in urban area.

Figure 2. Proportion of disabled population by residence in India, 2001-11

Source: C-Series, Table C-20, Census of India 2001 and 2011

Table 3. Disabled population by type of disability in India, 2011

Type of Disability	Persons	Males	Females
Total	**26,810,557**	**14,986,202**	**11,824,355**
In seeing	5,032,463	2,638,516	2,393,947
In hearing	5,071,007	2,677,544	2,393,463
In speech	1,998,535	1,122,896	875,639
In movement	5,436,604	3,370,374	2,066,230
Mental retardation	1,505,624	870,708	634,916
Mental illness	722,826	415,732	307,094
Any other	4,927,011	2,727,828	2,199,183
Multiple disability	2,116,487	1,162,604	953,883

Source: C-Series, Tables C-20, Census of India 2011

Figure 3. Disabled population by type of disability in India, 2011

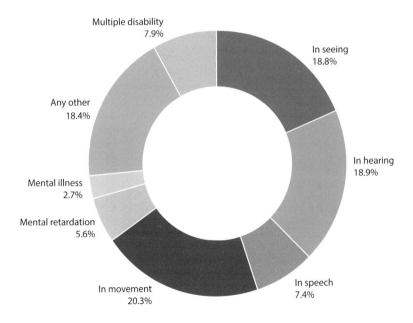

Source: C-Series, Tables C-20, Census of India 2011

Figure 4 . Proportion of disabled population in the respective age group in India, 2011

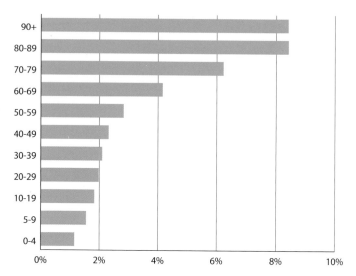

Source: C-Series, Table C-20, Census of India 2011

Figure 5. Disability by type and sex in India, 2011

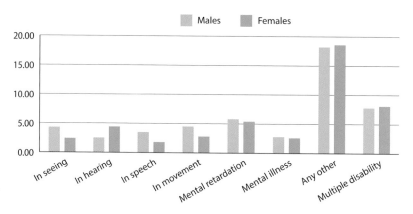

Source: C-Series, Table C-20, Census of India 2001, 2011

Information Literacy

The factor common to all with disabilities irrespective of their gender, age, caste, economic status etc. is the social ostracization and marginalization they face in their day-to-day lives. According to the World Bank (2007), children with disability are five times more likely to be out of school than children belonging to scheduled castes or scheduled tribes. When children with disability drop out of school, it leads to lower employment chances and subsequent poverty. Thus, the information literacy among them is dismal.

The World Bank (2007) report further states that, people with disabilities have much lower educational attainment rates, with 52% illiteracy against a 35% average for the general population. Illiteracy levels are high across all categories of disability, and extremely so for children with visual, multiple and mental disabilities. The National Policy on Education of 1986 played an influential role in bringing the issue of equality for children with special needs in the limelight. It stated that the "objective should be to integrate physically and mentally disabled people with the general community as equal partners, to prepare them for normal growth and to enable them to face life with courage and confidence".

The following four legislations in India are specific to people with disabilities:

- *Rehabilitation Council of India Act (1992)*: states that Children With Special Needs

- (CWSN) will be taught by a trained teacher.

- *Persons with Disabilities Act (1995)*: educational entitlement for all CWSN up to 18 years in an appropriate environment.

- *National Trust Act (1999)*: provide services and support to severely disabled children.

- *The 86th Constitutional Amendment (2007)*: free and compulsory education to children, up to 14 years. (Right to Education)

These legislations led to the formulation of the National Action Plan for Inclusion in Education of the Children and Persons with Disabilities (MHRD, 2004), and the National Policy for Persons with Disabilities in 2006 by the Ministry of Social Justice and Empowerment. Singal (2006) critically examined two Government reports: the Sargent Report of 1944 and the Kothari Commission (Education Commission, 1966). Both these reports recommended the adoption of a "dual approach" to meet the educational needs of these children. They emphasized on the integration of children with disabilities rather than their segregation from normal children, but also acknowledged that "many handicapped children find it psychologically disturbing to be placed in an ordinary school"

(Education Commission, 1966) and in such cases they should be sent to special schools.

The 1990s witnessed the incorporation of the term 'inclusive education' in various official documents and reports published by various institutions. In 2001 the Indian government launched the Sarv Shiksha Abhiyaan (SSA) with the target to provide quality education to children between the age group of 6-14 years. The provisions under the SSA for children with special needs are:

1. a cash grant of up to 1,200 Rupees per Children With Special Needs per year;

2. district plans for CSN that will be formulated within the above prescribed norm;

3. the involvement of key resource institutions to be encouraged.

The Sarv Shiksha Abhiyaan (SSA) lists 8 priority areas of intervention for inclusive education:

1. Survey for identification of Children With Special Needs (CWSN)

2. Assessment of CWSN

3. Providing assistive devices

4. Networking with NGOs/Government schemes

5. Barrier free access

6. Training of teachers on Internet based Education

7. Appointment of resource teachers

8. Curricula adaptation/textbooks/appropriate Teaching Learning Methods

Issues of Access and Enrolment

The data on the educational participation of children with disabilities is highly unreliable – both in terms of estimates in the school going age group and the actual numbers attending school. Mukhopadhyay and Mani (2002) quote a National Council of Educational Research and Training (NCERT) survey, suggesting that about 84,000 children with disabilities were enrolled in schools in 1998; and unpublished data gathered for the Ministry of Human Resource Development (MHRD) suggested that approximately 55,000 children with disabilities were enrolled in schools in 1999.

The model of funding used by SSA is the Child-based funding. This model is based on headcounts of CWD, as outright grant to regions, pupil-weighted schemes, or census funding based on total students and assumed share of CWD. This model is used widely across the world over. But, there are certain concerns with this model including:

1. the focus on the disability category of the child vs. actual learning needs and costs. Ultimately the system attains a mechanical shape rather than needs-based;

2. the model can be costly on individual basis ;

3. evidence from the EU suggests integration outcomes for CWD are worse that other approaches.

Higher Education Scenario for the Students with Special Needs

The authors of this article filed a Right To Application (RTI) application in four major institutes of higher learning of Himachal Pradesh. The primary data obtained is shown in the Table 4 below.

Table 4. Information received from institutions of higher education in Himachal Pradesh

Name of the Institution	Total No. of Books	Total No. of Journals	Educa-tional Resources in Braille	Educa-tional Resources in Sign Language	Special Seating Arrange-ment for PWD in Library
Himachal Pradesh University	220,174	Not Provided	Nil	Nil	No
Himachal Pradesh Agriculture University	88,286	Not Provided	Nil	Nil	No
Indian Institute of Technology, Mandi (Himachal Pradesh)	1,193	846	Nil	Nil	No
University of Horticulture and Forestry, Nauni (Himachal Pradesh)	47,086	17,285	Nil	Nil	No

It is evident from Table 4 that in spite of a huge number of books and journals available in all the educational institutions for the students, there was no special arrangement of seating or availability of books and journals in Braille for students with visual disability. Similarly, there were no learning sources for students with speech and hearing disability. Despite claims made by the Central and State governments in India for providing a platform for inclusive education, in all the four government institutions of higher learning, there is no provision of any kind to enable the students with disabilities to achieve better education. So this section of the society remains deprived of literacy and in turn information.

Recommendations

The education sector has been relatively progressive and quick in policy formulation when it comes to People With Disabilities (PWD). However, there is a struggle at the ground level to turn policy into effective practice. There is an urgent need to get the basics right: identify children with disabilities more effectively; create the relevant and accessible content; implement adequate outreach to teachers and children; and work through local opinion leaders to convince families that educating children with disabilities will make them independent.

Specific recommendations include:

1. **Identification of children with disabilities**
   In order to achieve this minimum outcome, it will be important to review the SSA systems for identifying children with disabilities entering the education system. The mismatch between Census Data and Ministerial sources must be avoided. The aids and appliances must be provided to the PWDs at the earliest as a right and not privilege.

2. **Accessibility to schools**
   This includes physical and geographic accessibility to, disabled friendly school premises and facilities as well as accessibility from the child's home, which brings in issues like transport system, toilets etc.

3. **Improving the quality of education**
   The efforts to make the content and format of the curriculum accessible to the learning needs of children with disabilities need to be intensified. Mere announcements and budget allocations won't help. Academicians must focus on assessing the daily activities and needs of disabled children.

4. **Changing the academic curriculum**
   The educational resources presently available are ridden with superfluous textual content. Extra-curricular and co-curricular activities, such as, games and sports, drawing and painting, craft and cultural activities should be an essential part of the curriculum. Vocational education can lead to gainful employment or entrepreneurship for the PWD.

5. **Financial incentives to CWD to facilitate their participation**

   The SSA has provision for financial funding for the CWD as well as institutions offering facilities for their education. However, there is an urgent need for a substantial increase in the financial aid at both the pupil and institutional level.

6. **Sensitizing the stakeholders**

   The attitudes of parents, communities and educators and policymakers must be such that they are sensitized to the needs of the students with special needs. Each one of them must ensure that the CWD are integrated into the mainstream and able to realize their potential. This can be effectively done with the active cooperation of the local panchayats and anganwari workers.

7. **Strengthening education institutions**

   A strong institutional relationship must be forged between the Ministry of Human Resource Development and Ministry of Social Justice and Empowerment. This would make sure that planning, financing and monitoring of the education of all children with special needs is done in a coherent manner. Public- private partnerships must be developed for speedy and widespread implementation of the schemes for PWD.

References

Education Commission. (1966). *Education and national development.* New Delhi: Ministry of Education.

Erb, S., Harriss & White, B. (2002). *Outcast from social welfare: Adult incapacity and disability in rural South India.* Bangalore: Books for Change.

Kuruvilla, S. & Joseph, A.I. (1999). Identifying disability: comparing house to house survey and rapid rural appraisal. *Health Policy and Planning.* 14 (2): 182-190.

Ministry of Human Resource Development. (2004). *Education for all: India marches ahead.* New Delhi: Government of India.

Mukhopadhyay, S. & Mani, M.N.G. (2002). Education of children with special needs, In Govinda, R. (Ed.) *India education report: A profile of basic education.* New Delhi: Oxford University Press.

National Council of Educational Research and Training (2005). *The national focus group on education of children with special needs. Position paper.*

NSSO (2003). *Disabled Persons in India, NSS 58th round (July – December 2002).* New Delhi: National Sample Survey Organisation.

Registrar General of India (2001). *Census of India* 2001. Available from: http://www.censusindia.net.

Singal, N. (2006). Inclusive education in India: international concept, national interpretation. *International Journal of Disability, Development and Education,* 53 (3), 351-369.

World Bank (2007). *People with Disabilities in India: From Commitments to Outcomes.* New Delhi: Human Development Unit, South Asia Region.

Towards a Framework of Media and Information Literacy Education for Children with Disabilities: A Global Entitlement

Vedabhyas Kundu

Notwithstanding the Right to Education Act, 2009 which tries to safeguard the rights of the children belonging to the disadvantaged groups, age old stereotypes and other factors continue to deny children with disabilities the opportunities to grow like other children. In a scenario where these children do not have easy accessibility to education, media and information literacy education seems to be a far-fetched idea. All forms of communications in the contemporary society are witnessing major technological and structural transformations. To ensure children with disabilities are an integral part of these transformations and are able to use tools of communications to realize their potential, a special thrust needs to be given to encourage media and information literacy programmes for them.

This article delves into approaches and methods of media and information literacy programmes involving children with disability. Article 7 of the UN Convention of the Rights of Persons with Disabilities states, "Necessary measures should be taken to ensure the full enjoyment by children with disabilities of all human rights and fundamental freedoms on an equal basis with other children."[1] Also the principles of the Global Alliance for Partnerships on Media and Information Literacy (GAPMIL) underline that women, men and boys, girls, people with disabilities, indigenous groups or ethnic and religious minorities should have equal access to media and information literacy[2].

This article by trying to develop a framework of media and information literacy programmes for children with disabilities will be an endeavour towards the fulfilment of Article 7 of the UN Convention and in sync with the GAPMIL framework.

Keywords: media and information literacy for children with disabilities, inclusive media and communication education, children's newspaper in Braille and Talking Paper

Introduction

A majority of young people with visual impairment like me do not get opportunity to participate in the public sphere. In this digital age, it is imperative that we enhance our communicative skills and ability to use different media. It is our right and entitlement and an essential component of an inclusive public sphere.

Jyoti Nagi, a young visually challenged singer

For young advocates of media literacy like Nagi, deeper understanding of the media and communication skills not only enables them to participate in critical public discourses but is crucial to expanding their self awareness and personality. "Media and communication literacy can contribute to our abilities to deal with many complex problems we fight in everyday life," Nagi opines. She and several others were interviewed as part of Expert Interviews conducted by the writer for this article. The aim was to gain insight and explore on the essence of media and information literacy in the lives of young people with disability and a framework needed for an inclusive MIL framework. The experts included those who have contributed in the area of disability. Besides, two young people – a visually challenged singer and a child editor of a children's newspaper which tries to encourage children with disability to become young reporters were also interviewed to get young people's perspective.

Concurring with Nagi, Kanupriya Gupta, Class X and Editor of the children's newspaper, *The Peace Gong* notes, "Children with visual impairment have equal rights like any other children to analyze issues concerning young people, come up with solutions and develop their own perspectives." She talks about developing an inclusive *Peace Gong* team where children from diverse backgrounds and abilities can come together to initiate dialogues and discussions. In this context, a Talking Paper is also developed so that visually challenged children can be reached. Media and information literacy training programmes are also conducted for children with disabilities which are discussed in a separate section later[3].

Meanwhile, George Abraham, the founding Chairman, World Blind Cricket Association and CEO, Score Foundation argues how media literacy can facilitate engagement of young people with disability in various socio-political issues. "This will help these young people in analyzing contemporary issues and also contribute in breaking stereotypes. Besides, it may open new livelihood opportunities which always seemed out of reach of people with disability," he adds.

For instance visually challenged young people can get opportunities as radio jockeys and radio journalists. With assistive technologies and new software, they can get opportunities as web content writers. Young physically challenged people with some assistance depending upon their disability too can take up many professions like journalism, web content writers etc.

Whereas the role of media literacy in strengthening public sphere and democratic participation has been underlined by Tornero and Varis (2010), Masterman (1985 & 2001) and Hobbs (1998), Abraham and Nagi's concern of how a vast majority of youth with disability are excluded from engaging in public discourses underlines the lack of opportunities available to the differently-abled youth.

Nagi describes this lack of space for many youth with disability like her to being excluded citizen. "How can we contribute to the democratic process if we do not have the required skills to take part in critical public discourses?" she asks. Nagi's observations underline the need to develop strategies to promote active citizenry amongst people with disability.

While the Expert Interviews conducted for this article amplifies Abraham and Nagi's contentions, it is also evident that media and information literacy education which is still to percolate down to a vast majority of young people is virtually an unheard subject for young people with disability. Weigand et al. (2013, p. 190-197) observes, "Only little attention has been paid to the specific aspects of information and media literacy suitable for disabled, and specifically for blind and partially sighted individuals."

Also notwithstanding the enthusiasm of young people like Nagi to be media literate, ensuring access to even basic education to a vast majority of children with disability (CWD) is one of the major challenges to their development. Ensuring access to quality education to all is a global priority and is amplified by the Goal 4 of the proposed Sustainable Development Goals[4]. It talks to 'ensure inclusive and equitable quality education and promote lifelong learning opportunities for all'. Goal 8 of the proposed goals talks of promotion of sustained, inclusive and sustainable economic growth, full and productive employment and decent work for all. By facilitating communication, media and information literacy training, the aims of the proposed goals can be realized with the enhancement of capacities of young people with disability.

Education of Children with Disabilities in India

The Right of Children to Free and Compulsory Education Act 2009 reinvigorates the rights of all children to free and compulsory education. An important step towards ensuring education for CWD was the Government of India's Sarva Shiksha Abhiyan (SSA) which underlined a zero rejection policy (Sarva Shiksha Abhiyan, 2007).

However, Singal (2009, p. 7) citing a World Bank Study of 2007 notes how "children with disability are five times more likely to be out of school than children belonging to scheduled castes or scheduled tribes." "Moreover, when children with disability do attend school they rarely progress beyond the primary level," she adds.

Even in the backdrop of efforts, by the Government and civil society, to facilitate education for CWD major challenges remain. It is not just appropriate education but also accessibility which is a significant concern. Kowsar et al. (2012, p. 1) writing for *The Peace Gong* talks about poor accessibility in majority of the schools and educational institutions. Kowsar, a student from Chuchot-Yokama, Leh, Jammu & Kashmir, India is physically challenged and shares her own predicament concerned that she could be a drop-out after high school:

> *The main problem is that after high school I have to join a new school where I can continue my studies. But there is no option for my parents because it is not possible for them to take me to school. There is no one in the family except my father who can take me to school but he is too busy in his work. I cannot travel myself to the new school.*

So while the SSA aims to adopt zero rejection policy, the reality on the ground seems to be different as hundreds of children like Samina are forced to quit education due to varied reasons. In such a scenario, introducing media and communication literacy programmes for CWD could be seen to be a difficult proposition. However, such initiatives are essential components of life skill education, means to promote self-awareness and facilitate active participation in the democratic process which necessitates critical discussions and action. This following sections, through Expert Interviews, and analysis of *The Peace Gong's* attempt to promote media and information literacy programme amongst CWD, aims to look at possible training structures.

Promoting Media and Communication Literacy amongst CWD

Expert Interviews

Jenkins et al. (2006, Executive Summary xiii-xiv) argues on the need for young people to acquire new media literacy skills in the changing media landscape. According to them these set of cultural competencies and social skills are significant to enable young people become full participants in the society. Jenkins et al. further note, "The new media literacies should be seen as social skills, as ways of interacting within a larger community, and not simply as an individualized skills to be used for personal expression."

The Expert Interviews reiterate the importance of development of language and communication skills in CWD. They also go on to stress on the different cultural and social skills discussed by Jenkins et al. Anil Mudgal, Secretary, Arushi, Bhopal, which is an organization working for people with disability, argues that limited exposure to various aspects of education is responsible for inadequate language skills in CWD. The Expert Interviews reveals the inhibition of CWD in the socialization process. J P Singh, Chairman, Amity Foundation for Developmental Disabilities notes, "The aspect of living together, playing together and studying along with peer have still not picked up and these children are left out in the schools and start feeling isolated. They do not come forward for any media activity because of their lack of vocabulary etc."

Major challenges in promoting media literacy programmes amongst CWD are connected to existing attitudes and stereotypes. Anupam Ahuja, Head, Department of Education of Groups with Special Needs, National Council of Education Research and Technology, New Delhi talks of restricted curriculum and exposure vis-à-vis CWD. She says:

> Teachers and educators involved with children with special needs generally feel that these children cannot grasp like others. So they try to restrict the training process and curriculum in any discipline they take up. These children are looked down as weird learners.

S R Mittal, Adjunct Professor, National Institute for the Visually Handicapped (NIVH) observes that a CWD had limited access to media as compared to any other children. He, however, underlines that wherever supportive environment was created, CWD can excel and show their real potential. He shares the initiative of NIVH to start a FM station, Hello Doon in Dehradun, Uttarakhand for the visually impaired. "Programmes for the FM station are mostly produced by visually impaired students," he says.

NIVH offers a one-year course in radio journalism for visually impaired people. According to a news story in *The Economic Times*, it is striving to initiate similar FM station in other states of the country. (*The Economic Times*, August 17, 2014)

"With language skills, visually impaired people can learn editing skills, can edit audio files, do practical reporting work and even write scripts for documentaries and films," Abraham talking about the salient components of media education programme.

Notwithstanding the need for extra support for training, most of the experts felt an inclusive approach to media literacy would be more fruitful than isolated training programmes. According to J P Singh, "The curriculum should be the same as for other children but methodology of communicating to a child with say visual impairment will change by way of providing necessary assistive devices."

An important component of the curriculum is digital literacy which would enable CWD to use the social media and other digital platforms extensively. Experts including Anupam Ahuja and J P Singh also point out the increasing centrality of mobile phones in shaping media and communication literacy amongst CWD. They also talk about how active communities of people with disability can emerge through digital platforms and how these are sites of dialogues and discussions of issues concerning them.

Arguing on the primacy of digital literacy, Jyoti Nagi observes:

> Young people like us can effectively connect with others and initiate social media campaigns. It will help us to access information from multiple sources and enable us to express in different platforms. Many of us have isolated learning experiences. With sufficient knowledge of the use of social media and digital communication technologies, we can develop models of participatory learning for young people with disability.

Analyzing *The Peace Gong's* Effort to Be an Inclusive Platform for Children

The Peace Gong child reporters led by Kanupriya have been facilitating several media and information training programmes. Sessions on understanding the media, how to be an effective communicator, interviewing techniques, researching, gathering information and constructing stories for the media are part of the training programme.

As stressed by the experts, Kanupriya also advocates an inclusive media literacy programme, "Through collective learning we can come up with innovative and creative ideas. I know sign language and Braille which helps me in communicating effectively with my peers with disability." She plans to bring her friends in school to work closely with CWD to put together an inclusive child media initiative and a *Peace Gong* edition in Braille.

As a volunteer since Class VII who records talking books, Kanupriya feels real inclusion can be promoted if regular children and young people learn Braille and sign language. "When we go out to take interviews or do research together, we are able to understand the dynamics of an inclusive team. It also gives my friends the confidence and determination to realize their potential," she adds.

With her knowledge of sign language, she plans to organize media training programmes for young people with hearing impairment. "We can invite a resource person and I can interpret the training programme through sign language," she says.

Rohit Trivedi, Assistant Professor, Sarojini Naidu Government Girls PG College, Bhopal and a resource person in the media training programme underline the importance of research skills for CWD:

> CWD have equal rights to be discoverer of information and use it to express their concerns. So media literacy programmes must give primacy to research skills as mostly CWD are not conversant with gathering informa-

tion and facts. They should be able to develop skills to distinguish reality and fiction, construct arguments, critically reflect on the information they gather and initiate dialogues.

Trivedi argues on the need to include media and information literacy programme as a compulsory component of life skill education for young people with disability.

He is clear that developing mere technical skills is not enough for CWD. He argues:

It is a misconception; unless the children go deeper using their research skills and critical thinking abilities they won't be able to negotiate with complex messages they might be getting from multiple sources. We have to challenge these children to go beyond their own personal concerns to larger concerns of the society.

For students with visual impairment like Gorelal Khuswaha and Monika Jha who have been part of the training programmes, it was an opportunity to learn new skills which could help them to advocate on concerns of people with disability with greater clarity and conviction. Shreekumar Thakre, another participant felt it was a unique exercise as through role plays they learnt how to conduct interviews and use different media like street plays, songs, social media and radio to create awareness on rights of children. All three now are keen to use different social media platforms to take up issues such as environmental pollution, issues of neglect of children etc.

Conclusion

The significance of media and communication education for CWD has been articulated through the Expert Interviews and the case study of *The Peace Gong*. The right of all citizens to media and information literacy was amplified in the UNESCO Conference on Media Education (media and information literacy) organized in Vienna in 1999 which also reiterated that "media education should be aimed at empowering all citizens in every society and should ensure that people with special needs and those socially and economically disadvantaged have access to it." In more recent time UNESCO, through use of various resources such as the *Media and Information Literacy Curriculum for Teachers* (2011), advocates for media and information literacy to be treated as composite concept cover media literacy, information literacy, digital literacy news literacy and other related literacies.

More discourses and deliberations are needed to develop effective media and communication training programmes for CWD. Action research and structured media and information literacy initiatives needs to be encouraged at different levels – both in an inclusive environment and also in special institutions. More efforts need to be made to encourage child media initiatives involving CWD. However, to make the process truly inclusive even children like Kanupriya needs to be motivated to learn Braille and sign language so that they can work effectively with their peers with disability.

References

'Hello Doon', FM station for visually-impaired seeks to expand reach. (2014); *The Economic Times*, August 17, 2014; http://articles.economictimes.indiatimes.com/2014-08-17/news/52901402_1_fm-station-doon-channel; retrieved on March 4, 2015.

Hobbs, R. (1998). Building citizenship skills through media literacy education in M Salvador and P Sias (Eds). *The Public Voice in a democracy at risk*. Westport, CT: Praeger Press.

Jenkins, H.; Purushotma, Ravi; Weigel, Margaret; Clinton, Katie; Robinson, Alice J (2006). *Confronting the challenges of participatory culture: Media education for the 21st century*. Chicago: The John D. and Catherine T. MacArthur Foundation.

Kowsar, Samina; Mir, Ireen Ahmad; Chakraborty, Arpan; Ali, Islam; Hossain, Akram (September 2012). Right to Education for Children with Disability in *The Peace Gong*; Vol 3, September 2012; Gurudev Rabindranath Tagore Foundation; Pg 1.

Masterman, L. (1985). *Teaching the Media*. London: comedia.

Masterman, L. (2001). A Rationale for Media Education, in Kubey, R. (Ed). *Media Literacy in the Information Age: Current Perspectives*. Information and Behaviour, 6. New Brunswick: N J Transaction Publishers.

Media and Information Literacy Curriculum for Teachers (2011); UNESCO; http://www.unesco.org/new/en/communication-and-information/media-development/media-literacy/mil-curriculum-for-teachers/

Sarva Shiksha Abhiyan (2007). Inclusive education in SSA. Available at: 164.100.51.121/inclusive-education/Inclusive_Edu_May07.pdf

Singal, Nidhi (2009). Education of children with disabilities in India; Paper commissioned for the *Education for All Global Monitoring Report 2010, Reaching the Marginalized*.

UNESCO Conference on Media Education (1999). Vienna.

Weigand, Monika; Zylka, Johannes and Muller, Wolfgang (2013). Media Competencies in the context of Visually Impaired People in Serap Kurbanogli, Esthers Grassian, Dianne Mizrachi, Ralph Catts, Sonja Spiranec (Eds), *Worlwide Commonalities and Practice: European Conference on Information Literacy*, ECIL 2013, Istanbul, Turkey; p. 190-197.

Notes

1 The UN Convention of the Rights of Persons with Disabilities articulates on the promotion, protection and ensuring of full and equal enjoyment of all human rights by all persons with disabilities. http://www.un.org/disabilities/convention/conventionfull.shtml

2 The Global Alliance for Partnerships on Media and Information Literacy was launched during the Global Forum for Partnerships on Media and Information Literacy organized from June 26-28, 2013. http://www.unesco.org/new/en/communication-and-information/media-development/media-literacy/global-alliance-for-partnerships-on-media-and-information-literacy/about-gapmil/

3 The *Peace Gong* is a children's newspaper published by the Gurudev Rabindranath Tagore Foundation, New Delhi where children up to 18 years of age can write. It tries to reach out to children from different parts of India and even abroad. It has a print edition, a Talking Paper and a web version (www.thepeacegong.org). Efforts are being made to put together a Braille Edition, both in English and Hindi. One can listen to some of the issues of *Peace Gong* Talking Paper in: https://www.youtube.com/watch?v=3wPQAxW4v9g & https://www.youtube.com/watch?v=lsaMv5UYhRU&feature=share

4 A major outcome of Rio +20 conference was the agreement of member states to develop a set of Sustainable Development Goals which would build on the Millennium Development Goals and converge with the post 2015 development agenda. As according to http://www.un.org/disabilities/default.asp?id=1618, "Disability is referenced in various parts of the draft proposal on the SDGs and specifically in parts related to education, growth and employment, inequality, accessibility of human settlements, as well as data collection and monitoring of the SDGs."

Advancing Knowledge Societies: Environment, Health and Agriculture

Ecomedia Literacy for Environmental Sustainability

Antonio López

Though media education and education for sustainability are often thought of as separate or disconnected subjects, they in fact share many of the same goals of empowerment, participation and critical engagement. When combined they align with the GAPMIL Plan for Action. But to make the link, it is necessary to recognize that media directly impact the UN's Sustainability Development Goals (SDGs), because media are interconnected with the environment in terms of their material impact on living systems (extraction of rare earth minerals, pollution from manufacturing, e-waste and CO_2 emissions from the data cloud); media affect how we perceive ecology (beliefs about how humans and living systems interact, framing of environmental policy in the news, and influence of consumerism that leads to resource extraction and waste); gadget usage influences our own sense of place, space and time (a necessary component of environmental awareness); and media engagement can positively contribute to sustainable cultural change and solutions. To address these issues, this article proposes that media education can be "greened" by incorporating the concept of green cultural citizenship from a framework called "ecomedia literacy." This curriculum model connects media with healthy living systems and is in alignment with the core principles of MILID and the UN's SDGs.

Keywords: sustainability, media education, eco-literacy, green cultural citizenship

Defining the Problem

It is fairly common for media educators and students to have difficulty seeing the relationship between media and environmental sustainability. There is a historical reason for this. In the 19th century the mechanistic paradigm of the Industrial and Scientific Revolutions separated technological progress from its environmental consequence, which is maintained today by a general perception that technology is disconnected and isolated from living systems. This is reflected in disciplinary silos (Patterson, 2015). For example, academia often divides environmental studies from the core disciplines of media, such a ssocial science, humanities or information science. These boundaries are then codified by the way universities, academic institutions, non-governmental organizations and

299

governments categorize fields and disciplines that define where media and environment are studied. Subsequently, research confirms that very few contemporary media literacy resources actually address environmental issues (López, 2014). However, media education should be holistic to incorporate connections, relationships and systems thinking so as to promote environmental awareness (Blewitt, 2009).

In reality, environmental issues and media are closely related, so it is not difficult to build in a rationale to incorporate sustainability into MILID curricula. The connection between media and environment can be divided into two broad categories: ecological footprint and ecological "mind print." In terms of media's ecological footprint, the material impact of media can be traced all along the production chain of our technological gadgets, which disproportionately and negatively impacts the developing world (Maxwell & Miller, 2012; Maxwell, Lager Vestberg & Raundalen, 2015). Smart phones, televisions and computers require rare earth metals (coltan, cassiterite, wolframite, gold) that are extracted from mining operations that have had a particularly devastating impact in African countries. These "conflict minerals" have destroyed biodiversity and exacerbated regional military conflicts (Alakeson, 2003). Once extracted, minerals and other resources are shipped, processed and assembled in developing nations like China. The production of electronic gadgets impacts the health of workers and poisons the water and air where they are produced (Maxwell et al., 2015). Once shipped around the world, gadgets are consumed and then disposed of at an alarming rate in poor countries (Vidal, 2013). In terms of cloud computing, on a global scale, server farms already produce as much CO_2 as the aviation industry, due largely to the fact that most energy they currently consume comes from coal-powered plants (Cubitt, Hassan & Volkmer, 2011). Unless large social networks such as Facebook, and search engines like Google, convert to renewable energy use, the total emissions of the global data cloud will double in ten years. As discussed below in more detail, all of these environmental problems are tied directly to the UN's SDGs.

Media's mindprint relates to how our understanding of the environment is largely influenced by media. Given the manner in which media are a kind of informal education, they affect our attitudes about how we define and act upon livings systems on multiple levels. Media shape and define our experience of the world by a) propagating an ideology of unlimited growth, b) reinforcing the view that nature is separate from humans, c) marginalizing alternative ecological perspectives, and d) favoring industry discourses surrounding environmental issues (Beder, 1998). In terms of our understanding of climate change, despite a scientific consensus that climate change is human caused, the majority of US citizens believe otherwise, and since 2009, that awareness has decreased (Oreskes & Conway, 2010). Part of this is explainable by the behavior of news media, which consistently under-reports environmental issues in favor of more sensationalistic news events and the shift towards "infotainment." Budget cuts have also reduced the number of full-time journalists reporting on environmental news at major news organizations, such as the New York Times and NPR in the United States. Other ways media's mind print impacts us is the manner in which media organizations depend on advertising for their revenue, and how ads promote unsustainable cultural practices, such as consumerism and waste.

In addition, our increased use of smart phones impacts our sense of place, space and time. Sustainability educators believe that environmental responsibility and action starts when humans learn to care about their habitats and develop a "sense of place" (Blewitt, 2006; Capra, 2005; Orr, 1992; Stibbe, 2009; Thomashow, 1995). Increasingly, travel and gadget usage has made many of us global citizens, but also have increased a sense of alienation and disconnection from living systems. Screens are also impacting our individual health, which is the most important environment we inhabit (Stevens & Zhu, 2015).

Finally, because solving environmental problems required diverse cultural perspectives and strategies, sustainability is closely linked with cultural and linguistic diversity (Davis, 2004; Hawken, 2007). According to the UN's SDGs, environmental solutions require global coordination and problem solving. By assuring access and culturally diverse expression as advocated in the GAPMIL Plan for Action, media can also have a positive impact on environmental sustainability.

Growing a Solution: Green Cultural Citizenship and Ecomedia Literacy

In general, there are two ways to look at the issue of media, environmental sustainability and MILID. First, it is necessary to encourage and advocate for a healthy media ecosystem that is socially just and environmentally sustainable. As indicated by the UN's SDGs, this means that the negative environmental impacts of media are not disproportionately borne by the poor or developing nations, and that ultimately media technologies are produced more sustainably for the benefit of all populations. Secondly, there is the broader issue of citizenship (as described by GAPMIL Plan for Action) and the ability of young people to critically engage unsustainable cultural, social and economic practices perpetuated by media.

To encourage environmental sustainability it is necessary to expand our understanding of citizenship to incorporate more specifically ecological issues. To this end, green cultural citizenship is intended to unite sustainability with citizen engagement to meet the UN's SDGs. This means learners are encouraged:

• To develop an awareness of how media are materially interconnected with living systems. As mentioned, media usage contributes to a variety of environmental problems, including biodiversity loss, water and soil contamination, CO_2 pollution, and the health of workers. This corresponds directly with the SDGs to ensure food security; healthy lives and wellbeing; sustainable water management; sustainable and modern energy; urgent action to combat climate change; and the sustainable use of terrestrial ecosystems.

- To recognize media's phenomenological influence on the perception of time, space, place and cognition. This links directly with the SDG of healthy lives and wellbeing.

- To understand how media systems and communications technology are interdependent with the global economy and development models, and how the current model of globalization impacts livings systems and social justice. This ties into many of the SDGs, including: ending poverty; gender equality; sustainable economic growth; resilient infrastructure and sustainable industrialization; reducing inequality between countries; and promoting justice and peace.

- To analyze how media form symbolic associations and discourses that promote environmental ideologies. In particular, this relates to the SDG to ensure sustainable consumption and production patterns.

- To be conscious of how media impacts our ability to engage in sustainable cultural practices and to encourage new uses of media that promote all of the SDGs.

It is important to recognize that green cultural citizenship entails key assumptions derived from technoliteracy and ecopedagogy. As conceived here, technoliteracy is not the same as learning how media technology works, but, rather, explores why communication technology exists and for what purpose (Kahn, 2011; Kellner & Kahn, 2005). This requires decentering Eurocentric norms around technology and progress that have contributed to the current global economic crises. Ecopedagogy calls for shifting from an anthropocentric perspective rooted in mechanism towards a more ecocentric worldview based on ecological-centered awareness (Grigorov & Matias Fleuri, 2012; Kahn, 2011).

Ecomedia Literacy

So, how can MILID educators work towards the goals of green cultural citizenship? To start, we need to educate ourselves about the relationship between media and the environment. This is not easy, because media educators are already pressured by external forces that are influencing the direction of education, which makes it more difficult to focus on environmental issues (López, 2014).

For example, there is an increased emphasis on digital media and information literacy that deemphasized a humanities approach to media literacy. This has led to more vocational oriented methodologies that lack critical engagement with technological media systems (Gutiérrez-Martín & Tyner, 2012). Moreover, because sustainability is complex and often relegated to the physical sciences, it can be difficult to grasp. Many educators can feel uncomfortable teaching a new subject (media are complex enough!) and need professional development. Clearly, there is a necessity for institutional support and training to help media educators develop this emerging field. However, we can at least map out some pathways towards an approach that would be less intimidating and more practical.

Assuming there is a desire among media educators and policy support to incorporate sustainability with MIL, there are methods and techniques that can make it possible. The following is a proposal that seeks to combine the goals of MIL and education for sustainability (EfS). This hybrid framework, ecomedia literacy, has the goal of aiding learners to understand how everyday media practice impacts our ability to live sustainably within Earth's ecological parameters for the present and future (López, 2014). The curriculum model is based on a backwards design method intended to work towards a solution based on an "enduring question" (Cloud Institute for Sustainable Education, 2011). For example, learners can be charged with answering the following guiding query: What constitutes a healthy media ecosystem? Or, What form does sustainable media take?

One approach to answering these questions is to use the ecomedia literacy framework's central heuristic, the Ecomedia Wheel. The Ecomedia Wheel is a figurative map of media as part of a greater ecosystem. That is, media are contextualized within an interconnected ecosystem of living and nonliving parts. At the center of the Ecomedia Wheel, which is like a circle divided into four sections, we designate a media text (such as an advertisement, news article, television commercial, website, etc.) or gadget (smart phone, tablet, computer, etc.) as a "boundary object" to be analyzed. Boundary objects are items that have a mutually recognizable form but change meaning according to context. A football is an example of a boundary object: everyone agrees that a ball with a particular shape constitutes a football, but its use will vary greatly according to context and social practices. Learners are then asked to explore the media object's use and meaning from four different perspectives: worldview, ecology, political economy and culture. Conceptually and theoretically, these four perspectives correspond with various lenses that inform media studies and environmental studies.

Worldview (phenomenology) relates to media's impact on our perception of time, space and place. Environmental educators advocate for learners to develop a sense of place in order to care for the living systems that they depend on and to become conscious of their living habitats. Learners can participate in a number of exercises to become aware of how media impact their experience of space, place and time by keeping media usage diaries, doing media fasts and making comparative analysis by experiencing places with and without media. For example, a learner can compare the experience of walking through a neighborhood or forest with no media device to the experience of doing the same route through the view of a video camera or smart phone. In terms of media texts, students can learn about how sound, color, shape, form and light are in fact nervous system stimuli and can be understood as physiological phenomena. This approach can broadly be defined as cultivating "media mindfulness," which is the ability to be conscious of how media impact our cognition.

Ecology (material conditions of media, environmental studies) identifies the material conditions of media, including extraction, production, e-waste, energy and emissions. Activities include environmental audits, which track and measure the ecological footprint of media (gadgets and texts). This incorporates a wide number of MIL skills.

Political Economy (critical theory, critical political economy) examines the ideological structure of the global economics system as it relates to media and gadget production. This also involves a kind of technoliteracy that critically engages the economic motives for technological systems. The research activities for this support the GAPMIL Plan for Action and the UN's SDGs.

Culture (hermeneutics, cultural studies, textual analysis, intercultural communication) focuses on the more classical activities of media literacy through semiotic and discourse analysis of media texts. In particular, learners can identify environmental ideologies (beliefs about how humans should act upon the environment) in media texts, but also use information literacy skills to verify environmental claims, such as those dealing with climate change. In addition, learners can map cultural behaviors and attitudes through social media to identify how belief systems are shared and spread. Intercultural dialog can be used to explore the relationship between different cultural perspectives concerning the use of technology and media in relationship to local ecological values.

Once learners engage the media object through the Ecomedia Wheel's four lenses, they can communicate their findings with online multimedia tools, such as Prezi (http://prezi.com). This final stage of analyzing the media object is based on Bateson's (2007) model of education for global responsibility. By using the Ecomedia Wheel, learners should able to:

- Create narratives of connection by using digital storytelling tools.

- Translate concepts between media and ecology disciplines by using ecological metaphors to describe media phenomena.

- Perform crossovers with ways of knowing through participant observation and social learning.

- Develop an ethical framework in order act upon these understandings and to make wise choices.

Conclusion

Because there are so few extant media literacy materials specifically related to environmental sustainability, the ecomedia literacy framework remains experimental and needs further testing and collaboration. To date it has been utilized in only a few contexts (Lopez, 2014). However, it does offer a model to combine the key objectives of the GAPMIL Plan for Action with the UN's SDGs.

References

Alakeson, V. (2003). *Making the net work: Sustainable development in a digital society.* Middlesex, England: Xeris Pub.

Bateson, M. C. (2007). Education for global responsibility. In S. C. Moser & L. Dilling (Eds.), *Creating a climate for change: Communicating climate change and facilitating social change* (pp. 281-91). Cambridge: Cambridge University Press.

Beder, S. (1998). *Global spin: The corporate assault on environmentalism.* Foxhole, Dartington, Devon; White River Junction, Vt.: Green Books; Chelsea Green Pub.

Blewitt, J. (2006). *The ecology of learning: Sustainability, lifelong learning, and everyday life.* Sterling, VA: Earthscan.

Blewitt, J. (2009). The new media literacy: Communication for sustainability. In A. Stibbe (Ed.), *The handbook of sustainability literacy: Skills for a changing world* (pp. 220). Totnes, UK: Green Books.

Capra, F. (2005). Speaking nature's language: Principles for sustainability. In M. K. Stone, & Z. Barlow (Eds.), *Ecological literacy: Educating our children for a sustainable world* (1st ed., pp. 18-29). San Francisco Berkeley: Sierra Club Books.

Cloud Institute for Sustainable Education. (2011). *EfS curriculum design workbook.* New York: Cloud Institute.

Cubitt, S., Hassan, R. & Volkmer, I. (2011). Does cloud computing have a silver lining? *Media, Culture & Society, 33*(1), 149-158. doi:10.1177/0163443710382974

Davis, W. (2004). A world made of stories: Saving the web of cultural life. In K. Ausubel & J. P. Harpignies (Eds.), *Nature's operating instructions: The true biotechnologies* (pp. 214-226). San Francisco: Sierra Club Books.

Grigorov, S. K. & Matias Fleuri, R. (2012). Ecopedagogy: Educating for a new eco-social intercultural perspective . *Visão Global, 15*(1-2), 433-454.

Gutiérrez-Martín, A. & Tyner, K. (2012). Educación para los medios, alfabetización mediática y competencia digital. *Revista Comunicar, XIX*(38), 31-39.

Hawken, P. (2007). *Blessed unrest: How the largest movement in the world came into being, and why no one saw it coming.* New York: Viking.

Kahn, R. (2011). Technoliteracy at the sustainability crossroads: Posing ecopedagogical problems for digital literacy frameworks. In P. Trifonas (Ed.), *Learning the virtual life: Public pedagogy in digital world* (pp. 43-62). New York: Routledge.

Kellner, D. & Kahn, R. (2005). Reconstructing technoliteracy: A multiple literacies approach. *E-Learning, 2*(3), 238-51.

López, A. (2014). *Greening media education: Bridging media literacy with green cultural citizenship*. New York: Peter Lang.

Maxwell, R., Lager Vestberg, N. & Raundalen, J. (Eds.). (2015). *Media and the ecological crisis*. New York: Routledge.

Maxwell, R. & Miller, T. (2012). *Greening the media*. New York: Oxford University Press.

Oreskes, N. & Conway, E. M. (2010). *Merchants of doubt: How a handful of scientists obscured the truth on issues from tobacco smoke to global warming*. New York: Bloomsbury Press.

Orr, D. W. (1992). *Ecological literacy: Education and the transition to a postmodern world*. Albany: State University of New York Press.

Patterson, R. (2015). *Greening africana studies : Linking environmental studies with transforming black experiences*. Philadelphia: Temple University Press.

Stevens, R. G. & Zhu, Y. (2015). Electric light, particularly at night, disrupts human circadian rhythmicity: Is that a problem? *Philosophical Transactions of the Royal Society of London B: Biological Sciences, 370*(1667). doi:10.1098/rstb.2014.0120

Stibbe, A. (2009). *The handbook of sustainability literacy: Skills for a changing world*. Totnes, UK: Green Books.

Thomashow, M. (1995). *Ecological identity: Becoming a reflective environmentalist*. Cambridge, Mass.: MIT Press.

Vidal, J. (2013, December 14). Toxic 'e-waste' dumped in poor nations, says United Nations. *The Guardian*.

Beyond Training the Trainers: Engaging the Grass Roots in China's Public Health Campaigns[1]

Cornelius B. Pratt & Ying Hu

This article presents theory-based strategies and tactics for protecting and enhancing public health through integrating the personal influence model at the grass roots (including nongovernmental organizations, local residents, online communities of interest, and local mass media) into wellness campaigns focused on China's response to its haze events. But China's fledgling media literacy programmes, its dearth of health-information participants, and the localness of individuals' social ties underscore the importance of community participation, multistep information flows, and the broader use of social networks that are increasingly becoming a common fixture in Chinese communities affected by haze events. That fixture serves as a vehicle for ensuring acceptance of individual responsibility in controlling air pollution and for placing governments on notice that they need to undertake actions free of corporate interference. This article concludes with recommendations for more efficacious intercultural dialogue and public-health practices in emerging, tradition-bound communities of interest.

Keywords: China, haze events, public health campaigns, nongovernmental organizations, the personal influence model

> *The majority of people fail to do their bit to help change the air quality for the better by doing what they can in their daily lives and acting as whistle-blowers on air pollution.*
>
> "Documentary on Smog" (*China Daily*, March 2, 2015, p. 9)

As governments worldwide stand ready to endorse and implement Post-Millennium Development Goals that, beginning in September 2015, are being rebranded as Sustainable Development Goals (SDGs), it is imperative that China continue to demonstrate its commitment to protecting and sustaining the environment (SDG 11) and to applying different approaches, models or theories toward achieving sustainable development (SDG 13). For the world's most populous nation, SDG 13 calls its attention to, among other things, environmental pollution.

Industrial air pollution and its associated clinical problems (e.g., Ostermann & Brauer, 2001) are partly a consequence of China's high-energy, sizzling economic and industrial growth and of the pervasive use of low-quality oil and gas. Air quality is so crucial to a nation's well-being that more than 63 percent of Chinese respondents say that the annual number of blue-sky days should be a criterion for assessing their governments' performance (Ma, 2014). The increasing severity of China's haze crisis is indicated in the country's first smog lawsuit filed February 20, 2014, against the government of Hebei province, which has some of the country's most polluted cities and whose air quality was rated "seriously polluted" for 320 days in 2013 (Zheng, 2014). In that lawsuit, plaintiff Guixin Li, a Shijiazhuang, Hebei province, resident, claimed, based on the knowledge he derived from his exposure to (traditional and digital) media discourses of haze events and their effects, that the negligence of his local government in controlling air pollution resulted in his poor health. Li is awaiting acceptance or rejection of his case by the district court.

The health challenges that confront the world's most populous country make it imperative that non-clinical measures supplement efforts geared toward ensuring less vulnerability to ill-health and toward attaining better overall health. Therefore, this article proposes theory-based strategies and tactics for protecting and enhancing public health through integrating the personal influence model at the grass roots (including nongovernmental organizations [NGOs], local residents, online communities of interest, and the mass media) with wellness campaigns focused on responding to China's ever-raging haze crisis. The acquisition of media and information literacy (MIL) competencies, as a form of personal influence model that provides impetus to public health campaigns, specifically that on controlling air pollution, is proposed. And it emphasizes community participation, multistep information flows, and social networks as a beachhead to intercultural dialogue and community empowerment for responding strategically to a national crisis: haze and its effects on public health.

Research indicates an overwhelming interest in developing lifelong information-literate learners and better media educators and trainers (e.g., Ponjuan, 2010; Stern & Kaur, 2010); however, little attention has been directed to grass roots engagement in China's health and wellness programmes. This article attempts to fill that gap.

Cognizant of the public-health risks of pollution, global health communities have initiated programmes to ameliorate some aspects of China's public health challenges. Since September 2003, when UNESCO convened its first international Information Literacy Meeting of Experts in Prague, The Czech Republic, there has been a groundswell of global efforts to develop, implement and evaluate plans geared toward enhancing information literacy. In late October 2008, for example, UNESCO organized workshops to train trainers in information literacy (Pagell & Munoo, 2008, 2010; UNESCO, 2008). Those workshops had major pedagogical strengths: they outlined teaching objectives, methods and course objectives; identified course materials; and specified tactics for recruiting course participants. Even so, the nature of their audiences – paraprofessionals and institutions – left a void that this article attempts to fill: responding strategically to China's audiences' (traditional and digital) media literacy needs (knowledge, skills and competencies) in deciphering health and wellness programmes in an attempt to ensure public safety from the health effects of the haze crisis.

A Theory-Based Health-Campaign Proposal

For China's multicultural nation-state still largely rooted in traditional, collectivistic practices, the personal influence model is a refreshing departure from (across-the-board) orthodoxies and from a cache of (ritualized) platitudes. How so? The model has at least four key elements (Cohen & Bradford, 2005). First, it identifies the culture-sensitive salience of a national issue to communities. Encouraging citizen buy-ins on limiting (social) practices inimical to haze-reduction efforts or on discontinuing such practices for the national interest requires balancing citizen interest with the national interest. Examples are China's revered funeral rites and Spring Festival events that require smoke-emitting practices that have now been banned by the government, yet still undertaken sporadically in violation of such bans.

Second, the model diagnoses carefully others' interests. Personal interests that are threatened by government actions will require careful balancing of communications to acknowledge, accommodate, and even celebrate the salience of such interests.

Third, it assesses one's resources, ensuring that government agencies and grass-roots organizations are sufficiently resourceful to engage in persuasive communication for behavior change.

Fourth, it cultivates relationships by building on the ground mutual relationships and networks that are crucial to developing and disseminating effective public-health messages.

Those actions will determine the appropriate intercultural, values- and interests-based approach or a combination of approaches – rational persuasion, inspirational appeal, grass roots consultation, ingratiation, personal appeal, coalition, or relentless pressure (Cohen & Bradford, 2005) – toward galvanizing communities of interest for controlling haze events. The public absence of a central authority in itself engenders community participation, multistep information flows, and the use of social networks that are increasingly becoming a common fixture in Chinese communities – urban and rural.

309

Media and information literacy is closely related to the personal influence model, particularly when one considers both as a tool and process of empowerment at community and national levels. Table 1 outlines how they are related and how each can enhance sustainable change.

Table 1. Linking the Personal Influence Model to media and information literacy

The Personal Influence Model	Media and Information Literacy
Identify culture-sensitive salience of a national issue to communities	Understanding the need for, create and communicate information and media content with relevance to the local as well as national level
Balance citizen interest with the national interest	Describing and harmonizing citizen interest and national interest, as identified by citizen (consumer) in media and information content
Encourage citizen buy-ins and engage in two-way symmetrical flow of information	Encouraging media- and information-literate citizens to receive effectively information, particularly as a two-way symmetrical process, and specifying relevance of the information to behavior outcomes vis-à-vis haze events
Diagnose carefully others' interest(s)	Respecting, recognizing and appreciating diversity and plurality of interests in information and media content
	Having the ability to search for information or media content through multiple information and communication platforms, about others' interest, evaluating this information and acting positively upon it by using it to facilitate dialogue between the "other" and me or us
Assess one's resources to ensure that stakeholders such as governments and community organizations have the wherewithal to enable them to communicate effectively for behavior change	Demonstrating that media- and information-literacy competencies enable citizens to conduct relevant fact finding on resource availability; using access to information laws and regulations to request information where these laws apply
	Applying MIL competencies to ensuring effective use of media, social networks, libraries, as well as using other repositories of information and communication platforms for informed decision making, on individual actions and choices
	Encouraging citizens to create and disseminate user-generated content on relevant health or social issues
Foster (personal) relationship building on the basis of mutual understanding and outcomes of engaging multiple social networks	Demonstrating knowledge, skills, and attitudes to interact and communicate with others across, say, interests, perspectives, borders, cultures. Use social networks, media, ICTs for exchanges

The appeal of the personal influence model, combined with media and information literacy, to China's public health campaigns is further underscored by the country's socialized health care services, which are largely government owned and managed (Hung, Rane, Tsai & Shi, 2012; Yang, 2013; Zhao, 2006), resulting in government rhetoric that may not always meet the information literacy needs of the population. Also, China's media literacy education is fledgling; the inadequacy of social participation (Cheung & Xu, 2014; Tan, Xiang, Zhang, Teng & Yao, 2012) further underscores the need to direct more attention to grass-roots engagement in its health and wellness programmes. All of this requires a health-communication plan of action that is informed by problem and opportunity statements, a subject to which we now turn.

Problem and Opportunity Statements

An international visitor walks on Chang'an Avenue, in Beijing; a local resident bicycles on Jiefang Boulevard, in Wuhan, Hubei province; and a pedestrian strolls on Chunxi Road, in Chengdu, Sichuan province, all in areas of the country with disparate levels of economic and industrial development. Yet, all three parties have a common experience: straining to breathe freely through their nose masks. To protect world leaders and their delegations from environmental pollution during the November 2014 Beijing summit meeting of the Asia-Pacific Economic Cooperation (APEC), the central government, among other actions, banned the ritual burning of flowers at the Babaoshan Revolutionary Cemetery, in Beijing; declared an APEC Golden Week, a six-day vacation to reduce congestion in the city of 21 million people; closed factories; and restricted the entry of trucks into Beijing (Tatlow, 2014). That outcome had been dubbed "APEC blue," in reference to blue skies that were apparent only when APEC delegations were in Beijing.

This public health issue suggests that information, knowledge (symptoms of and preventive measures against air pollution), and awareness of haze events are critical to understanding air pollution and reducing its effects on the individual. How resourceful are citizens in coping with the outcomes of haze events? Granted, governments play a key role in the extent to which haze events are manifested. To what extent, for example, are environmental laws and regulations on industrial pollution enforced (rigorously)? An indication of a renewed government enforcement of existing laws and regulations is provided by Chinese courts' ruling in 2014 on 16,000 cases on environmental violations (Chen, 2015). That figure is nearly nine times that of the previous year. Civil cases seeking damages from pollution rose by more than 50 percent between 2013 and 2014.

Problem Statements

PS_1: Local and central governments are perceived publicly as paying lip service to a national-health crisis.

PS_2: Local and central governments are perceived publicly as conniving with manufacturing industries that contribute significantly to air pollution.

PS_3: The public is oblivious of the panoply of its responsibility in controlling air pollution.

PS_4: There is limited multiple flows of information and knowledge, leading to limited public awareness and limited individual and collective action and dialogue on haze events.

Opportunity Statements

OS_1: China's local and central governments are committed to fostering and sustaining a safe, healthy environment.

OS_2: Chinese governments' capacity to (a) establish partnerships with NGOs and with other communities of interest and (b) cooperate with the public can be harnessed for an efficient enforcement of regulations on environmental pollution.

OS_3: Public interest in air pollution is a raison d'être for its response to it.

OS_4: China's digital information environment is increasing access to both social and traditional media, leading to growing opportunities for enhancing its citizens' media and information literacy.

Health-Campaign Goals, Strategies and Tactics

Goals

1. To increase public understanding of air pollution and of governments' role in reducing it.

The rationale for this goal, as indicated in this article's epigraph, is that public understanding is two-pronged: that reasonable *knowledge* and *awareness* of haze and its effects play a major role in their control by, for example, encouraging the public to detect and report symptoms and to seek proper and timely interventions – all within the context of sharing testimonies within social networks and benefiting from increasing media and information literacy.

2. To engage further various communities of interest (e.g., NGOs) in reducing air pollution.

The rationale for this goal is that the financial and public health toll of haze events makes it imperative for a citizen role in reducing the magnitude of a public health crisis that imposes economic, environmental and health burdens on a nation and its people. Critical health literacy, for which media and information literacy is a sine qua non, is now more participatory, more empowering, more bottom-up, and more respectful of local needs than was the case in China (Wang, 2000). Consequently, several of China's NGOs are also promoting public awareness of health issues. One such organization is Darwin Nature Knowledge Society, which, in 2011, launched "I Monitor Air Quality for My Motherland" to encourage the public to monitor air quality in their neighborhoods and to post air-quality data on its website. Citizens in Wuhan and Zhengzhou contributed significantly to such efforts.

3. To demonstrate the impact of personal influence on a national-health issue.
The rationale for this goal is that technology- and nontechnology-mediated social networks serve as pervasive conduits for exercising persuasive appeals to engage citizens in behavioral actions consistent with limiting the impact of a health crisis on a nation and its people. Therefore, social media, one-on-one linkages, mass media, and access and exposure to health-communication campaigns on a variety of culture-sensitive platforms will widen the scope of a health appeal on a national health issue and result in significant desired behavior change (Dai, Hao, Li, Hu & Zhao, 2010; Mo et al., 2014; Wang, 2000). A former China Central Television anchor and reporter, Jing Chai, in March 2015 launched a 103-minute, self-funded documentary, "Under the Dome," to raise public awareness on the public health effects of haze. Such grass-roots citizen involvement in a national crisis, as illustrated by Chai's one-person national effort, has opened the floodgates to a heightening public discourse on it.

Objectives

1. To present publicly, during the next 12 months, governments' accomplishments vis-à-vis the health crisis attributed to haze.

2. To demonstrate, during the next 12 months, governments' transparency and trustworthiness in their response to the impact of air pollution on public health.

3. To demonstrate by the end of the campaign the value of the personal influence model as a theoretical foundation for health campaigns.

4. To improve, during the next 12 months, Chinese publics' MIL skills and competencies.

5. To facilitate, among grass roots communities, during the next 12 months, a number of intercultural dialogues and town-hall-style meetings on government actions and challenges to date.

Strategies and Tactics

Strategy 1: Encourage a public understanding of the importance of government initiated public-safety actions.
    Tactic 1: Disseminate information on the importance of haze
events to the government.
    Tactic 2: Provide third-party endorsements of government efforts.
    Tactic 3: Share with public specific data on haze events, by year.
    Tactic 4: Use (personal) stories (or testimonies) to demonstrate
a public understanding of governments' efforts in
controlling air pollution.

Strategy 2: Demonstrate to the public the credibility (or trustworthiness) of
governments in their actions on haze events.
    Tactic 1: Share with the public specific evidence on the autonomy
of government agencies' public-safety actions.
    Tactic 2: Disclose publicly instances of government-industry
connivance on actions vis-à-vis haze events.

Strategy 3: Emphasize critical exposure to and analysis of several media
platforms among Chinese citizens.
    Tactic 1: Adopt standard pretest-posttest measures of MIL
competencies for select Chinese citizen samples and
for select media fare on haze events.
    Tactic 2: Engage media-exposed citizens one on one for individual
or collective assessment.

Strategy 4: Apply the personal influence model to air pollution management.
    Tactic 1: Provide local citizens' testimonies as they relate to their
individual actions to reduce the effects of air pollution.
    Tactic 2: Document the effects of grass roots organizations on
public behaviors vis-à-vis haze events.

Prescriptions

The importance of grass roots involvement in resolving China's haze events is predicated on building a citizenry of ardent, knowledgeable consumers of media products: messages, discourses, audiovisuals. That translates into ensuring that citizens are developing the skills to learn from the media through selective exposure, critical reading, and analysis. Publics will then be able to, as Aguaded-Gómez, Tirado-Morueta & Hernando-Gómez (2015) state,

> question content and produce their own, which enables them to gain
> a greater understanding of the language and transforms them into
> citizen readers who are more judicious and critical in their continuous
> and daily dealings with the media. (p. 660)

Accomplishing those outcomes also requires that citizens' discerning skills and their literacy be at a level conducive to effective media engagement. This article, therefore, also recommends that public education campaigns on the ever raging haze crisis focus pari passu on citizen preparedness to engage critically media fare, on public awareness and understanding of governments' actions in controlling air pollution, on the public's social obligation to contribute to that control, and on the overarching importance of the public – not only the trainers – as cross-cultural partners in ensuring the effectiveness of health campaigns and of intercultural dialogues on health issues.

Finally, from an institutional perspective, it behooves local and central governments to match words with actions and with public expectations; that is, to demonstrate that officials are not on the take or that their agencies are not at the beck and call of industrial behemoths, after all.

References

Aguaded-Gómez, I., Tirado-Morueta, R. & Hernando-Gómez, Á. (2015). Media competence in adult citizens in Andalusia, Spain. *Information, Communication & Society, 18*, 659–679. doi: 10.1080/1369118X.2014.985244

Chen, T.-P. (2015, March 13). China sees more cases against polluters. *The Wall Street Journal*, p. A11.

Cheung, C. K. & Xu, W. (2014). Promoting media literacy education in China: A case study of a primary school. *International Journal of Adolescence and Youth, 19*, 1-3 (Topical PhD Thesis: Short Account). doi: 10.1080/02673843.2013.821078

Cohen, A. R. & Bradford, D. L. (2005). *Influence without authority* (2nd ed.). Hoboken, NJ: John Wiley.

Dai, J., Hao, Y., Li, G., Hu, D. & Zhao, Y. (2010). 'Love Teeth Day' campaign in China and its impact on oral public health – the twentieth anniversary. *British Dental Journal, 209*, 523-526. doi:10.1038/sj.bdj.2010.1039

Documentary on smog by individual insightful. (2015, March 2). *China Daily*, p. 9.

Hung, L.-M., Rane, S., Tsai, J. & Shi, L. (2012). Advancing primary care to promote equitable health: Implications for China. *International Journal for Equity in Health, 11*, 1-5. doi: 10.1186/1475-9276-11-2

Ma, L. (2014, March 11). Add blue-sky days to performance appraisal: Survey. *China Daily*. Retrieved from http://www.chinadaily.com.cn/china/2014npcandcppcc/2014-03/11/content_17339311.htm

Mo, D., Luo, R., Liu, C., Zhang, H., Zhang, L., Medina, A. & Rozelle, S. (2014). Text messaging and its impacts on the health and education of the poor: Evidence from a field experiment in rural China. *World Development, 64*, 766-780. doi:10.1016/j.worlddev.2014.07.015

Moore, P. (2002). An analysis of information literacy education worldwide. White Paper prepared for UNESCO, the U.S. National Commission on Libraries and Information Science, and the National Forum on Information Literacy. Information Literacy Meeting of Experts, Prague, the Czech Republic. Retrieved from http://portal.unesco. org/ci/en/ev.php-URL_ID=19633& URL_DO=DO_TOPIC&URL_SECTION=201.html

Ostermann, K. & Brauer, M. (2001): Air quality during haze episodes and its impact on health. In P. Eaton & M. Radojevic (Eds.), *Forest fires and regional haze in Southeast Asia* (pp. 195-226). New York: Nova Science.

Pagell, R. A. & Munoo, R. (2008). Information literacy for the information literate: UNESCO information literacy training the trainer workshop, Wuhan, China, October 2008. Retrieved from http:// www.slideshare.net/rpagell/il-for-il-rajen-ruth-111008

Pagell, R. A. & Munoo, R. (2010). Information literacy for the information literate: A model and case study from the Wuhan UNESCO training in the trainers in information literacy program. *The International Information & Library Review, 42*, 84-90.

Ponjuan, G. (2010). Guiding principles for the preparation of a national information literacy program. *The International Information & Library Review, 42*, 91-97.

Stern, C. & Kaur, T. (2010). Developing theory-based, practical information literacy training for adults. *The International Information & Library Review, 42*, 69-74

Tan, Q., Xiang, Q., Zhang, J., Teng, L. & Yao, J. (2012). Media literacy education in mainland China: A historical overview. *International Journal of Information and Education Technology, 2*, 382-385.

Tatlow, D. K. (2014, November 8). In Beijing, clearer views hide real life. *The New York Times*, pp. A4, A6.

UNESCO. (2008). Training the trainers in information literacy portal. Retrieved from http://portal.unesco.org/ci/en/ev.php-URL_IDZ25623& URL_DOZDO_TOPIC&URL_SECTIONZ201.html

Wang, R. (2000). Critical health literacy: A case study from China in schistosomiasis control. *Health Promotion International, 15*, 269-274.

Yang, W. (2013). China's new cooperative medical scheme and equity in access to health care: Evidence from a longitudinal household survey. *International Journal for Equity in Health, 12*, 20-32.

Zhao, Z. (2006). Income inequality, unequal health care access, and mortality in China. *Population and Development Review, 32*, 461-483.

Zheng, J. (2014, February 27). Smog suit by resident a long shot, experts say. *China Daily*. Retrieved from http://www.chinadaily.com.cn/china/////2014-02/27/content_17308022.htm

Notes

1   The authors acknowledge the invaluable comments and suggestions offered by reviewer Alton Grizzle on an earlier version of this article. Grizzle also provided the framework for linking the personal influence model directly to media and information literacy, as presented in Table 1. He is a Programme Specialist in the Media Development and Society Section of the Freedom of Expression and Media Development Division, Communication and Information Sector, UNESCO, Paris.

News Kills: Media Literacy and Health Education

Li Xiguang, Zhao Pu & Ouyang Chunxue

In mid-December 2013 and early 2014, series of infant deaths were wildly reported in the Chinese media which blamed Hepatitis B vaccine for causing the deaths and demonized Hepatitis B as 'killing vaccine'. But scientists later reported that the so-called "killing vaccine event" was a coincidence. But most Chinese media and reporters refused to correct their factual mistakes and they insisted on linking that infant mortality to the vaccine, which almost destroyed public confidence in the much-needed vaccination program for all Chinese newly-born babies. In the market-driven and highly commercialized media environment, most Chinese people lack both health education and media literacy. The Chinese media companies tend to take advantage of public ignorance of media and health literacy. In recent decade, the media have repeatedly used some isolated cases of infant mortality to attract attention by exaggerating, sensationalizing and even fabricating stories about the country's vaccination program. This article offers an extensive analysis of how media manipulate public opinion, fabricate crisis, and instigate public panic in the context of media commercialization using hepatitis B vaccination as a case study.

Keywords: media literacy, health education, media fabrication, media sensationalization

Introduction

Chronic infection of hepatitis B virus (HBV) poses serious public health threat around the world, potentially causing adverse clinical outcomes including premature deaths from hepatic decompensation, cirrhosis, as well as hepatocellular carcinoma (Cui & Jia, 2013). Infection of HBV can cause chronic liver disease and infection, and increase the risk of death from cirrhosis of the liver and liver cancer. The situation is particularly true in China, where 120 million people are chronically infected, and 30 million people suffer from chronic hepatitis, and the annual toll of the deaths due to HBV-related diseases is about 300,000 individuals (Zhu, Wang & Wangen, 2014).

China is a highly endemic area of hepatitis B. Since mother-to-child transmission was proven to be a leading cause of high infection rate of HBV, Chinese government initiated a nationwide HBV vaccination program in 1992 and later offered free HBV vaccination for all newborns in 2005 (Wang & Jia, 2011). Infants and young children, who are most prone to develop long-term complications following HBV infection, have been given high priority. Because of these relentless efforts to curb HBV transmission, the HBV prevalence among children had been reduced to 1.0% according to the latest nationwide survey in 2006 (Liang et al., 2013).

In mid-December 2013 and early 2014, several cases of infant deaths were reported after taking hepatitis B vaccination. Food and drug regulators started to investigate the cause of those deaths. Before there was any solid evidence that the vaccination caused the problem, the media pointed fingers at the "deadly" or "killing" hepatitis B vaccination for causing those deaths.

After thorough investigations, Chinese scientists and the authorities later claimed that the so-called killing vaccination events were merely coincidences. World Health Organization also issued a statement that China's vaccines are produced and regulated in accordance with international standards, and the hepatitis B vaccination program is vital in safeguarding children against the illness. But most Chinese journalists insisted on connecting those deaths to the vaccine, destroying public confidence in HBV vaccine and tens of thousands of families refused to vaccine their newborns.

According to a survey conducted by the Chinese Center for Disease Control and Prevention in December 2013, twenty percent of parents refuse to let their children receive a hepatitis B vaccination, and nearly thirty percent showed hesitation. Panic triggered by those false reports led to a thirty percent drop in hepatitis B vaccination rate in December. Moreover, public panic over vaccination safety also led to a 15 percent decline of vaccinations for other diseases. If the situation exacerbates, according to the official, an estimated 400,000 to 500,000 children will be susceptible to infectious diseases.

Media Commercialization in China

Prior to the economic reform in the early 1980s, news media in China were mostly seen as party propaganda apparatus, disseminating state policies, decisions and actions to the general public (Tang & Sampson, 2012). Since 1980s, press commercialization in China has been part of the broad transformation of the whole society when Deng Xiaoping's opening-up policy began to execute. Many market-driven newspapers and magazines started to emerge in their pursuit of economic self-interest (Zhao, 2000). As of 2014, there are nearly 1,900 newspapers and over 9,000 magazines in China, and profits of commercials account for the main income of these media companies (Cui, 2014).

In the highly commercialized media environment, "mass entertainment", instead of "factual information" has become the key element of journalism in China. In order to attract readers' attention, most media organizations would resort to reporting scandals or sensational events, at the expense of their credibility.

With the increasing interactions between the Internet and traditional media in the past few years, business has taken over the newsroom. Shen Hao, a promising journalist, publisher of the 21st Century Business Herald, was detained in 2014, guilty of extortion in exchange for cover-ups and payments for news. The newspaper owners had to pay his newspaper hefty "protection fees" to avoid negative news coverage.

Media Event: News vs. Science

Under current Chinese journalism education system, most journalists lack the necessary scientific trainings and access to interdisciplinary study in journalism schools, especially in the arena of public health reporting, the majority of health journalists have never gone through any health reporting training. They tend to rephrase the story via a more sensational but totally unscientific way. Whenever a medical event emerges, journalists would report it from the scandal angle instead of the scientific angle. Media makes more profit by selling sensation.

"Those children hurt by vaccinations" headlined a lead story highlighted at one of the most popular portals, sohu.com, on June 24, 2013.

Due to lack of health literacy and scientific training, reporters tend to sensationalize news story without checking the facts. In the Internet era, media organizations, especially website portals, sensationalize the headlines, or fabricate stories with the aim of increasing traffic and hits. When more death cases were found in Shenzhen in the mid-December 2013, *Beijing Nightly* covered the issue, but changed the news language from scientists' words "suspected death cases for vaccine" into "killing vaccine". After the news was released, the phrase "killing vaccine" started to spread among Chinese tweeters –Weibo, the most popular twitter-like social network site, like wild fire. The public demanded the central government to release more information. Some Weibo users blamed the government for attempting to cover up negative reporting about health problems, just as they did during the SARS crisis in 2003. Chinese government was harshly criticized for hiding the seriousness of the SARS virus and early efforts to fight the virus were slowed by poor information released by the national health department.

"疫苗致死" 增至7例 北京新生儿未用 "叫停疫苗"

2013/12/25 7:29:04　来源:北京晚报 作者:贾晓宏

原标题: "疫苗致死" 增至7例 北京新生儿未用 "叫停疫苗"

新华社电 记者昨天从广东省疾控中心证实,从11月至今,该省共报告4例疑似接种由深圳康泰生物制品股份有限公司生产的重组乙型肝炎疫苗 (酿酒酵母) 后死亡病例。这意味着加上国家食药监总局此前公布的湖南、四川两省案例,全国疑似 "疫苗致死" 病例已增至7例。

广东省疾控中心 4例疑似 "疫苗致死" 病例

广东省疾控中心介绍,这4例病例分别发生在中山、江门、深圳、梅州等地,其中中山市病例11月29日经过中山市预防接种异常反应调查诊断专家组调查,诊断结论为重症肺炎,与疫苗接种无关。另外3例正陆续进行尸体解剖以明确死亡原因。由于尸检需要30个工作日才能得出具正式报告,目前仍只能列为疑似病例。

记者注意到,除中山、深圳两例广为人知外,江门、梅州两例并未见诸公开报道,此前也未有相关部门公布。

"The number of 'killing vaccine' cases keep rising, Beijing newborns did not use killing vaccine", *Beijing Nightly*, December 24, 2013.

Due to immense pressure from the press as well as public through social media, Chinese public health departments at all levels decided to suspend the use of all hepatitis B vaccines while medical experts in the field of vaccines or public health urged news outlets to differentiate between "possibility" and "certainty". China's Ministry of Health and CFDA (China Food and Drug Administration) hosted a press release and explained all possible reasons that might lead to those deaths and insisted that it is far too early to determine the cause of death before the official investigation concluded. They also invited WHO to join the investigation.

"Health Hype" and Health Education

News media plays a crucial role in the dissemination of health information in influencing public debate regarding health issues or promoting public health (Wallack, Dorfman, Jernigan & Themba, 1993). Driven by profits from commercials, most health journalists choose to attract readers' attention via posting sensational articles or pictures, photos of violence etc. Signorielli (1993) describes this phenomenon, i.e. health news exaggerating and entertaining when reporting health-risk issue for the purpose of commercial profits, as "health hype".

In China, the most powerful news reporting is the one that successfully influence the public's sentiments. To capture people's minds means to capture people's appeal. In this case, media tend to use drama to amplify people's emotions. Coverage of health crisis is often sensational, full of worst-case scenarios and instigating language.

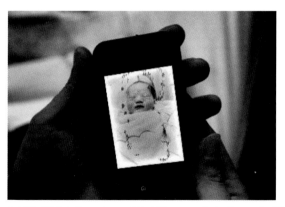

Subtitle "This is the only proof that his son really had come to this world",
Modern Express, December 24, 2013.

On the 2nd page of *Modern Express,* a metro paper in Nanjing, Jiangsu, the reporter covered the scene where one of the newborns died after taking vaccination in this way.

> *"It's pulmonary hemorrhage. There is no hope for saving your baby. We are very sorry for your loss."* The chief doctor waved his head and sighed.
>
> *"But he is still breathing! Save him!"* his (the baby) father insisted.
>
> *"It is actually the air we pressed in. Sorry, sir."* said the doctor.
>
> *"But his head is so warm!"*
>
> (*Modern Express,* January 24, 2014)

Soon after this coverage was released, anger rapid spread over the Internet, and many netizens blamed the hospital and pharmaceutical companies for killing the baby, and expressed deep regret for all the parents who had lost their children due to the "deadly vaccine". "Deadly vaccine" became the second trending topic on Sina Weibo overnight on Wednesday, after "Merry Christmas", with most postings voicing worries over product quality control.

A few days before this report was published, *Qianjiang Nightly*, another metro paper in Hangzhou, had covered another story headlined in a more sensational and even cruel way, "Babies' bodies were exhumed for test, and the parents are waiting for official response". Once published, netizens vented their rage on Weibo using languages such as "Go to hell, bloody doctors" or "Poor baby, I swear I will not vaccine my child next time." "It is too dangerous to live in China, say no to local vaccines, for the sake of our lives!"

Irrational angers accumulate at the local BBS, *Eighteenth Floor*, December 26, 2013.

Some people attempted to defuse the tension by voicing on the local BBS "Eighteenth floor", saying that "there is no solid evidence that these vaccines have real problems. We should calm down and be more reasonable". Netizens immediately responded to those who support the government and scientists and even threatened to blacklist them from the BBS. Fueled by the sensational reporting of the media, the public would rather believe that the government is covering up for pharmaceuticals, than to believe in the authorities who are more experienced in handling these issues.

News media is the main source of health information, and the general public relies on news media for information on health issues, even more than they rely on physicians (Covello & Peters, 2002). Acting as the core health-related information source for the public in China, news media is to blame for the prevailing lack of health literacy and irrational tendencies towards health institutes of most Chinese people. It is proven by numerous studies that media is capable of changing health beliefs and behavior, informing on public health issues while providing frames or agendas that are consistent with the media's benefits or core values.

The media may influence an individual's tendency to overestimate the risk of some health issues while underestimating the risk of others, ultimately influencing an individual's health choices (Berry, Wharf-Higgins & Naylor, 2007). In other words, since most people have no time to sort out the complexity behind the public health issues, news media act as the "interpreter" and intermediary between what people should concern themselves with and what not.

The news media have decisive power over which health-related topics reach the public and what are the most pressing health-related issues of the day. Since most medical journalists in China lack professional knowledge, unbalanced and inaccurate news coverage of diseases may cause the public to overestimate health risks such outbreaks like SARS in Asia or Ebola in Africa, while underestimate fatal and deadly diseases such as cancer and diabetes in their own country, which are more noteworthy but not as "newsworthy" as those diseases which can not attract as much attention as an endemic.

Figure 5. Mortality rate of main diseases in China, 2013.

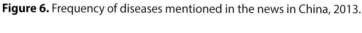

Source: *China Health and Family Planning Statistical Yearbook 2013*

Figure 6. Frequency of diseases mentioned in the news in China, 2013.

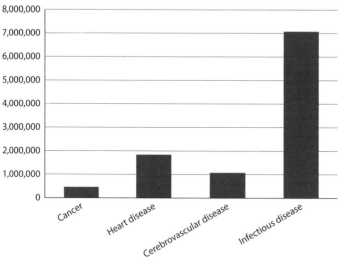

Source: Baidu Index, 2013

Besides unbalanced health reporting, another reason why news media have not been qualified as an ideal source for promoting public health education is that journalists work on deadlines, but scientists work at the pace of scientific process. Many of the problems in reporting health risks arise from the constraints of deadlines. Reporters do not have enough time or energy to master the nuances of scientific and medical issues. Since few reporters have the scientific background or expertise to evaluate complex scientific or medical data within a tight time frame, news media always fail to provide background information, which is crucial for the public to put the health crisis in perspective, therefore fail to take appropriate measures to prevent the outbreak.

Discussion and Conclusion

With China heading into an aging society, media coverage of public health issues has increased substantially in recent years. Fuelled by "attention economy", news media in China have abandoned their responsibilities as the main source of unbiased, accurate health information for the public, and establish frames that can create fear and misconception that there exists real and serious risks that need to be addressed not only by the public, but also by policy makers. News media uses the frame "health hype" to put pressure on government authorities to take drastic measures to manage the crisis.

Scholars have pointed out that news media fueled unnecessary fears during the SARS epidemics in 2003 and in other cases, by exaggerating the risk and overacting to the threat (Vasterman & Ruigrok, 2013). Even so, the average level of health education among most Chinese audience is still low, and the media therefore can still manipulate collective emotions by triggering huge and fast trending news stories, which may overthrow any possible balanced and rational voices from the experts and scientists.

This case study proves that China in general is in great need of health education to raise health literacy.

References

Berry, T. R., Wharf-Higgins, J. & Naylor, P. J. (2007). SARS Wars: An Examination of the Quantity and Construction of Health Information in the News Media. *Health Communication*, 21(1), 35-44. doi: 10.1080/10410230701283322

Covello, V. T. & Peters, R. G. (2002). Women's perceptions of the risks of age-related diseases, including breast cancer: reports from a 3-year research study. *Health Communication*, 14(3), 377-395. doi: 10.1207/S15327027HC1403_5

Cui, Y. & Jia, J. (2013). Update on epidemiology of hepatitis B and C in China. *Journal of Gastroenterology and Hepatology*, 28, 7-10. doi: 10.1111/jgh.12220

Liang, X., Bi, S., Yang, W., Wang, L., Cui, G., Cui, F., Wang, Y. (2013). Reprint of: Epidemiological serosurvey of Hepatitis B in China – Declining HBV prevalence due to Hepatitis B vaccination. *Vaccine*, 31, J21-J28. doi: 10.1016/j.vaccine.2013.08.012

Tang, L. & Sampson, H. (2012). The interaction between mass media and the Internet in non-democratic states: The case of China. *Media, Culture & Society*, 34(4), 457-471. doi: 10.1177/0163443711436358

Vasterman, P. L. & Ruigrok, N. (2013). Pandemic alarm in the Dutch media: Media coverage of the 2009 influenza A (H1N1) pandemic and the role of the expert sources. *European Journal of Communication*, 28(4), 436-453.

Wang, Y. & Jia, J. (2011). Control of hepatitis B in China: prevention and treatment. *Expert Review of Anti-infective Therapy*, 9(1), 21-25. doi: 10.1586/eri.10.143

Zhao, Y. (2000). From commercialization to conglomeration: the transformation of the Chinese press within the orbit of the party state. *Journal of Communication*, 50(2), 3-26. doi: 10.1093/joc/50.2.3

Zhu, D., Wang, J. & Wangen, K. R. (2014). Hepatitis B vaccination coverage rates among adults in rural China: Are economic barriers relevant? *Vaccine*, 32(49), 6705-6710. doi: 10.1016/j.vaccine.2013.06.095

Role of Agricultural Information Literacy in Agricultural Knowledge Mobilization

Inder Vir Malhan

A number of end users and even those involved in transfer of agricultural knowledge are not effectively searching and profitably using the existing agricultural information in India. There are therefore knowledge gaps between what agricultural best practices actually exist in the country and what is by and large being practised at farmers' fields. Agricultural information literacy can play a crucial role in agricultural knowledge mobilization and bridging the knowledge gaps. This article presents a collaborative information literacy model for India including the partnership of public libraries, agricultural extension departments, and other stakeholders that can potentially enhance the practices of knowledge based agricultural work in India.

Keywords: agricultural information literacy, farmers' empowerment, agricultural knowledge mobilization

Introduction

India is one of the major players in production of food grains, horticulture produce and milk. The indigenous system of medicine namely Ayurveda is also by and large plant based as a large number of medicinal plants exist in India. Because of the existence of different environmental and climatic conditions in different regions, the country has enormous diversity of plants and field crops ranging from condiments in Kerala, sandalwood forest in Karnataka, saffron in Kashmir, apple orchids in Himachal Pradesh, mangoes in Uttar Pradesh and tea in Assam. A sizeable Indian population is engaged in agriculture and almost seventy percent of the rural population is dependent on agriculture for their livelihoods. The country has achieved self sufficiency in food production to a great extent by green revolution, white revolution and blue revolution. By improving bilateral ties with other countries and other nations, India is making efforts for initiatives ameliorating agricultural sector and improving the income of farmers.

Indian agricultural sector is facing several challenges, such as rising temperature, growing soil salinity, lowering ground water level, increasing pollution in rivers and waterways, decreasing size of farms, conversion of fertile farm land into urban areas, and increasing cost of agricultural inputs. Besides crop damage by national disasters, enormous quantity of food grains and horticulture produce is also wasted every year because of the lack of adequate storage and food processing facilities. Food grain production in India per hectare area and milk production per animal is low as compared to a number of other countries mainly because of knowledge gaps of global best practices.

Agricultural Knowledge Gaps

To enhance agricultural productivity in India, every farmer is required to be provided with the best possible existing knowledge, motivation and environment that facilitate enhanced production. Our overall agricultural productivity is, in fact, a combined balance sheet of contribution of individual farmers. The agricultural productivity level of various farmers even in the same geographical area may vary because farmers in India have asymmetric access to existing agricultural knowledge. The mantra for increasing crop yields is to render help to every farmer by transferring and imbedding state-of-the-art agricultural knowledge and best practices in his work and fields. Knowledge gaps are, by and large, detrimental to enhancing agricultural productivity. The transfer of latest agricultural knowledge from agricultural labs to land is one of the neglected areas of Indian agriculture. "We have a huge gap between what is produced on research stations and demonstration fields and the average actual production. And that gap can be up to 200%. This means that at least in theory there is a potential for doubling yields if recommended practices and crop varieties are followed" (Bhattacharya, 2008). Generation of new agricultural knowledge is thus not as much a problem as its communication to end users. "According to National Sample Survey Organization Report, 60% of farmers in India have no access to agricultural technology" (Suryamurthy, 2005). This raises a pertinent question that whom do we serve by generating agricultural knowledge through publically funded research. What makes a difference in the productivity and economic well being of farmers is knowledge and awareness of best practices and varieties of seeds, etc. "I planted the permal variety [of rice] in my fields last year while my neighbour Jasmeet Singh opted for muchhal while I got a price of Rs. 750 per quintal for my produce. Jasmeet's crop fetched him a rate of Rs. 2,200," said Joginder Singh, a farmer from Jeevan Nagar Village of Sirsa (Sushil, 2008).

The problem is not only transfer of newly generated knowledge at agricultural research institutions, but also diffusion of best practices developed and established by some innovative farmers to other farmers. For instance Parkash Singh Raghuvanshi singlehandedly developed a number of high yielding nutritious and disease resistant varieties of wheat paddy, pigeon pla (*tur dal*) and mustard which can also withstand adverse weather changes. "Every variety, I developed has a yield of 20-40 percent more than the ones available in the market" says Prakash Singh (Ashish Kanwal, 2011). Setting paddy stubble on fire is both an environmental pollution issue as well by killing microorganisms in the soil hampers productivity too. A villager at his workshop developed a machine called shredder-chopper not only alleviated the need for burning paddy stubble but also helps to mix straw with soil to prepare soil for the next crop. "This machine designed by Gurtej Singh Channi of Siriwala Village has been recommended because of its appreciable results on the ground" (Bariana, Sanjeev Singh, 2014). This indicates that generation of new knowledge is not only the prerogative of high fliers, a number of innovative farmers develop from their experiential knowledge their own way of solving problems at hand. The major challenge in a vast country like India is how to transfer the best possible knowledge available at research labs to grass root innovative farmers and how to organize, and mobilize this knowledge for widespread use. The mobilization of agricultural knowledge resources and their appropriate use requires information literacy skills at all levels. This will enable various stakeholders to build their capacities to actively and collectively find information about knowledge resources and mobilize that knowledge for enhanced productivity and knowledge based problem solving and for research work practices.

Information Literacy and Knowledge Mobilization

Millions and millions of farmers in India are struggling with poverty because of illiteracy and lack of information literacy skills. Their inability to find information that may help them to improve their economic status to come out of the clutches of deprivation, is keeping their lives glued to poverty. In view of the growing volume of multi-media sources of information, even the illiterate farmers can get access to new ideas in their local languages to further mobilize such knowledge resources. An organization namely 'Digital Green' asks successful farmers to make videos for other farmers not only to facilitate farmers' access to need based and relevant agricultural knowledge, but also to help assimilate that knowledge through 'show how' video content. "Since its inception in 2008, Digital Green has produced 2,800 videos, in 20 languages, reached 2,200 villages and 130,000 farmers in eight Indian States and four African countries... The 'Digital Green' team is upbeat as they claim that their approach was found to be 10 times more cost effective and uptake of new practices, seven times higher compared to traditional extension services" (Chandra, Kavita Kanan, 2014).

Improving the farmers' economic status and adoption of sustainable best agricultural practices must go hand in hand. "A recent study, undertaken in the states of Karnataka, Madhya Pradesh and Orissa, estimated that an average farmer who adopted the new practices for rice cultivation and livestock featured in [Digital Green] video would see an annual income gain of \$294" (Chandra, Kavita, 2014). If such efforts can make difference in farmers' lot, agricultural practices if linked to systemic and effective knowledge resource centres, and if farmers are motivated to learn new things, the combined effect will definitely result in increased agricultural productivity.

Agricultural information literacy is a skill which all stakeholders in the agricultural professions at all levels must acquire, but farmers must learn how to learn for putting agricultural knowledge to practice. Having knowledge and competency of how to effectively search and profitable use information is important but we must have, quality filtered, best information resources that can ensure appropriate positive actions. In addition to knowledge resources pertaining to state-of-the-art agricultural technologies, databases of best practices, lessons learned, success stories and other similar content may be created. At individual level, every Indian farmer has curiosity to know, and a story to tell. But bringing them to systemic process of information seeking to augment their knowledge and enhance their productivity is a big challenge. Information providers and information literacy educators must also intimately understand their concerns and contexts in which they seek information. They should see how farmers can best be linked to information resources and engaged in information seeking, evaluation, and information use processes. They should also understand the socio-cultural contexts and landscape of their work practices and situations for which they seek information. The major problem area is lack of knowledge of existing agricultural knowledge resources. When the farmers don't know about these resources, they cannot take benefit of such resources.

While imparting information services to farmers, communication technologies and devices commonly used by them should be taken into consideration. As mobile telephony is very common and social media is also getting grounded in farming communities, information exchange through such media will be helpful for them. Training some farmers as trainers in information literacy skills will have positive effect. If delivery of training is made interesting and musing, when new knowledge enters the portal of a village, it gets diffused easily though customized manner in a conformist sense by news makers and information brokers.

Indian agriculture is facing many questions, such as "can we grow apples in Andhra Pradesh, blackberries in Bengal, olives in Assam, moringa in Maharashtra, Brazilian nuts in Bihar, *cordyceps simensis* in Kerala?" Answers to such questions are in agricultural knowledge bases and information repositories to provide access to latest agricultural information resources and motivate practitioners to venture into risk free new agricultural endeavours.

Information literacy is an essential skill for lifelong learning, self learning and accessing agricultural information resources. A massive effort is required in India to train agricultural farmers if we are seriously concerned to mobilize agricultural knowledge resources and bridge the knowledge gaps in agricultural sector. Some efforts are being made here and there in some states of India to empower people to access information. For instance, in the state of Kerala, which has 100 percent literacy, one person of every family is being imparted computer literacy under project Akshayla.

To empower farmers and other stakeholders in the field of agriculture, public libraries, agricultural university libraries, mass media channels and extension departments must work in tandem as they have the common objective of improving the lot of people through channelization. We are in the ocean of agricultural information. There is so much to search and learn, then we must learn how to search, access, and strategically use information that matters in our lives and work practices.

References

Barniana, Sanjeev Singh, (2014). "Sowing Crops without burning stubble; Bathinda farmers users new machine, shredder chopper to sow potatoes. *The Tribune,* November 3, p. 5.

Chandra, Kavita Kanon, (2014). "Enter Harbingers of social change; a look at innovative entrepreneurs who use technology to effect social engineering. *The Tribune, Spectrum,* March 31, p. 1.

Kanwal, Ashish, (2011). *Agricultural Industry Survey,* Available at http://www.agricultureinformation.com/mag/

Suryamurthy, R., (2005). ICAR revamp to benefit farmers. *The Tribune,* September 27, p. 2.

Sushil, M., (August 1, 2008). Farmers dump parmal for muchhal, *The Tribune,* August 1, p. 7.

Contributors

Adebola Adewunmi Aderibigbe
Department of Communication/Performing Arts, Bowen University, Iwo, Osun State, Nigeria. adebolaalert@gmail.com

Anjuwon Josiah Akinwande
Department of Mass Communication, Babcock University, Ilishan Remo, Ogun State, Nigeria. anjuwon2013@yahoo.com

Jose Reuben Q. Alagaran II
Professor, Miriam College, Philippines. jralagaran@gmail.com

Tomás Durán Becerra
PhD candidate, Universitat Autònoma de Barcelona (UAB), Spain. tomasduranb@gmail.com

Dilara Begum
Librarian, Head of Library, East West University, Dhakka, Bangladesh. dilalab@gmail.com

Santiago Tejedor Calvo
Researcher and lecturer, Universitat Autònoma de Barcelona (UAB), Spain. santiago.tejedor@uab.cat

Sherri Hope Culver
Associate Professor, School of Media and Communication, and Director, Center for Media and Information Literacy (CMIL), Temple University, Philadelphia, USA. shculver@temple.edu

Senada Dizdar
Department of Comparative Literature and Librarianship at Faculty of Philosophy in Sarajevo, University of Sarajevo, Bosnia and Herzegovina. senadadizdar@gmail.com

Alton Grizzle
Programme Specialist, Communication and Information, UNESCO HQ, Paris, France. a.grizzle@unesco.org

Lejla Hajdarpašić
Department of Comparative Literature and Librarianship at Faculty of Philosophy in Sarajevo, University of Sarajevo, Bosnia and Herzegovina. lejla.hajdarpasic83@gmail.com

Forest Woody Horton, Jr.
Library and Information Consultant, Washington, DC, USA. f.w.hortonjr@att.net

Jagtar Singh
Professor and Head, Department of Library and Information Science, Punjabi University, Patiala, (Punjab), India. jagtardeep@gmail.com

Joan Yee Sin
University Librarian, University of the South Pacific, Laucala Campus, Suva, Fiji. sjoan.yee@usp.ac.fj

Tessa Jolls
President and CEO, Center for Media Literacy, Director, Consortium for Media Literacy, Malibu, USA. tjolls@medialit.com

Harinder Pal Singh Kalra
Associate Professor, Department of Library and Information Science, Punjabi University, Patiala, India. hpskalra@gmail.com

Sujay Kapil
Research Scholar, Central University of Himachal Pradesh, Dharmshala, India.
kapilsujay@gmail.com

Tibor Koltay
Professor, Head of Department and Course Director, Department of Information
and Library Studies, SzentIstván University, Jászberény, Hungary.
Koltay.Tibor@abpk.szie.hu

Vedabhyas Kundu
Programme Officer, Gandhi Smriti and Darshan Samiti, New Delhi, India.
vedabhyas@gmail.com

Li Xiguang
Honorable Dean, Southwestern University of Political Science and Law; Professor
and Director of Tsinghua University International Center for Communication;
Director of Tsinghua University Institute of Health Communication, Beijing, China.
xiguang@tsinghua.edu.cn

Antonio López
Assistant Professor of Communications and Media Studies, Department of
Communications, John Cabot University, Rome, Italy. alopez@johncabot.edu

Inder Vir Malhan
Professor, Head of Department of Library and Information Science, Dean of
Mathematics, Computers and Information Science, Central University of Himachal
Pradesh, Dharamshala, India. imalhan_47@rediffmail.com

Neelima Mathur
Executive Producer, Researcher and Writer at SPOTFILMS, Trustee & Trainer
at FORMEDIA, New Delhi, India. Neelima.mathur@gmail.com

Syarif Maulana
Lecturer, Faculty of Communication and Business, Telkom University, Bandung,
Indonesia. syarafmaulini@gmail.com

Kyoko Murakami
Director, Asia-Pacific Media and Information Literacy Education Centre, Program
Manager, CultureQuest Japan, and Lecturer, Hosei University, Japan.
mkyoko5@nifty.com

Marta Portalés Oliva
Predoctoral Researcher, Department of Journalism and Communication Sciences,
Faculty of Communication Sciences, Universitat Autònoma de Barcelona (UAB),
Spain. marta.portales@uab.cat

Ogova Ondego
Director, Creative and cultural entrepreneur, Nairobi, Kenya. oondego@gmail.com

Chunxue Ouyang
PhD candidate, Tsinghua University School of Journalism and Communication,
Beijing, China. annouyang@aliyun.com

José Manuel Pérez Tornero
Director, Department of Journalism and the Gabinete de Comunicación y Educación
(UAB), Spain. josep.manuel@uab.cat

Cornelius B. Pratt
Temple University, Philadelphia, USA. cbpratt@temple.edu

Manukonda Rabindranath
Dean, School of Journalism, Mass Communication and New Media, Central
University of Himachal Pradesh, Dharmshala, India. mrabindra2002@yahoo.co.in

Mia Rachmiati
Functional Staff, Center for Development of Early Child, Non-formal and Informal Education, Bandung, Indonesia. mia.rachmi@gmail.com

Thomas Röhlinger
Founder and Editor in Chief of Radijojo World Children's Media Network (since 2003), Berlin, Germany. roehlitom@yahoo.de

Jun Sakamoto
Professor, Director for Librarian training course, Faculty of Lifelong learning and Career studies, Hosei University in Tokyo, Japan. sakamoto@hosei.ac.jp

Ibrahim Mostafa Saleh
Chair of Journalism Research and Education Section, University of Cape Town, South Africa. Ibrahim.Saleh@uct.ac.za

K. S. Arul Selvan
Associate Professor, School of Journalism and New Media Studies, IGNOU, New Delhi, India. ksarul@ignou.ac.in

Adebisi O. Taiwo
Lecturer, Department of Media, Communication and Social Studies, AfeBabalola University, Ado-Ekiti, Nigeria. toksbis2k2@yahoo.com

Sally S. Tayie
Lecturer, College of Language and Communication, Arab Academy for Science, Technology, and Maritime Transport, Cairo, Egypt. stayie@aucegypt.edu

Jordi Torrent
Project Manager, Media and Information Literacy, United Nations Alliance of Civilizations (UNAOC), New York, USA. jordit@unops.org

Kathleen Tyner
Associate Professor, Department of Radio-Television-Film, University of Texas, Austin, USA. ktyner@utexas.edu

Carolyn Wilson
Instructor and Program Coordinator, Faculty of Education at Western University, London, Ontario, Canada. cwils66@uwo.ca

Anubhuti Yadav
Associate Professor, New Media, Indian Institute of Mass Communication, Aruna Asaf Ali Marg, New Delhi, India. anubhutiy@gmail.com

Ying Hu
Central China Normal University, Wuhan, Hubei Province, China. musichy@gmail.com

Zhao Pu
PhD candidate, Tsinghua University School of Journalism and Communication, Beijing, China. zhaopu13@mails.tsinghua.edu.cn

1.